CONTEMPORARY THEOLOGIES OF MISSION

CONTEMPORARY THEOLOGIES OF MISSION

ARTHUR F. GLASSER
DONALD A. McGAVRAN

BAKER BOOK HOUSE
Grand Rapids, Michigan 49506

ISBN: 0–8010–3790–5

Library of Congress Catalog Card No.: 82–73530

Printed in the United States of America

Unless otherwise indicated, the Scripture quotations are from the Revised Standard Version, copyrighted 1946, 1952, 1971, and 1973 by the Division of Christian Education of the National Council of the Churches of Christ in the United States of America. The other translations cited are the King James Version (KJV), the New American Standard Bible (NASB), the New International Version (NIV), and the New English Bible (NEB).

Contents

Acknowledgments

$\mathbf{W}$hen this manuscript was in the rough stage we contacted ten evangelical leaders deeply involved in a variety of strategic church ministries. We asked them to evaluate critically our approach to the complexity of the current debate on the Christian mission and to share with us their reactions. They have been most diligent in this service and we would like to record herewith their names and express in this fashion our heartfelt appreciation for their invaluable assistance:

Dr. Daniel W. Bacon, U.S.A. Director, Overseas Missionary Fellowship

Dr. Clyde Cook, President, Biola University

Dr. Ronald A. Jenson, President, International School of Theology, Campus Crusade for Christ

Dr. Louis L. King, President, The Christian and Missionary Alliance

Rev. Paul McKaughan, Coordinator, Mission to the World, The Presbyterian Church in America

Dr. R. Keith Parks, President, Foreign Mission Board of the Southern Baptist Convention

Dr. David L. Rambo, President, Nyack College and the Alliance Theological Seminary

Dr. Eugene Rubingh, Executive Secretary, Christian Reformed World Missions

Dr. Warren W. Webster, General Director, The Conservative Baptist Foreign Missionary Society

Dr. Vernon R. Wiebe, former General Secretary, Mennonite Brethren Missions/Services

We count ourselves most grateful to the Lord Jesus Christ for friends such as these. They have uniformly expressed themselves as being in hearty accord with the dominant thrust of this study. The final form of the manuscript reflects our diligent efforts to respond positively to their counsel. Their support has encouraged us no end.

Arthur F. Glasser
Donald McGavran

Introduction

Arthur F. Glasser

Christians are agreed that the church has a mission to the world, a mission that reflects the love of God for all peoples and nations. However, when it comes to defining the precise nature of this mission, one finds great differences of opinion among those who profess to be His followers. The mandate in the Scriptures seems clear: Christians are to proclaim to all peoples the Good News of the kingdom. Through Jesus Christ, God has made it possible for men and women everywhere to come under His rule and live for His glory. Disciples are to be made and gathered together into communities where God is known, loved, and served. Indeed, the message of the church is Jesus Christ and the dynamic of the church is the Holy Spirit. And it is to labor at this demanding task until Christ returns.

But this mandate must be "theologized," that is, conceptualized in such a way that it becomes meaningful and motivational to the people of God. Every generation must do this. True, it has been contended that some of the periods of greatest missionary obedience have not been accompanied by supporting theological reflection. But this contention is not quite accurate, for the church has often "theologized" without using those formal categories characteristic of Western systems of theology. We will not debate this matter.

What we desire to point out is that our day is characterized by two contradictory streams touching the Christian mission. On the one hand, we are witnessing tremendous worldwide missionary activism. Never before have so many missions and missionaries been so fruitfully engaged in making Christ known. On the other hand, never has the church had to cope with so many articulate voices advancing theologies of mission not only hostile to this activity but challenging its very validity. Inevitably, this latter stream is having a negative influence on many denominations formerly in the vanguard of Protestant missionary advance. Persuasive theorists increasingly call for the dismantling of mission structures and the

7

recalling of missionaries. They argue that the resources of the churches should be redirected into channels unrelated to the task of making Jesus Christ known where He is not known and planting congregations where none now exist. And all this at a time when evangelicals on the frontiers of mission advance are finding greater numbers of individuals, indeed whole segments of society, more receptive to the gospel than ever before. Obviously, there is no simple explanation for this paradox that, in a day of unprecedented receptivity, strident voices declare the day of evangelization has passed!

All those who are theologizing on the Christian mission confess that Jesus is Lord. As a result, we must take them seriously; they deserve to be heard. Even the most radical conceptualization of the Christian mission is worthy of serious study, provided, of course, it be evaluated in the light of the total witness of Scripture—our only infallible rule of faith and practice. For this reason, we are boldly entering this arena of debate to listen and then respond to the contemporary missiological theologizing of major segments of the church, whether conciliar, Roman Catholic, Orthodox, Pentecostal, or evangelical. In so doing we shall not engage in stale polemics. Our desire is to explore the forces and reasonings behind each of the competing theologies of mission of our day. And we trust that our interpretive response will prove both insightful and constructive.

A study of this sort needs a time frame. Initially, we thought that it might be useful to begin with the World Missionary Conference convened in Edinburgh in 1910. That conference marked the beginning of the modern era of ecumenical mission. However, because the serious issues to be reviewed in this study began to surface in strength only in the late 1950s, we became increasingly inclined to regard the 1961 absorption of the International Missionary Council by the World Council of Churches following the Third Assembly in New Delhi, India, as our starting point. Indeed, a good case can be made for 1961 marking the missiological watershed of our generation.

During the past two decades the theological crisis over the nature of the church and her mission has become acute. This crisis has in large measure been precipitated by questions concerning the nature of religious authority and by vast changes in the world in which this mission is to be carried out. The relative diminishing presence of the church in a world whose population is rapidly expanding has been regarded by some not as a challenge but as a rebuke to the "triumphalists" with their vision of a world coming to Christ. The new-found sense of dignity and freedom among many African peoples makes it necessary that Western churches drastically revise their missionary methodology which fitted an earlier day but is now outworn. The struggle for social justice in Latin America has pressed the churches to evaluate critically their understanding of the gospel, namely, that men and women are saved by faith in Jesus Christ and then are given power and desire to act justly. Then, too, the increasing bankruptcy of Marxism and Maoism in those vast areas of the world where they have been ruthlessly applied has brought confusion to their uncritical apologists in the West, the "secular" theologians. And always in the background loom the threat of thermonuclear war, the unresolved energy crisis in the industrial West, the growing poverty and hunger in the underdeveloped nations, the unwillingness of Jews and Arabs to reconcile their differences in the Middle East, and the politicalization of ancient ethnic faiths. Moreover, there has developed in recent times a new respect for individual conscience and for the inherent worth of every culture; and pluralism is now regarded by many as an acceptable—even desirable—fact of life. As a result, those who carry out the Great Commission's mandate to teach all peoples must be especially careful not to destroy something of value in the process.

That there is a crisis of faith in the churches over the issue of religious authority none will deny. For confirmation one has but to trace the changing attitudes toward Scripture held in the World Council of Churches from its inception in 1948 until the present.[1] Suffice it to say, these churches appear unable to agree on this issue other than to affirm that Jesus Christ is Lord and that the Bible has only a "derived authority" because of "the diversity amongst or even contradiction between biblical writers."[2] In contrast we—the authors—adhere to the position held by many down through the long history of the church, that "the Old and New Testament in their entirety are the only divinely inspired, truthful and authoritative written Word of God, without error in all that it affirms, and the only infallible rule of faith and practice."[3]

An investigation into the contemporary theologies of mission will inevitably have to grapple with the perennial missiological questions. In our day these have been given added emphasis because of the impact of secularism, Marxism, and scientific pantheism, but they are not new. Throughout the long history of the church, the writings of the apologists as well as the Greek and Latin Fathers are surprisingly replete with explorations of the missiological issues raised by the encounter between the church and the religious pluralism of their world.

Here the answers depend exclusively on whether the Bible is regarded as God's one authoritative revelation—at the same time "God's Word" and

1. Richard C. Rowe, *Bible Study in the World Council of Churches,* Research Pamphlet 16 (Geneva: World Council of Churches, 1969).

2. Ellen Flesseman–van Leer, ed., *The Bible: Its Authority and Interpretation in the Ecumenical Movement,* Faith and Order Paper 99 (Geneva: World Council of Churches, 1980), pp. 47, 40.

3. "The Lausanne Covenant," Section 2.

"voiced by humans"—or as simply one of many "revelations of God" or the religious insights of humans. One's definition of mission and theology of mission will be formed in accordance with the convictions held on this point. Conciliar and liberationist theologies of mission are on one side of the watershed. Evangelical and Roman Catholic theologies of mission are on the other side.

There are a number of issues with which the four major theologies of mission must constantly deal in one way or another. Although we shall not approach these issues topically, our readers will face them constantly as we move from one system of theology to another. Each major system gives—or implies—its own set of answers to these issues:

1. *God's Revelation and Other Religions.* Since Scripture clearly teaches that God has spoken and acted, finally and decisively, in Jesus Christ for the salvation of men and women, what is the relation between revelation and all other religious systems? Do they represent only unrelieved blackness, God-forsakenness, and human rebellion? Or do they have "religious value"? If so, what are the nature and extent of that value?

2. *The Salvation of the Human Race.* Since Jesus Christ clearly taught that the salvation of His people was made possible by His death, burial, and resurrection, and by this alone, what is the relation between His redemptive work and the eternal destiny of those who have died without ever hearing the gospel? Or of those who, while ignorant of this message, have perceived the divine through "common grace" and have cried out, "God, be merciful to me a sinner!"

3. *God in History.* Since the God of revelation is the God over the nations, does it not follow that He has been at work among them, sorrowing over their idolatry and making them ready for the coming of the gospel? What then is the value of each separate culture? To what degree are its components the work of humans? Are any components made by God? Consequently, should some of its elements be "baptized" and incorporated into the churches being planted in its midst? And should some elements be rejected as worldly and forbidden to the people of God?

4. *The Church's Apostleship.* A central purpose of the church in every land is to glorify God through obedience to the missionary mandate. What form is this obedience to take? What is the church's collective responsibility touching the selection, training, and sending forth of laborers? What is the individual Christian's responsibility? How shall church and Christian "bring about obedience to the faith for the sake of his [Jesus'] name among all the nations" (Rom. 1:5)?

5. *The Church's Structural Problem.* Since the Lord has given various gifts to His church (apostles, prophets, evangelists, pastor-teachers) to make possible the individual and corporate participation of His people in the ongoing of the Christian mission, what is the relation between the

church's congregational structures and those mission structures within its life, whether voluntary or authorized, whose objective is to support or extend the mission as it moves out to the regions beyond? Are both equally "church"? And further, what is the relation between these mission structures and the congregational structures they bring into being?

In our day it is widely recognized that the modern missionary movement was made possible by and followed European colonial expansion. As a result, the church was able to break free from its Western base and spread to every continent and nation. Despite the vast amount of good it has been able to accomplish throughout the world, there are many today who persist in identifying the Christian mission with Western imperialism. Evangelistic activities are denigrated as a form of Western arrogance clothed with a self-styled cultural superiority. Indeed, in some quarters to speak of mission in anything like positive terms is to conjure up the image of something that has long since lost its relevance. To be sure, this perception of mission is biased and simplistic, but it is widespread. It is understandable, but unwarranted. In times past, when there were few Christians in most parts of the world and those very largely illiterate, the missionary was properly a teacher and a parent. Now, wherever strong churches and well-educated leaders are abundant, that initial parental care is neither needed nor as a rule tendered. Mission moves on to unchurched populations—to the three billion who have yet to believe. Well-established churches in all lands should be—and increasingly are—carrying on their own mission and being teacher and parent to small bands of new Christians.

We rejoice over all the good that missionaries have been able to achieve and trust that in our generation we shall do as well and be as fruitful. We do not stand in judgment of their work (1 Cor. 4:5).

And we do not feel pressed to peer into the future and predict the ultimate direction of any of the impulses that have come to various segments of the church from New Delhi (1961) onwards. At present, for instance, the ecumenical movement appears to be divided between two visions: the classical vision with its focus on historic issues between communions and confessions, and the secular, this-worldly vision dominated by questions of peace and justice. We cannot say that denominationalism has had its day and is on the wane. Indeed, if anything, the tempo of multiplication of indigenous forms of Christianity (denominations and churches) seems to be increasing, not diminishing, not only in the Third World but in the West as well. And although those churches that confine the Christian movement to the struggle for social justice tend to empty their pews in the process, we are confident that biblical Christians everywhere will continue to be socially concerned in the days ahead—though, to be sure, many difficulties will be encountered in removing or reforming oppressive structures and deeply entrenched oligarchies.

Furthermore, despite the many positive gains that Vatican II brought to the Roman Catholic Church, we do well to keep in mind that in the years since this instrument of *aggiornamento* (updating) was fashioned, not a few ardent spirits within that tradition have pressed its affirmations to extreme ends. In fact, a post–Vatican II crisis of major proportions has been created. Some schools of Roman Catholic mission theology have subsequently undergone "more radical change in the last fifteen years than in the previous century."[4] Witness the drastic shrinkage of Jesuits by a third during this period, the polarizing debates precipitated by Karl Rahner's highly speculative theory of "anonymous Christians," and the church's diminishing sense of missionary obligation brought about by the issuance of the papal encyclical *Redemptor hominis* by John Paul II in 1979. And yet, the steady growth of the *Communidades Eclesiales de Base* or "Base Communities"—over 100,000 of these informal house congregations exist, mostly in Brazil but increasingly all over Latin America—clearly indicates the growing vigor of Catholic laity. Moreover, the streams of charismatic vitality pouring into this church in other parts of the world cannot but be vital signs of the Holy Spirit's presence and renewal activity in its midst.

Finally, we have not mentioned those innumerable Christians scattered throughout the Soviet Union and Eastern Europe, China and North Korea. During the early decades following World War II little was known other than that they were suffering. One could only surmise as to their experience within political environments hostile to religious freedom. But now their voices are beginning to be heard in the West. And the witness is to God's faithfulness to His people and a surprising increase in their numbers. We are finding that they have much to say to Christians throughout the non-Communist world, especially to those who live in less openly hostile, yet equally destructive environments. They speak of the power and grace of God to redeem the despairing, giving them songs of deliverance. Invariably, they find it utterly incomprehensible that anyone outside the Communist world would contend that Marxism has something to contribute to the humanization of society. Just the reverse.

So then we commend our essays on contemporary theologies of mission to your sober reflection. There are four of these theologies: conciliar, evangelical, Roman Catholic, and liberationist. In regard to each, our general pattern has been first to reconstruct its historical background replete with documentation (Glasser), and then to describe and discuss its theology (McGavran). The fast-flowing currents of modern thought and the rapid movement of events in the world have made the former task fascinating. How these various theologies of mission—so different—arose

---

4. Gerald H. Anderson and Thomas F. Stransky, eds., *Christ's Lordship and Religious Pluralism* (Maryknoll, NY: Orbis, 1981), p. 110.

from the common biblical base is hard to understand, until one sees what really happened. The latter task has been made easier in some respects and more difficult in others by the fact that this is the first attempt to describe accurately the various theories and theologies of mission which dominate the last third of the twentieth century. We have also explored certain subjects which play a significant role in today's creative—and confused—thinking on missions; for example, "Religious Liberty and Theology of Mission."

We conclude with the apostle Paul's brotherly counsel to a younger Timothy: "Think over what I say, for the Lord will grant you understanding in everything" (2 Tim. 2:7).

Abbreviations

CELAM	General Conference of Latin American Bishops
CWME	Commission on World Mission and Evangelism
DWME	Division of World Mission and Evangelism
EFMA	Evangelical Foreign Missions Association
IFMA	Interdenominational Foreign Mission Association
IMC	International Missionary Council
LAM	Latin America Mission
SCM	Student Christian Movement
SFMF	Student Foreign Missions Fellowship
SVM	Student Volunteer Movement
WCC	World Council of Churches
WSCF	World Student Christian Federation

1

What Is Mission?

Donald McGavran

A major cause for the tremendous decline in missionary sendings on the part of the mainline denominations and the older missionary societies is the spreading confusion concerning the word *mission*. Any good enterprise is called a mission. Television viewers remember the series called "Mission Impossible," in which the heroes and heroine carried out thrilling and difficult adventures.

Before we can have any theology of mission at all, we must define "mission" exactly, so that it does not mean everything and nothing. The extensive reinterpretation of "mission," which has been going on in church circles for twenty-five years and is still going on today, makes it impossible to think accurately or biblically about "mission-in-general." In this chapter we shall describe the main views of mission now being advocated and implemented. The colossal revolution in the midst of which we live, which affects every aspect of life, makes it imperative for anyone who would think exactly about mission to recognize the many variations. We must always ask, In what sense is the word *mission* being used? Everyone is agreed that "mission" can mean a missionary agency, but great uncertainty arises when the word is used to describe tasks instead of structures.

In the early stages, theology creates mission. If in studying the Bible Christians come to believe that God wills the salvation of all the peoples of earth and commands Christians to surge out in effective world evangelization, they send out missionaries. In later stages, the mission activities being carried out generate their own theologies of mission. Sometimes the world situation leads Christians to say, "In this kind of a world, God would have us do thus and so." In this chapter, speaking to the contemporary situation, we shall note the varied circumstances which create different kinds of mission and different theologies of mission.

Various Kinds of Mission

Let us turn to the radically different concepts of mission current today. As we look at Christian mission, which has formed such a large part of

15

the life of the Western churches for the last hundred years, we see that
missionaries—cross-cultural workers—have engaged in thousands of
activities. We shall describe briefly several aspects of the tremendous missionary enterprise. Always to be remembered is that *mission is a vast enterprise made up of many kinds of missions,* many kinds of activities, carried on
cross-culturally by many kinds of Christians. A great diversity in motives
has led to many kinds of mission. David Livingstone went to Africa, moved
in part by desire to make Christ known, in part by the urge to explore,
and in part by a resolve to end the slave trade. In his day some British
leaders began to call Christian missions "the cement of the British Empire."
The motive behind agricultural missions, to make greater productivity
available to the poor peoples of Asia and Africa, moved considerable
numbers of missionaries. The Presbyterian Sam Higginbottom, who
founded the Agricultural Institute at Allahabad, India, is one instance.
Yet another motive is that of the Wycliffe Bible Translators. They purpose
to reduce many oral languages to writing, and translate a portion of the
Bible into each.

Official statements of many boards during the last twenty-five years are
illuminating examples of the diversity which exists in the concept of mission. For example, "Mission Is Unity" and "Worship Is Mission" have often
been proclaimed. Those motivated by a passion for church mergers,
liturgical advance, or indigenization of worship forms believe sincerely
that they are thereby carrying out mission.

There are a number of factors which help determine the kind of mission actually carried out. Among them is the kind of support people are
willing to give. For example, many missionaries and their boards have
found that support for orphans can be readily raised, as witness the rise
of World Vision in recent years. Leprosy victims have great promotional
power. Christians are touched with pity and give generously. Medical services are so greatly needed, and are such a valuable aid in convincing
strangers that Christians are genuinely interested in their welfare, that
medical missions have flourished. Evangelistic missions among the resistant frequently turn into philanthropic missions (partly because money is
more readily raised for philanthropy).

Another factor strongly influencing the kind of mission carried out is
the size and nature of the churches which are being planted. For example,
sweeping people-movements to Christ resulting in denominations of 50,000
or 500,000 demand certain kinds of activities, and generate certain kinds
of missions. Small movements resulting in denominations of 1,000 or
5,000 require other kinds of missions, while nongrowing, tiny denominations of a few hundred, richly served by missionaries decade after decade,
require still another kind of mission.

The kind of mission which traditionally was best supported and whose activities therefore became the most common created what I have called the mission-station approach. Most missionaries were engaged in these activities and spoke concerning them in tens of thousands of sending congregations. Someone who wishes to know the sort of activity carried on by typical missions might scrutinize the budget distribution of a mission reflecting the mission-station approach.

A common theology of mission arose as this most common pattern of missionary activity sought for theological justification for what it was doing or what it believed should be done. A hundred years ago the mission was theologically justified as the outpost of world *evangelization*. That the gospel was for decades rejected by the Muslims, Hindus, and Confucianists was to be expected. The services rendered and the life of the small Christian community which gradually arose were ways of commending the gospel. Theologically mission was evangelism by every means possible.

After World War II, as the evangelistic purpose waned, other theological justifications for cross-cultural work were born. Johannes Hoekendijk defined mission as proclamation, fellowship, and service—*kerygma, koinonia,* and *diakonia*. His theology of mission went back to the first chapters of Acts where the apostles proclaimed the gospel, founded churches (*koinoniai*), and engaged in *diakonia*. The extensive services carried on by most missions, their evangelistic work, and their Christian community life were seen as three equally important ends of mission. Evangelism from being the chief end became one of three important ends. The three activities were justified theologically—God required them, not as means to an end but as ends in themselves.

Similarly after World War II, when leaders of the Latin American churches saw the enormous gap between the rich and poor, and came to believe that Christians should do something to effect a juster distribution of land and income, they began taking direct action to achieve that end. Then a theology of liberation, based on those biblical passages which were understood to support such action, was formulated. Mission was direct action to achieve more justice in human relationships. Theology of mission was the affirmation, based on biblical passages, that God wants justice on earth, and that those carrying out direct action to achieve it are doing God's mission.

In similar fashion all kinds of human needs, on many different levels, were addressed by missionaries and by church leaders. Mission therefore gradually became all kinds of outreach, all kinds of mission work. Theologies of mission gradually became biblical justification of these varied good activities.

Mission today is, by conciliar churches, defined in many ways. "Everything done outside our four walls" and "everything the church does for nonmembers" are the ways that Richard Niebuhr defined mission. "A capacity in any job to find and help people with the grace of Christ" is the way J. V. Taylor, bishop of Winchester, describes not missions, but "evangelism." If *evangelism* is so widely defined, how much wider would *mission* be?

When mission is defined so that vague generalities like "help people with the grace of Christ" capture the stage, two undesirable theological outcomes may be expected. First, it is affirmed that the *supreme* purpose of God is to create a better world. Passages which tell us that the Lord Jesus came to preach the gospel to the poor are interpreted to justify the gospel of the full dinner pail. Since the affluent parts of the world are coming to have a bad conscience about the enormous numbers of the very poor, and since many secularized Christians are a bit doubtful about the soul and eternal life, the new theology of mission which affirms that social reconstruction and other temporal improvements are the desperate need of the hour and are pleasing to God at this time, achieves a very wide acceptance. Second, since most persons touched by any one Christian are his or her immediate neighbors, "mission" is theologized as the church acting "evangelistically" in its own locality, that is, being a good neighbor.

It is important to point out that there are also potential dangers when missions become integrated with churches abroad. In all missions the steady goal has been the establishment of self-supporting, self-governing, and self-propagating congregations and denominations. As soon as strong denominations have been established, control and leadership have properly been transferred from missionaries to church leaders, and from missions to churches.

When this occurs, some Christians start asking, "Should not the mission agency now disappear?" Missions have ceased to exist in Zaire, I was told when visiting that country in 1977, though hundreds of missionaries and millions of mission dollars were still at work there. When John Gatu of East Africa in the early seventies suggested that in some circumstances a moratorium on missions might be a good thing, a huge debate on "moratorium on missions" erupted all over the world. And that at a time when three-fourths of the human race had yet to believe on Jesus Christ and most of them had yet to hear of Him in any way which would enable them to believe. Such a moratorium would have destroyed the only vehicle which can carry the gospel across cultures.

As we look back on the last fifty years, we see the rise of younger churches in nation after nation. Sometimes the transfer of leadership from mission to church took place over a thirty-year period. Sometimes it took place in a year. Sometimes the transfer resulted in a new burst of growth on the part of the church. Usually, however, it was followed by a period of small growth or of shrinkage as the church learned how to manage itself. Missions usually disappear by stages. A leadership is trained for the new congregations. The institutions and the property are then deeded to the national church. A few missionaries stay on to help the church they have founded. Finally the missionaries go and their local mission structure is torn down.

Unfortunately, not only does the organization called the mission disappear (a positive occurrence when a strong church has been established), but the function of the mission to proclaim Christ to those who have not heard and to found Christian congregations in new segments of non-Christian society is no longer carried out (a calamity). If, while there are thousands of unreached people, the missionaries turn over authority and go home, the whole purpose of world evangelization is thwarted. Often the young church does not reach out to others and evangelize. If, however, the missionaries, after turning over authority, do not return home but go on to some new field in that land and carry on the process all over again, then the mission is *not* integrated with the younger church, but continues in the urgent evangelization of regions beyond.

When the mission disappears and the missionaries go home, it often happens that efforts to carry out the Great Commission also disappear. There is no longer a theology of mission; only a theology of the church remains. The strong denominations which used to carry on mission then turn to other enterprises which claim their attention. Frequently they call these "mission," but the theologies justifying them are radically different from the theology justifying world evangelization.

Regardless of administrative adjustments between founding fathers and emergent churches, every church (African and Asian as well as European and American) should send out missionaries to proclaim Christ and persuade men and women everywhere to become His followers and members of His church. A theology of this kind of mission must not disappear! Indeed, we must continue to hold it before the church. A theology which focuses on the actual communication of the Good News of Christ and on the multiplication of cells of His baptized believers among the three billion still unreached must be seen as *a paramount concern of God.*

The New Kind of Mission

The World Council of Churches, which was founded in 1948, has made a point of integrating mission with the established church. This has tremendously affected the meaning of the word *mission*. In 1961 in New Delhi, the International Missionary Council became the Division of World Mission and Evangelism (DWME) of the World Council of Churches. By 1966, the DWME had had a considerable change of staff and framed a theology of missions which deliberately set forth the making of a new world order as the contemporary task of mission. Mission was the bringing in of a new humanity. It was the outlawing of all forms of oppression and distress. The Fourth Assembly of the World Council of Churches (Uppsala, 1968) laid special stress on this new perspective: "We have lifted up humanization as the goal of mission. . . . In another time the goal of God's redemptive work might best have been described in terms of man turning toward God. . . . The fundamental question was that of the true God. . . . Today the fundamental question is much more that of the true man."[1]

This formulation was conceived in Europe and North America by those who were concerned with what their powerful churches ought to be doing toward making the world a better, more righteous and peaceful place in which to live. In effect they were asking what they could do in a world full of poverty and hunger. We rejoice in their expression of Christian concern, but are distressed by their lack of interest in evangelism. The reason for this lack of interest is that most of the citizens in Eurica (Europe and North America) claimed to be Christians already. Thus European and North American Christians were not vividly conscious of the need to bring peoples from spiritual darkness to the Light of the world, Jesus Christ. Representatives of the Third World churches, mindful that their nations had been ruled (and in many cases robbed) by Europe, welcomed this reconceptualization of mission as primarily social action.

Moreover, the churches of Eurica were inevitably concerned with their own problems. While perhaps 90 percent of the people in parts of Eurica had been baptized in infancy and maybe even confirmed in adolescence, only 3 or 4 percent attended church, and only 1 or 2 percent partook of communion. Roman Catholics counted great sections of industrial France as mission territory because of the very small numbers there who attended mass. The Eurican church faced, its leaders said, a post-Christian era. It was a guilt-ridden church which as late as the Fifth Assembly of the World Council of Churches (Nairobi, 1975) went through elaborate and sincere acts of public penitence. It was this Eurican church which turned away from the evangelization of the world. "Have we not lost our empires?" they asked. "How can we evangelize sovereign nations? Rather, we should be working to rectify the injustices of the world, outlaw its poverty, and reduce its diseases. The church must cease to be selfishly concerned with the church. It must be concerned with the world. Humanization everywhere, not evangelism and church growth, is mission today." In short, a radically new kind of mission was advocated.

It is easy to understand how Europe could set forth this new definition, for that continent is filled with churches. But the "new mission" Uppsala proposed says very little indeed to those many nations where the church

---

1. *Drafts for Sections: Uppsala '68* (Geneva: International Review of Mission, 1968), p. 34.

is a tiny percentage of the total population and is powerless to affect national policies. Where Christians comprise but 2 percent (or even less) of the population, the task of the church is clearly evangelism, that is, bringing men and women into an authentic life-giving, society-redeeming relationship to the Lord Jesus Christ. Indeed that is the first task of the church everywhere, even in Europe.

If the church is going to disciple the three billion non-Christians and lift to genuine commitment the seven hundred million nominal Christians, it must define the goal of mission as enabling multitudes to receive eternal life through Jesus Christ. And it must believe that the greatest single step it can take toward a new world order is to multiply in every segment of every society cells of the redeemed, in living contact with the Triune God, in utter dependence on His revealed Word.

This traditional (and biblical!) approach to mission was rejected by the leaders of the conciliar churches. Consequently, they developed a "new mission" which they declare is necessary in this new age. In this new mission, they call for everything but sinner-converting, church-multiplying activity. *Presence* is the most desirable form of mission—simply being there as a witness to the love of God in Christ. Proclamation of Christ is replaced by dialogue with men and women of other ideologies and other religions. We talk not to them, but with them. We learn from them. They learn from us. In addition, books have been written on the "missionary structure of the congregation." By this phrase is meant that every congregation should act in a Christian manner *in its own neighborhood.* The need to send missionaries to places where the church does not exist has ended. The church—it is erroneously said—is now everywhere; so, if it simply acts everywhere as it should, sufficient mission will be carried out. Nothing more is required. Other leaders have talked a great deal about *involvement with the world.* Rejoice in secularization, they announce. What the church needs is *conversion to the world*! One noted leader has declared that we must "enworld" the church and cease being so concerned with it.

In short, the new kind of mission influential church leaders in Europe and North America have proposed is this: Cease being concerned so much with the church. Play down the sort of evangelism which is designed to enlarge your church. The order is God–world–church, not God–church–world. Rejoice in the desacralization of society. Act like Christians in the world. Become kind and neighborly. Work hard at the new social order which must come about. God is at work more outside His church than in it. Yield to the Holy Spirit and let the old forms die. See God in the revolutionary surges of our time—especially in the work of artists and even of atheists. Forget conversion and baptism. Stress people becoming kindly and serving others. Belong to the servant church, not the triumphant church. No more denominational extension, no more multiplying of your kind of congregations—just a great deal of quiet Christian presence and of genuine Christian conduct.

Some leaders have gone further. They are convinced that a tremendous revolution is taking place. Who knows where the revolution is taking us, they exclaim. Go along with it. God is in it. It is reaching for a juster society. About twenty-five years ago a prominent professor of missiology in a famous seminary said to me: "God is judging the church today as He did Israel in Isaiah's time. With the destruction of the temple, the temple form of worship went into a dark tunnel. Some hundreds of years later the synagogue form of Judaism, so well illustrated in the New Testament, emerged. Just so the church is going into a dark tunnel. What will emerge is yet to be seen."

Evangelization having disappeared, this Eurican remedy has been applied around the world. The Division of World Mission and Evangelism of the World Council of Churches called "changing the industrial structures of society" evangelism. Budgets for evangelism have dwindled and sometimes disappeared. In 1964 the *International Review of Missions* published a sharp criticism of Evangelism-in-Depth on the grounds that it was church-centered rather than concerned with remaking the social order. Most missionaries of boards affiliated with the World Council of Churches have become specialists who have nothing to do with multiplying churches. If churches are to be multiplied, it will have to be done by the national church—not by missionaries. The age of world evangelization is over. At the same time, it is mysteriously maintained that such specialists are "evangelistic in the true sense of the word."

Once evangelism was defined as "bringing to bear the grace of Jesus Christ on the needs of men and women everywhere," evangelism intended to lead men and women to belief in Jesus Christ as God and Savior inevitably diminished and, in many cases, ceased altogether. The desperate need of people for eternal life was *not* recognized as a genuine and crucial need. Hence, the new kind of mission neglected evangelism.

The theology which will support and require this wide, imprecise kind of mission is necessarily broad and vague. Mission becomes unity. Unity becomes mission. Evangelization is changing the structures of society. Conversion means any kind of turning from faulty structures to those which promise more good. The world becomes more important than the church. Indeed, the church is held to be purely instrumental. Sections of the Bible which seem to support these new concepts of mission are freely quoted. Amos is a favorite authority. Paul is not. Only part of John 3:16 is quoted. The clause "whoever believes in him should not perish" is often not mentioned. Proof texting becomes the order of the day. The central thrust of the Bible is studiously avoided.

The World-views of Modern Society

We have been describing the many varied kinds of mission which have arisen, but much more needs to be said, especially in light of the revolutionary changes which have taken place in the world-views of modern society. The basic question concerns the kind of universe we live in. There are several fundamental world-views. Some communities hold only one; but most communities, particularly in the developed nations, are composed of adherents of several different world-views. Men and women may belong to the church and seemingly have a biblical view, but in reality their lives are governed by an entirely different set of values. For example, more than nine-tenths of the population of Scandinavia are members of the Lutheran Church, yet most Scandinavians are highly secular. In Italy, most members of the Communist party with its Marxist set of values and consciously atheistic world-view are baptized Roman Catholics and insist on having their infants baptized.

The Biblical World-view

First we look at the biblical world-view, which held sway in Europe and America till the early twentieth century. According to the biblical view the universe was created by God. Human beings have both bodies and souls. The Bible is God's revelation, giving them the ultimate standard of right and wrong. The church is respected. To be a member is a good thing—even in the opinion of many who choose to remain out of it. Since the European nations which adhered to the biblical view ruled over large portions of the rest of the world, it was reasonable to believe that all nations would come to this view of the universe sooner or later. Missionaries were sent out by denominations and missionary societies holding this view, and their labors were regarded in this light. Missions were pleasing to God, the Maker of heaven and earth, and were therefore good.

The Secular World-view

Second, there are many who reflect a consciously secular view of life. The modern secular view arose as the principles of science began to be taught as a part of the educational process through which all boys and girls passed. Science, of course, is neutral. But the world-view formed on the basis of science, the view which is properly called scientism, is not neutral. It is a radically different religion. It denies that God created the world and all that is in it. The human race, it holds, was not created but evolved from lower forms of life. Evolution, not creation, is taught in hundreds of thousands of schools as the only possible view. Books and magazines discuss at great length other planets on which life may have evolved, but they never speak of planets on which God might have created

other intelligent beings in His own image. Nor do they discuss the likelihood that since God is one, the world-views and revelations of God on
those far-off planets would be substantially the same as those the Bible
sets forth.

Secularism in the modern world holds that the human being has no
soul. Consciousness ceases when one dies. There is no heaven and no
hell. The afterlife is a figment of the imagination. Marx called religion an
opiate for the masses by which the upper classes make them content with
their wretched lives. During the twentieth century, secularism became
very widespread, not only in Eurica, but in some sections of Latfricasia
(Latin America, Africa, Asia) also. Japan today, for example, is a highly
secularized nation. Iran has not only rigorous, Khomeini-type Muslims,
but also large numbers of very secular Muslims. How could it be otherwise
with tens of thousands of Iranians studying in Europe and America and
imbibing secularism/scientism every day in their university classes?

Christian mission, to the secularist, is a good activity if it serves the
human race, runs schools, builds hospitals, heals the sick, wipes out diseases, helps spread the knowledge of a better, more productive way of
life, and, in general, helps make the world a better place in which to live.
But missions which proclaim Jesus Christ as God and only Savior, and
persuade men and women to become His disciples, seem to secularists a
fanatical sectarian process. Many secularists believe such forms of missionary activity ought to be discouraged. Others are willing to let them
continue, however, since religious liberty requires that all must be free to
hold and propagate their view, no matter how nonsensical.

Whether they were conscious of it or not, whether they accepted it or
not, many Christians carrying on world evangelization in a heavily secularized society were influenced by secularism/scientism. This was inevitable because the dogmas of secularism struck at the very roots of classical
Christian missions. As a result these missionaries began to rethink the
traditional approach to mission. Some dedicated their lives to a much
reduced concept of mission. They used the same sacred words, but gave
them new meanings. They added certain activities which would appeal to
secular donors who were members of the sending denominations. They
eliminated certain emphases, certain attitudes to non-Christian religions,
and certain goals and expectations. A new kind of mission was devised.
But because it used the same words, operated under the same general
umbrella, and was rather vague in its expression, it was not often recognized as radically different.

The Marxist World-view

Third, we come to the Marxist world-view, which is not only thoroughly
secular, but purposes to bring in a classless society. Marxism intends to

build a new social order in which there will be neither rich nor poor. "From each according to his ability and to each according to his need" will be the undergirding principle of that utopia. Since Marx taught that there is no future life, and no authoritative revelation from God in any religion, and since the good life means the good life here and now, the good toward which Marxism works is this-worldly improvement.

Marxism has been enormously influential. As European empires began to break up following World War II, it became apparent that a new world order was coming into being. The imperial age was gone. The democratic-Christian order might be going too. Communism might someday rule the world. Capitalism seemed doomed. A world in which there were no rich and no poor seemed within grasp. The overwhelmingly urgent work of the church should therefore be to help bring in that better world, that new social structure. The Life and Work Movement, carried on by very good Christians, felt keenly and voiced constantly that in these revolutionary times Christians ought to be working hard at bringing in the new world order. Some of them called it the kingdom of God. They had only to read the Gospel of Matthew to find plenty of passages which (if slightly misconstrued) indicate that Jesus had just such a utopia in mind. In Matthew, there are in fact approximately fifty references to the kingdom of heaven.

We must not imagine that at this point Christians were copying the Marxists. Rather, the church has always been at work benefiting society. Transformed people seek to transform their society. Marxism has simply taken this basic drive in the biblical faith and directed it strictly to a this-worldly end.

That the rise of Communism and its growing world empire stimulated many Christians to social action cannot be doubted. The enormous advances which modern technology has made possible also helped the process along. Warm houses, plenty of food, electricity, flush toilets, modern medicine, and high degrees of comfort ought, Christians thought, to be enjoyed by everyone. Helping to realize these goals came to be regarded as mission.

The Rise of Various Theologies of Mission

When missionaries went out in 1880, they and their supporters shared a common world-view (biblical). Even so, as we have seen, they carried out many different kinds of mission. Following World War I the first shift in approach took place and missionaries began to operate from different world-views. An example which comes readily to mind is a North American missionary of some note who worked in central India. At a 1935 session of the Mid-India Christian Council, he maintained, in open meeting, that missions centering on conversion were now outmoded and should be replaced by missions which were ready to reconceive Christianity in the light of the valid insights and practices of Hinduism. In 1935 he was in a minority, but his point of view continued to spread. Indeed, given the popularity of the secular and Marxist schools of thought, it is hard to see how it could have failed to spread. Of course, this was more true in some denominations than in others.

The ground rules for mission were being changed. There was disagreement as to the ultimate authority for Christian mission: Was it the Bible taken as God's revelation? Or was it the Bible viewed as bearing witness to the truth in some mysterious way (without being truth)? Or was it an inborn common sense and urge toward goodness in the human race as a whole? Was the goal toward which mission ought to work that all should hear of the Lord Jesus Christ and as many as possible accept Him, or was it rather to help men and women live the good life here on earth? Was the goal to spread cells of the redeemed throughout the world, so that by feeding on the Word of God written and being dependable members of Christ's body Christians might leaven society as far as it could be leavened? Or was the goal to bring into being a better world order in which men and women would find the good life, while following any one of a dozen different religions or ideologies? *A radically different kind of mission would necessarily be formed on each of these radically different bases.*

Each new kind of mission would then inevitably set forth a different theology of mission to justify its activities. Thus many different theologies of mission would arise. Sometimes they would be recognized as different; but for the most part, since they used the same sacred words (e.g., mission, evangelism, conversion, salvation), many (if not most) Christians would not be keenly aware of the radically different kinds of mission. That is exactly where we are today. Many kinds of new mission are being advocated and carried on, while their supporters often think they are aiding the cause of classical mission.

The Biblical Definition of Mission

In this book we cleave to the classical biblical way of regarding mission. We define it strictly as *"carrying the gospel across cultural boundaries to those who owe no allegiance to Jesus Christ, and encouraging them to accept Him as Lord and Savior and to become responsible members of His church, working, as the Holy Spirit leads, at both evangelism and justice, at making God's will done on earth as it is done in heaven."*

The three billion souls (shortly to become four billion) who live outside the reach of any Christian congregation at all must be the special concern of contemporary Christian mission. Unbelievers living in societies where the church is strong call for one type of evangelism, but those who live in as yet unevangelized areas of the world constitute an entirely different mission problem and should be given highest priority. Our definition of mission does not narrowly confine mission to verbal announcement of the gospel. It accepts the practice of the last 150 years that a great variety of activities may be used to communicate the gospel across linguistic and cultural barriers to those who have yet to believe:

Education	All these are mission when their purpose is so
Literacy Programs	to witness to Christ that men and women may
Agriculture	know Him, love Him, believe Him, be found in
Medicine	Him, become members of His church, and cre-
Presence	ate in the segments of society they control, a
Dialogue	social order more agreeable to God.
Proclamation	
Social Action	

Our definition of mission rejects any activity, even that of verbal proclamation of the name of Jesus, which does not unshakably intend that the unredeemed should choose to become disciples of Christ, bound together in congregations, indwelt by the Holy Spirit, and resolved to live the corporate life as Christ would have them live it.

We hope that our readers will make special study of the confusion as to what is mission and will have the Great Commission in mind whenever they use the word *mission*. Part of the contemporary problem is that many leaders of the church (trying desperately to hold the various ideas of mission together) maintain that all these ideas are good and are equally mission. A weak "lowest common denominator" definition of mission results. It includes everything and means nothing.

We believe that a great deal of diversity is necessary. Christian mission meets thousands of situations and must speak to each in a somewhat different way. Yet at all times the clear biblical goal of discipling all the peoples of the earth has to be maintained. The diversity must neither include approaches and goals which cannot be validated by Scripture, nor destroy the priority which the Bible gives to discipling *panta ta ethne* (all the peoples).

We wish to be clear on this point. We do live in a new world. Beyond doubt, a new international world order is being formed. New days do require new emphases. New light will break forth from the Bible. As is written in stone over the door of Zwingli's church in Switzerland, "If you give the Word of God to the people of God, God will speak to His people through it, the word they need for their day."

New light may come from many sources. The wonderfully innovative human mind sees many new things. The old religions and ideologies contain many good teachings. After all, it was Greek polytheism which created some of the most beautiful statues the world has ever seen. But whether human insights—modern or ancient—are good, beautiful, and true, must be judged by God's revelation in the Bible and in His Son our Savior. There lies the ultimate authority. The Bible must not be twisted to fit insights from Mao, Khomeini, Plato, or John Dewey. Unless the Bible is the only authority for a theology of Christian mission, Christian mission (if carried on at all) will be nothing but one long series of current emphases—whatever happens to come to the surface as nations and peoples interact.

Informed Christians today must see the difference in the various concepts of mission and theologies of mission. A theology of mission which focuses on propagation of the gospel is one thing. A theology of mission which focuses on increased rice production is an entirely different matter. We particularly hope that our readers will not be derailed by the superficial and false charge that mission focusing on propagation of the gospel is exclusively concerned with individual salvation and cares little for a just society.

The word *holistic* is commonly used today. We are told that mission must be holistic. It must be concerned with the whole individual and the whole society. It must be concerned with the body as well as the soul. It must fight for just labor laws and an equitable distribution of land, and against multinational corporations. The difficulty with some such pronouncements is that 95 percent of the stress is laid on temporal improvements and (maybe) 5 percent on eternal salvation. Any such proportion is not holistic at all. True holism has ever marked the mission of the church. Remember our Lord's statement in Matthew 10:28, "Do not fear those who kill the body, but are unable to kill the soul; but rather fear Him who is able to destroy both soul and body in hell" (NASB). The body is important. The Lord Jesus healed and fed bodies, but He clearly taught and demonstrated that the soul is more important.

Followers of Christ, when they are indwelt by the Holy Spirit, seek first to be in Christ, that is, to believe in Him, to be baptized in His name, and to become a part of His body, the church. Then, inevitably, He causes them to seek a better social order and to change their society. This may be the family, the kindred, the neighborhood, the village, or the city and state. For some it may be the international social order.

This process can be seen in the past labors of missions. Whenever missions have planted churches successfully, improvements in the areas of health, education, agriculture, justice, and freedom have followed. The church is the most powerful instrument known for the alleviation of social ills.

As we begin our study of theologies of mission, it is imperative that we have a correct perspective on the many good activities now being advocated and carried on. If they are all called mission, there is no way to avoid confusion. Then mission becomes, as Richard Niebuhr said, everything the church does outside its walls. When that happens, mission as world evangelization is necessarily assigned a minor place. It becomes one of multitudinous good works. And our theology of mission boils down to the platitude that God wants Christians to do their duty or to bring in the kingdom of God on earth. God is, no doubt, bringing in His kingdom. Johannes Verkuyl defines mission as "the salvific activities of the Father, Son, and Holy Spirit throughout the world, geared to bringing the kingdom of God into existence." Any such wide definition which includes everything done by God and mortals toward a better world necessarily creates a theology of mission which touches on every good thing God and mortals do toward bettering the human lot. We are friendly toward every good thing people do, but we refuse to call all of them Christian mission. We prefer the classical definition. Christian mission is all activities whose basic purpose is to disciple all the peoples of earth. We are pleased when friends carry on other godly activities—Christian education, study of the Bible, social action, church mergers, the public worship of God, the healing of diseases, and so on. We pray that God will bless them. But we hope that they will not muddy the waters by calling all these good things Christian mission.

2

The Whole-Bible Basis of Mission

Arthur F. Glasser

N ever in history has there been so much evangelical activity seeking to make Jesus Christ known, loved, and served throughout the world. And yet the church has never been so harassed and troubled by voices calling for the reduction or abandonment of these activities— and for the reconceptualization of its message and mission in terms of social justice, international peace, racial integration, and the elimination of poverty. Since there is validity to all these varied activities, it can be said that the Spirit is struggling within the churches that they might more fully rise to the complex challenge of their worldwide mission.

It is this struggle within the church that concerns us. It is not only the struggle for its spiritual integrity—whether or not it shall truly enthrone Jesus Christ as Lord of all aspects of its life and contend for the historic biblical faith committed to its care. It is also the struggle for a comprehensive understanding of its mission to the nations.

Our concern is that the church once again listen to the Word of God— the Word written, the Word incarnated, and the Word expounded. We believe that only if the church understands the total revelation of God concerning the mission of His people, will they offer to Him the heart, strength, time, and resources essential to carrying out His will among the nations. This means the Old Testament witness as well as the New. We acknowledge the authority of the Old Testament because Jesus was very closely bound to it. He knew no other Word of God and He knew no other God than the God of the Old Testament. Then too, we desire to listen anew to what He particularly said about the missionary task—which has at its heart discipling the peoples of earth—and to review the very specific ways in which the apostolic church sought by word and deed to carry it out.

All Scripture makes its contribution, in one way or another, to our understanding of mission. This is our thesis. In our day, evangelicals are finding that the biblical base for mission is far broader and more complex than any previous generation of missiologists appears to have realized. Gone are the narrow presuppositions of the early Pietists whose missionary understanding had but a single focus: an overwhelming concern for the spiritual condition of "the heathen" living outside the pale of *corpus Christianum*. And it has become increasingly difficult to defend the still-limited basis of the modern missionary movement which supplemented this concern with appeals to the Great Commission—in the tradition of William Carey and Hudson Taylor. Nor can a credible broadening of that base be achieved by appealing to selected texts on such related themes as the "sending" character of God, the compassionate compulsion of the Spirit, the example of the apostolic church, and the relationship between missionary obedience and the second coming of Christ. These themes are certainly worthy of serious reflection, but one cannot build a comprehensive biblical theology of the Christian mission on isolated texts.

Indeed, in our day, there is a growing impatience with all pragmatic approaches to the missionary task that arise out of a selective, proof-text use of Scripture—despite their popularity among activistic evangelicals in the years immediately following World War II. This impatience has been heightened by overtones from the conciliar debate on mission following the 1961 New Delhi Assembly of the World Council of Churches. From that time onward it became increasingly apparent to evangelicals that serious-minded Christians in WCC-related churches, who supported an approach to mission that was disturbing to say the least, were likewise using proof texts. This inevitably raised questions. Was something basically wrong with the extractive use of Scripture? Did not this method of constructing foundations for the missionary task tend to produce incomplete approaches? Was there not the need for an overall approach to Scripture that would allow each part to make its contribution, so that the total concern of God for the nations might be understood? We became convinced of this need, and will attempt to meet it in part in this chapter.

The Unifying Theme: The Kingdom of God

All are agreed that Jesus Christ gave His church a worldwide mission. The "good news of the kingdom" is to be preached throughout the whole world, as a testimony to all nations; and then "the end will come" (Matt. 24:14). This mission, rightly understood, defines the relation of the people of God to the peoples in whose midst they dwell and to whom they are sent. A right understanding of mission focuses on the kingdom of God—the Good News Jesus announced and displayed to His generation.

Paul Minear notes that "the deepest cry which the Holy Spirit arouses in man is the yearning cry for heaven, for direct contact with God's throne, for the victory of God over His demonic enemies, for an invitation to the marriage feast of the Lamb."[1] Johannes Verkuyl adds that the church would be remiss if it failed to attend to this heart-rending cry and ignored the evangelistic task of extending invitations to this marriage. But then he goes on to state that the Bible in its totality confronts us with far more than the crucial dimensions of personal salvation: "Missiology is more and more coming to see the kingdom of God as the hub around which all mission work revolves. One can almost speak of a consensus developing on this point."[2]

The Old Testament and the Kingdom of God

Actually, the kingdom of God is one of the central, overarching themes of the Bible. Although it is explicitly a New Testament theme, we are deeply persuaded that the Old Testament can also be best understood from this perspective. In the Old Testament God discloses Himself and His outgoing activity: as Creator He establishes the world and fills it with His creatures; as Governor He watches over it for His good pleasure; as Redeemer He reveals His forgiving love for His people; and as Guide He points the way to His ultimate purpose "to unite all things in [Christ], things in heaven and things on earth" (Isa. 43:4–7; Eph. 1:10). The Old Testament affirms again and again that God desires to destroy all evil and bring to an end every grief that plagues the human race. Without the Old Testament's contribution to our understanding of the eternal purpose of God touching individuals and nations, the New Testament portrayal of the "already," the "not yet," and the "consummation" of the kingdom will appear incomplete and inadequate. The revelation of the love of God in Christ cannot be fully grasped apart from the Old Testament. Even the lordship of Christ can be best understood if informed by Old Testament concepts of kingship.

God's kingship is both universal and covenantal. After He created the heavens and the earth by His Word and after He created the human race in His own image and likeness, it was inevitable that He would exercise a loving and preserving control over His creation. This can be described as His universal kingship. He is the source of all authority and He has decreed His ultimate triumph over all things, particularly the nations (Ps. 22:28–29). The New Testament also teaches the universal kingship of God (Rev. 1:6; 19:6).

1. Quoted in Johannes Verkuyl, *Contemporary Missiology: An Introduction*, trans. and ed. Dale Cooper (Grand Rapids: Eerdmans, 1978), p. 203.
2. Ibid.

However, in the Old Testament we also find God's kingly rule identified with a particular people with whom He established a covenantal relationship. When the record of universal history (Gen. 1–11) ended with the scattering of the fallen human race (the tower of Babel), God graciously purposed through one people to bring this fragmentation to an end. Indeed, when He called Abraham out of Ur of the Chaldees, He took the first step in His purpose to achieve the redemption of the fallen human race. Hence the significance of His promise that by Abraham and his seed all the nations of the earth will bless themselves (Gen. 12:1–3).

God constituted the seed of Abraham, Isaac, and Jacob as His peculiar possession after liberating them from Egyptian bondage and securing their willing acceptance of His covenant at Sinai (Exod. 19–20). From that time onward His moral governance over them embraced the pledge of guidance and provision, instruction and blessing. If they obeyed, they could count on His faithfulness to this pledge. However, if they became rebellious and disobedient, they could anticipate His chastening.

Over the years God disclosed Himself to His people by mighty acts and spoken words. And they came to understand that His rule was spiritual and irrevocable, and included the guarantee of an imperishable communal existence, a messianic expectation, and an eternal salvation. When God revealed through Daniel that "the saints of the Most High [would] receive [His] kingdom, and possess the kingdom for ever and ever" (7:18), He sent their minds soaring. Here was an unconditional promise of ultimate triumph under the banner of "one like a son of man" (7:13). He would enable them in the last day to share in God's total and final victory. Understandably, the Jewish people have never forgotten this promise! As Johannes Bavinck summarizes:

> Israel was thus strongly under the impression that its history was not a particular affair of no concern to anyone else, but that God utilized its history to deal with other nations, rather with the whole world. Israel's defeats and victories, its greatness and subjugations, its wonderful deliverances, and its heavy sufferings are all included in God's plan for the world. God stretches out his arms to all the world in such events.[3]

Hence, in the Old Testament it is not uncommon for God to be addressed by His people as their King (Ps. 10:16). They regarded Yahweh as enthroned in their midst, dwelling between the cherubim in the innermost sanctuary of the tabernacle, and later in the temple in Jerusalem (Num. 7:89; Isa. 37:16). His throne was the mercy seat. His presence thereon pledged His faithfulness to His covenant. They would triumph over their enemies!

3. Johannes H. Bavinck, *Introduction to the Science of Missions,* trans. David H. Freeman (Philadelphia: Presbyterian and Reformed, 1960), p. 15.

There are both differentiation and intimate correlation between God's universal kingship and His kingly rule over His people. As Creator and Redeemer He will finally and fully triumph in human history. As Yahweh, faithful to His covenants, He will bring His people to their golden age of salvation. The one depends on the other. First, the Israel of God must be a redeemed people. And second, the peoples (*goyim, 'ammim*) that have long resisted God's will must be totally divested of their pretensions, their autonomy, and their dominion. Indeed the ruin and downfall of all God's enemies (Isa. 26:21) are prerequisite to His being established as "King of kings and Lord of lords" (Rev. 19:16). And it is only at the last day—the time of God's judgments—that "Jerusalem shall be called the throne of the LORD, and all nations shall gather to it" (Jer. 3:17). Following this eschatological summons to all peoples to seek the Lord, the people of God will finally see the new heavens and the new earth (Isa. 65:17). Only then will they enjoy the enduring peace and justice mortals have always sought, and the economic security that has always eluded human experience (Mic. 4:3–4).

Despite this oft-repeated prospect of the final triumph of God in human history, the record of the Old Testament represents almost unrelieved failure on the part of Israel. The kingly rule of God met with little appreciation and even less response. Yahweh lavished His love on His people but received little or none in return. In the end His judgments fell on them and the bitterness of exile overtook them. In their own strength they found it very difficult to live under His direction and for His glory amidst the enslaving idolatries of the day. They were constantly surrounded by rival claims to knowledge, security, and power attractively packaged by ancient and respected cultures. Again and again they faced total catastrophe as they allowed themselves to be lured into syncretistic adaptations to the religions around them, and thus departed from their God. They survived only by His grace. Each successive deliverance revealed His faithfulness and His power, as Liberator, Healer, and Guardian. Over the years they were taught what is demanded of those who would confess God as their sovereign King.

The *sine qua non* for understanding the Old Testament is to take full measure of this record of failure. One must ponder deeply the somber details of Israel's persistent apostasy and from this frame of reference review the hopes and expectations so vividly set forth by the prophets— that despite Israel's failure God would ultimately realize His covenantal goal with His people. Only thereby can one begin to appreciate the uniqueness of Jesus Christ, that "other Israel." By a totally obedient life, by a truthful witness to His generation, and by the substitutionary atoning surrender of His life in death, He would establish a new and unbreakable covenant of grace and salvation (Jer. 31:31–34; Ezek. 39:25–29).

Old Testament Perspectives on the Kingdom

Five major perspectives on the coming of the kingdom can be traced within the long history of Israel's experience with God in the Old Testament. Each one is an intimation of what will be developed in fulness in the New Testament.

First, God is sovereign in His kingship. His rule over individuals and nations is always righteous and just. His power and His goodness, His holiness and His judgments, His patience and His mercy are always prompted by a loving concern for the best interests of His creatures. No one steeped in Old Testament truths is likely to become preoccupied with "second" causes. It is God and God alone who is the cause of all creation. And this God is the moral Governor of the universe.

Second, God's sovereign rule demands personal commitment. This commitment is to Him personally, and to His righteousness. He has decreed no acceptable alternative other than that He be loved with all heart and soul, strength and mind. There can be neither king nor kingdom without subjects, and the righteous God demands righteousness on the part of all who would be in covenantal relationship with Him. His people—the true children of Abraham—must practice justice, love kindness, and walk humbly with Him (Mic. 6:8). Those who become careless in their allegiance experience much sorrow and loss (1 Sam. 13:14). Even so, His loving-kindness is never withdrawn despite His chastening, and He is always faithful to His covenant.

Third, God's subjects must constitute a "servant" community. He is not solely concerned with individuals, but with families, peoples, and nations. Hence, He presses social obligations on His people. He delights to dwell in their midst that through them His rule might extend to all aspects of their social order.

He reveals Himself as opposed to racism, nationalism, and whatever else demeans people. His prohibition of marriage with strangers was partly political, mainly religious, and certainly not racial (Exod. 34:12–16; Deut. 7:3–4; Ezra 9:1–2). Apart from the infrequent occasions He used His people to bring judgment on certain nations (Deut. 7:1–5), He stands against aggressive war. Enforced poverty, the abuse of political power, the neglect of "the stranger within the gates," likewise come within the circle of His concern. Indeed the Old Testament can often surprise us by suggesting approaches to many of the problems confronting the church in our day. God is concerned over the struggle for social justice, for He is strongly moved by the cries of the oppressed, particularly when His people collectively make no effort to relieve their anguish.

Fourth, God's sovereign rule is relentlessly resisted and opposed by His people, by the peoples that do not know Him, and by the unseen powers.

One feels the humiliation of God. His gifts are either despised or irresponsibly wasted, His love appears squandered on an ungrateful people, and His will is opposed again and again. This discloses the inveteracy of human evil and the implacable hostility of Satan and his hosts. God knows the full measure of human ignorance, apathy, selfishness, greed, and cowardice. The amazing thing is that God is never overcome by evil, although He often bears the shame of the failure of His people (Jer. 34:16; Ezek. 39:7).

Fifth, God's sovereign rule is always directed toward the future. He is never totally preoccupied with the present. Again and again His prophets pointed to the coming day of the Lord, when His righteousness will be fully triumphant, when "the earth will be filled with the knowledge of the glory of the LORD, as the waters cover the sea" (Hab. 2:14). He is the God of hope, of victory, of salvation. His ultimate goal for human history is never lost sight of. Thus, despite the dark shadows which cover most of Old Testament history, He enabled His people to face forward, looking for "the consolation of Israel" and "the redemption of Jerusalem" (Luke 2:25, 38). Their firm belief was that the beneficent purpose of God would finally be realized and that His kingdom would be fully established.

So then, the Old Testament contribution to our understanding of the mission of the church is incalculable. Despite its tragic record of human frailty and open rebellion against God, the Old Testament enables one to believe in the unseen reality of the kingdom of God above history, the providential power of God within history, and the consummation of His kingdom in the last day, beyond history.

Jesus Christ and the Kingdom of God

"When the time had fully come, God sent forth his Son" (Gal. 4:4). There is a sense in which the sending of Jesus into the world is not unrelated to the Old Testament pattern summarized by Jeremiah: "From the day that your fathers came out of the land of Egypt to this day, I have persistently sent all my servants the prophets to them, day after day" (7:25). And yet, the sending of Jesus was unique. The fallen condition of the human race was so acute and the need for redemption so great that only the incarnation of God and the atonement of the cross could avail to provide for the salvation of His people. Previous sendings set the stage for this final sending or mission, and the advent of Jesus the Christ marks the great hinge of human history.

The tragedy, of course, is that because Israel had not profited from her failure under the old covenant, she was largely unable to discern the Servant of Yahweh when He came into her midst. Not that there was insufficient evidence of His coming. When John the Baptist suddenly appeared in the style of Elijah and assumed the long-prophesied role of the herald of the Messiah, many were stirred. How could it have been otherwise, when he announced in no uncertain terms the coming of Israel's long-deferred hope: the kingdom of God! To the well-instructed, this could mean only that God was about to intervene and act redemptively on behalf of His people. The expectations of the majority, however, were that the Messiah would deliver them from the grievous yoke of imperial Rome.

Our Lord's three years of ministry provoked much searching of heart. The first year saw Jesus and John engage in a ministry of renewal. Both spoke of God, of righteousness, of sin, and of repentance. Both announced the imminent coming of the kingdom. Then the unexpected happened: John was imprisoned and in the weeks that followed Jesus did nothing to release him. Instead, He saw in this imprisonment the end of the old era, and straightway inaugurated the messianic era (Luke 4:18–21; 16:16). In the synagogue in Nazareth He boldly projected Himself into the role of the Servant of Yahweh. He fed the hungry, healed the sick, gave sight to the blind, caused the lame to walk, and delivered the demon-possessed. That second year was characterized by these messianic signs, the crowds that hung on His words, and His parabolic exposition of the nature of the kingdom. The third year saw the mounting opposition which culminated in His crucifixion.

This opposition arose because the words of Jesus offended the great majority of the people. When Jesus stated that the kingdom of God represented primarily the salvific activity of God—the moral and spiritual rebirth of the human race—and not the overthrow of Rome and the end of oppression and unjust taxation, the leaders of the Jews lost their patience. They were largely concerned with a kingdom of this world, not something spiritual and ethical. Actually, Jesus' kingdom—the saving and ruling presence of God over His people—was so different from what they wanted that they sought to destroy Him as an impostor. They could not see that by this kingdom God was entering the human scene in ways unprecedented and altogether new.

The Jews hardly regarded the cross—a common and most cruel means of executing criminals—as a redemptive triumph. They did not know that God was in Christ, reconciling the world to Himself (2 Cor. 5:19). Nor could they conceive that the cross marked a cosmic triumph in which all principalities and powers were disarmed, the works of the devil destroyed, and the world conquered (John 16:33; Col. 2:15; 1 John 3:8). They could not believe that Jesus of Nazareth was the Lord of human history, and they failed to realize the implications of His empty tomb and bodily resurrection. Even His disciples were slow to believe that He was indeed the

Lord of glory, and that all human history would be consummated with
the final manifestation of His kingdom.

We should underscore the precise nature of the kingdom of God. Its
distinctions are many. First, for the present it is devoid of all dimensions
of outward glory. It is a buried treasure—a priceless pearl—and its acquisition is worth any cost or sacrifice (Matt. 13:44–46). Second, its form is
hidden. It represents the hiddenness of God, working in the hearts of His
people scattered throughout the evil world of time and place. Jesus used
the phrase "the mystery of the kingdom" (Mark 4:11) to represent God's
present invasion of Satan's kingdom to release people from bondage (Luke
11:14–22); and He added that those who enter His kingdom through
repentance and faith enjoy, in part, a foretaste of the age to come. They
enter into life (John 3:3); they receive both the forgiveness of sins
(Mark 2:5) and God's righteousness (Matt. 5:20). And they discover that
all the criteria for success in this world (size, possessions, achievements,
ego, brilliance, and noise!) have been discredited in His kingdom of love
and selfless service.

Third, the only acceptable response that can be made to God's gracious
gift of the kingdom is to put oneself consciously and deliberately under
Christ's rule and embrace this new pattern of values and service. This
involves repentance, faith, and submission. Those who do not "obey the
gospel of our Lord Jesus . . . shall suffer the punishment of eternal
destruction and exclusion from the presence of the Lord and from the
glory of his might" (2 Thess. 1:8–9).

It was these distinctives that particularly offended many Jews. They
could not see how the messianic age could come in mystery form. They
brushed aside as mere verbiage Jesus' affirmation that the kingdom was
already present in His own mission before its final apocalyptic consummation. They had been taught that the kingdom of God, when it came,
would require no human involvement. It would be an abrupt divine erup-
tion upon the human scene in the last day. Hence, when this Galilean
rabbi preached the necessity of a repentance-and-faith response to His
person before the kingdom rule could become operative in their lives,
they drew back. Even Nicodemus—that most open-minded teacher in
Israel—was completely mystified when Jesus told him that he needed the
regenerating work of the Holy Spirit in his heart, or he would not even
see much less enter the kingdom of God (John 3:3, 5).

It is significant that Jesus also spoke of the future consummation of
the kingdom. Indeed, He deliberately instructed His disciples to pray for
that day when the will of God shall be carried out on earth even as it is
in heaven (Matt. 6:10). But He did not dwell on this, lest it engender the
sort of apocalyptic preoccupation that encapsulates one in a dream world
of persistent expectations, constant revisions of one's "prophetic" charts,

and growing impatience ("How long, O God?"). Jesus wanted His contemporaries to realize that the kingdom of God had truly come, and that its spiritual urgings were every bit as forceful as the final apocalyptic display of power that will compel every knee to bow and every tongue to confess that Jesus is Lord.

In the parables Jesus spoke of the Good News of God's present rule over His people as seed sown in good soil. Fruitfulness depends on how His kingdom is received (Matt. 13:3–8). Its coming does not abruptly disrupt the present order. The sons and daughters of the kingdom—the true children of Abraham—multiply throughout the world, alongside the children of the evil one. And this will be the situation at the time of God's final harvest of the nations (Matt. 13:24–30; 36–43; Rev. 14:15). The kingdom is like mustard seed—it is not physically imposing in its beginnings, but it grows and eventually fills the earth. It is like yeast, permeating the dough in which it has been placed, making it rise with gentle, irresistible power (Matt. 13:31–33). It is like a banquet where the poor and needy become the favored guests and find new perspectives of justice and freedom, fellowship and love (Luke 13:29; 14:15–24).

There is one discordant note found in the public teaching of Jesus: the scandal of His crucifixion. "And he began to teach them that the Son of man must suffer many things" (Mark 8:31). The crucifixion was necessitated by the terrible alienation between the holy God and the sinful human race. Nothing is so intolerable to the human race as God's holiness and nothing is so intolerable to God as human sinfulness. Jesus knew that He would be deliberately destroyed ("Away with him, away with him, crucify him!"—John 19:15). But He also knew that if it is the folly of the human race to put the best of God's children to death, God will turn the tables and use this same folly to reconcile the world unto Himself.

Let it be granted that Satan gathers all the powers of this world together against the Lord's Anointed. Let it be granted that when these hostile forces are mobilized the leaders of Israel, the inheritors of all God's promises, will be in the front ranks. Let it be granted once again, that Roman law and order will become the cowardly and obliging accomplices of Jewish intrigue. And let it be granted, that Satan will persuade the frightened disciples to renounce their Master, or else will reduce them to silence, and that one of the Twelve will turn traitor . . . let all that be granted. Nevertheless, in the midst of all these apparent victories, won by the prince of this world, his ultimate defeat is hidden. He is merely the instrument of a higher purpose . . . and the victory of Jesus becomes . . . his giving his life as a ransom for many.[4]

4. Suzanne de Diétrich, *God's Unfolding Purpose: A Guide to the Study of the Bible*, trans. Robert McAfee Brown (Philadelphia: Westminster, 1960), pp. 183–88.

With the resurrection, Jesus' redemptive triumph became fully apparent to His disciples. Indeed, had the resurrection not taken place there would have been no Christian church and no worldwide missionary movement. But they now knew that both sin and death had been conquered, and they were now ready for the climax of Jesus' earthly ministry: His authorization and command that as witnesses of His resurrection they proclaim to all segments of the human family the forgiveness of sins (Luke 24:44–49).

In the forty-day interval between His resurrection and ascension Jesus brought to a climax His instruction concerning the kingdom of God (Acts 1:3). He did this by bringing together three great streams of truth. First, He opened the Old Testament to His disciples through providing His person and work as a hermeneutical key (Luke 24:25–27). And they were encouraged to count on the continuing illumination of the Holy Spirit to guide them into its truths and into the matters yet to be revealed to chosen apostles (John 16:12–15). By intimation He showed the indissoluble unity of the biblical revelation and obligated His followers to condition all thought and practice to the witness of the apostles and prophets (Eph. 2:20). Second, He commissioned His disciples to proclaim worldwide the Good News of the forgiveness of sins and the possibility of coming under the rule of the King through repentance and faith. They were to make disciples of every segment of the human family (Matt. 28:18–20). His lordship is universal; He must reign until He has put all His enemies under His feet (1 Cor. 15:25). Third, He told His disciples that they were incapable of carrying out this Great Commission on their own. They had to wait for the outpouring of the Holy Spirit. Having stated this, Jesus had completed His earthly ministry (Luke 24:49–53).

Apostolic Teaching and the Kingdom of God

The ascension of Jesus marks the beginning of the reign of the risen Christ. He is now "highly exalted" and the time has come for the magnification of His name and the confession of His lordship (Phil. 2:8–11). Having earlier been "lifted up" on the cross, He now is "lifted up" in glory and begins the work of drawing all people to Himself (John 12:32). By the cross He overcame death; He will now deliver His people from the dominion of darkness and transfer them into His kingdom (Col. 1:13). Although His sovereignty is now hidden from the world and known only to His people, the day is coming when He shall return in power and glory (Acts 1:11). Then every eye shall see Him (Rev. 1:4–7).

The first act of the enthroned King in glory was the creation of the church by the sending forth of the Holy Spirit. This took place on the day of Pentecost in the midst of Jesus' disciples and was in part the issue of their waiting and praying (Luke 11:13). Suddenly the Spirit was there in their midst, fusing them into one body and enabling each and every one to bear witness in a miraculous fashion to Christ's ascension. By their utilization of many languages they were able to demonstrate what the glorious kingdom will be like that final day when the human race, fragmented and defiled by sin, will once again be united in God. "Pentecost marks the beginning of the vast reassembling of the scattered children of God, which the prophets had hoped for and foretold" (Isa. 2:2–3; John 11:49–52).[5] Indeed, Peter specifically identified Pentecost with Joel's prophecy concerning the last days, when all the people of God participate in the confession of His mighty acts. The eschatological summons of the nations had begun. The exalted Christ was the central point about which they began to gather and the Great Commission was thereby demonstrated to be the climax of Jesus' teaching on the kingdom.

It was the apostle Paul who later gave the theological rationale for this interpretation of the Old Testament prophecies concerning the nations. We recall how as a rabbinic Jew he had sought to serve the God of his fathers. He was concerned about sin, righteousness, and judgment. But when he was confronted by the risen Christ on the road to Damascus, he learned that he needed to make a complete break with his futile efforts to justify himself before God through struggling to keep the law. The way to God's presence was through repentance and faith, apart from the law.

When Paul grasped the full implications of this great truth—justification by faith—he began to see that if salvation can be bestowed on the Jews apart from the works of the law, then salvation is universal in its scope and becomes God's gift to all who repent and believe. In Ephesians 3 Paul develops the missiological implications of this gracious provision. He builds his argument on the word "now" (v. 10). *Now* is the time for the inclusion of the Gentiles in the redemptive purpose of God. This is the final stage in His redemptive timetable: the period of the Gentile church. During this era the church is to proclaim the gospel to the peoples of every tribe, tongue, and nation. This is the central priority: today is the day of salvation. Tomorrow Christ's glorious return will usher in the day of judgment.

The Acts of the Apostles records the beginnings of the age of the church. Among other things it contains the record of the first great schism, when the believing church, despite its efforts to continue as God's saving remnant within Jewry, found itself increasingly rejected by Jews and increasingly welcomed by Gentiles. Synagogue separated from church and the cleavage remains till this day. This points up the mystery of unbelief, as well as the mystery of Israel "after the flesh." Down through the cen-

5. Ibid., p. 219.

turies since Pentecost, Israel has continued a suffering presence, exposed to the world's rejection, yet tenaciously clinging to its determination to be a people apart in the midst of the nations. Whereas Paul affirms that it was Israel's hardness of heart that opened the way for salvation to be taken to the receptive Gentiles—and sees in this Israel's unwitting involvement in the redemptive purpose of God—he emphatically states that this rejection of the witness to the Christ is only temporary (Rom. 11:11, 25). Israel shall yet turn to the God of grace and glory, for "the gifts and the call of God are irrevocable" (11:29). "When the pagan world has found its way to the Father's house, Israel will find its way back home, and its return will be a resurrection from the dead. In the apostle's thought, Israel's return to faith will mark the end of time" (11:15, 25).[6]

So then, the baptism of the Spirit on the day of Pentecost was outwardly marked by the same signs of the kingdom that had characterized Jesus' earthly ministry. There were authoritative preaching (Acts 2:37–41; 4:33), the bestowal of the forgiveness of sins (Acts 2:38), the healing of the sick (Acts 3:1–11), and victory over the powers (Acts 4–5). The reigning Christ was the Liberator and Guardian of His people. The Good News of the kingdom meant freedom for the individual believer to live in true community with all of "like precious faith." This meant the spontaneous sharing of material goods with those in need, and reflected the joint participation all had in the Christ in their midst (Acts 2:37–47; 4:23–37). Their acceptance of baptism reflected their involvement in the covenantal stream that identified them as the children of Abraham, and their celebration of the Lord's Supper renewed and nourished their awareness of union with Christ and with one another. They were indeed "of one heart and soul" (Acts 4:32).

It may strike one as strange that the phrase "kingdom of God" is only infrequently found outside the first three Gospels. How are we to account for this? We need to keep in mind the chronological sequence in God's revelation. First, the apostles had, in addition to Jesus' teaching, the reality of His exaltation as Lord and Christ and the activity of the Holy Spirit in their midst. This naturally influenced their references to the kingdom. Second, the author of the Acts, who uses the phrase seven times, increasingly identifies it with the grace of God in salvation which Jesus accomplished by His death and resurrection. The author of Acts uses the term *kingdom* as symbolic of such divine blessings as salvation and eternal life. Third, as the apostles entered the Gentile world they inevitably had to contextualize their message so that it made sense to non-Jews. Kingdom language as Jesus used it could sound politically subversive. Although Pilate had Jesus put to death because the Jewish leaders tricked him into

6. Ibid., p. 242.

doing so, he doubtless saved his own face by making it appear that Jesus was a Zealot. Hence the inscription on the cross: "Jesus of Nazareth, the King of the Jews" (John 19:19).[7] Actually in Thessalonica the apostles encountered difficulty because they proclaimed "another king, Jesus" (Acts 17:7–8). In adapting language and thought forms to make the message clear to Gentiles, it is not surprising, then, that Paul defines "kingdom" not as material abundance—"food and drink"—but as "righteousness and peace and joy in the Holy Spirit" (Rom. 14:17). In this he does not depart from the essence of Jesus' thought; for the kingdom (God's rule over people) is an inner reality to Jesus' followers (the redeemed), made possible by the presence and power of the Holy Spirit in heart and life.

This brings us back to what we earlier noted as the Old Testament's five major perspectives on the coming of the kingdom. In the New Testament Epistles we find these perspectives developed in fulness because of all that Jesus accomplished by His death, burial, resurrection, and the sending of the Spirit.

First, God is sovereign in His kingship. This is now specified to embrace the confession of Jesus as Lord. We preach not ourselves, but Jesus Christ as Lord—this is the heart of the Good News of the kingdom (Rom. 10:9–10; 2 Cor. 4:5). Jesus is the Vice-Regent of the Father: He has conquered all His foes; He has obtained salvation for His people; He now works by the power of the Holy Spirit; His present rule over the redeemed but adumbrates His coming rule over all. The worship of anyone but Him is utterly abhorrent and totally futile. He is Lord of all.

Second, God's sovereign rule demands personal commitment—the sort that arises from a transformed, regenerated heart. The church not only makes the truth of Christ's lordship known throughout the world; in its proclamation of salvation through His name, it issues the call to repentance and faith, the call to conversion—to the deliberate dislodgement of oneself from the solitary throne in his or her heart, so that Christ Himself might be enthroned thereon by the Holy Spirit. Concerning this salvation the New Testament is more explicit: "Any one who does not have the Spirit of Christ does not belong to him" (Rom. 8:9). Indeed, the Christian life involves nothing less than being conformed to Christ (Rom. 8:29). It is for this reason that the missionary mandate is so explicit: not merely the proclamation of the historic fact that "Christ died for our sins in accordance with the Scriptures" (1 Cor. 15:3), but also the need for "making disciples"—the sort of persuasive evangelism that pleads with one and all to be reconciled to God by receiving Jesus Christ (John 1:12; 2 Cor. 5:20). Only those who are new creatures in Christ shall enter the kingdom of God.

7. See Oscar Cullmann, *The State in the New Testament* (London: SCM, 1957), pp. 24–49.

Third, God's subjects must constitute a "servant" community. The church is not the kingdom although the two are intimately related. When Jesus told Peter He would build the church (Matt. 16:18–19), He was speaking of His gathering together a community of the redeemed. They would become a participating fellowship in the sense that as individuals they would submit to God's rule, accept His salvation, and then seek to live and worship in loving, serving humility toward one another. Once united to Christ and to each other, they would lose the right to a separate existence apart from the group. They would exercise the responsibility of discipline within the group to insure it remained Christ-controlled. The Lord in their midst would not only be mighty on their behalf, but through them would also reach out to the unconverted in service and witness.

On the other hand, the kingdom is not the church. It represents the action and rule of God by which He builds and sustains the church. It is prior to the church in the sense that the realities of the kingdom constitute the Good News committed to the church. But the kingdom is always God's. Although the church is of divine creation—in essence it is the body of Christ—it always represents, in part, the human response to the kingdom. Although often flawed, its corporateness is what gives it significance. And its role in society is that of a "serving presence." The rule of God over the lives of its members—also flawed, because God never takes away their free will—challenges them in every aspect of life to affirm His lordship and reflect His concern. Because of this, Christians have come to see that as sons and daughters of the kingdom they have to exceed the Old Testament concern for justice in human society. As the "Lausanne Covenant" (1974) clearly states: "Evangelism and socio-political involvement are both part of our Christian duty. For both are necessary expressions of our doctrines of God and man, our love for our neighbor and our obedience to Jesus Christ."[8]

Fourth, God's sovereign rule is relentlessly resisted and opposed by His people, by the nations that do not know Him, and by the unseen powers. The New Testament is a record of conflict and suffering. Jesus learned obedience through what He suffered (Heb. 5:8). And the church, too, has to experience the sifting of Satan (Luke 22:31) and the testing of fire (1 Peter 1:6–8), that it might be perfected. All this is a mystery. Indeed, the church is a curious mixture of grandeur and misery, and it shall know attacks from within throughout this age. This conflict arises particularly from the cosmic struggle which Christ joined at His cross—when He disarmed the principalities and powers (Col. 2:15). It will continue until He has "put all his enemies under his feet" in the last day (1 Cor. 15:25).

8. "The Lausanne Covenant," in *Let the Earth Hear His Voice,* ed. J. D. Douglas (Minneapolis: World Wide, 1975), p. 5.

This means that Christians are under the obligation of their King to fulfil the role of prophet and reformer in society. He would have them become advocates and defenders of the poor, bearing witness to their misery and calling for the removal of those exploitative actions that have forced them to be poor. Naturally, for Christians to be effective in this demanding role, they must first be victorious in the inner world of their hearts, overcoming the temptations to pride, jealousy, self-righteousness, covetousness, and lust. Through gaining victory over themselves, they will experience Christ's freedom and become indifferent to public opinion and to personal danger. They will then be in a position to recognize that

> the powers are incarnated in very concrete forms. Their power is expressed in institutions or organizations. . . . The battle against these material powers must be fought by Christians. . . . The spiritual warfare they are summoned to is concerned with injustice, oppression, authoritarianism, the domination of the state by money, the exaltation of sex or science, etc. . . . they are to wage the warfare of faith, their only weapons those Paul speaks of: Prayer, the word of God, the justice of God, the zeal with which the gospel of peace endows us, the sword of the Spirit. . . . And if they think this is easy, it is because they know nothing about life in Christ. [Eph. 6:10–18][9]

Indeed the New Testament greatly amplifies the Old Testament understanding of the spiritual warfare precipitated in this fallen world by the advent of the kingdom of God.

Fifth, God's sovereign rule is always directed toward the future. As the church faces the future, it will know much conflict and suffering. This will continue throughout the age because of the church's apostolic calling. Jesus Christ was the first "sent one" (apostle—Heb. 3:1) and He had to endure the cross if He was to liberate the human race from all bondage. The church—both in its congregational structures and in its mission structures—is commissioned to "complete what is lacking in Christ's afflictions for the sake of his body" (Col. 1:24). Individual missionaries—men and women—will particularly know this suffering as they continually remind the church of its essential missionary nature and evangelistic task. They will keep striving to reach out beyond its borders to bring into the church and into God's kingdom the whole world for which Christ died but which does not yet acknowledge Him as King.[10]

And this missionary task will be completed. God will call out His people from the nations. The question is often asked: What delays the return of

9. Jacques Ellul, *Violence: Reflections from a Christian Perspective,* trans. Cecilia Gaul (New York: Seabury, 1969), pp. 163–65.

10. Ronald Bocking, *Has the Day of the Missionary Passed?* (London: London Missionary Society, 1961), p. 24.

Christ? In response some have argued that God delays the day of judgment because He is merciful, not willing that any perish, but that all come to repentance (2 Peter 3:9). Others point to the unfinished mission of the church, arguing that the element which restrains, which prevents the utter collapse of human society and the invasion of Antichrist, is the work the church must do to extend the gospel (2 Thess. 2:6–8).[11] In any event, what concerns us is that God Himself, the Ruler of world history, will finally triumph. The satanic empire will be overcome and the kingdom of God will be fully manifested in power and glory. On this the New Testament is most explicit. The apostle Paul declared that God "has fixed a day on which he will judge the world in righteousness by a man whom he has appointed, and of this he has given assurance to all men by raising him from the dead" (Acts 17:31). This is "our blessed hope, the appearing of the glory of our great God and Savior Jesus Christ" (Titus 2:13). When it takes place, the church in its completeness will know that its missionary purpose has been finally realized. Then, all creation will behold the triumphant Christ delivering the kingdom to God the Father, having destroyed every rule and every authority and power (1 Cor. 15:24).

11. Oscar Cullmann, "Eschatology and Missions in the New Testament," trans. Olive Wyon, in *The Theology of the Christian Mission,* ed. Gerald H. Anderson (New York: McGraw-Hill, 1961), pp. 51–54.

3

New Mission

A Systematic Reinterpretation of the Concepts of Mission

Donald McGavran

Students of contemporary theologies of mission cannot avoid serious consideration of the massive and worldwide program to change the course of Christian mission, the nature of Christian mission, and the theology of Christian mission. Looking at the radically new world which we now see racing ahead to ever new forms and presenting problems which have never been encountered before and thus demand fresh solutions, many Christians have come to the conclusion that a radically new form of mission is required. Indeed, most Christians in most countries of the world would agree that we face new days and must at least devise new programs.

Ernest Hocking, back in 1933, felt this way. In his *Rethinking Missions* he declared that the days of Christianizing the world were over. In the future each religion would reconceive itself in the light of the other religions. The end result, he confidently affirmed, would be something very like the Christian religion, but would not come about by people leaving their own religion to become members of Christ's body, the church.

Till the mid-sixties, each missionary society set its own course, determined its own theology of mission on a biblical base, and allocated missionaries and funds in accordance with its own understanding of God's will and its own assessment of the situation it faced. There were, of course, many variations which arose from denominational, national, or biblical roots. Thus German missions were slightly different from British, and British from American. Roman Catholic missions differed from Protestant and Baptist from Episcopalian. Yet all were united in a common belief that the great goal was to win men and women to faith in Jesus Christ with consequent forgiveness of sins, the gift of eternal life, and gradually thereafter the reformation of society. All were calling men and women from darkness to light and from death to life.

The great gatherings also and the great movements, such as the Student Volunteer Movement, influenced most missions. Political events, such as the tremendous growth of European empires and the establishment of European rule in countries like the Congo or Burma, influenced where missions could go and what they could do. The many-sided missionary movement touched the sending denominations in hundreds of ways and radically changed the international situation. Long before secular modern society began to speak of "one world," the missionary movement was talking about and working toward one world—that intended by God.

Nevertheless, despite these international influences, the essence of mission activity was in most cases derived from biblical foundations. Missionaries went out to obey Christ and preach the gospel to every creature. They intended to carry out the Great Commission and disciple all peoples. They necessarily won converts and established churches. Clusters of ongoing congregations arose and were gradually formed into branches of the church—denominations. The missionaries did this not because any government or sending church told them to, but because this is what God has clearly commanded. The Holy Spirit impelled them to Christian mission of this sort. The dogma popularized by the Student Volunteer Movement—that the great purpose of Christian missions is to establish self-governing, self-propagating, and self-supporting churches—was seldom questioned. The basic purpose was the same for all missions.

While the basic purpose and the long-range goal were the same, the short-range goals were decided by each missionary society and, indeed, by each mission on the field. How much money and how many missionaries were devoted to evangelism, medicine, education, famine relief, agricultural improvement, and so on, depended strictly on the needs of the situation and the judgment of the missionaries concerned. In short, under the overarching basic purpose which arose from biblical foundations, missions were *inner-directed* and remarkably independent and autonomous. Each did what it, under God, thought right. Each missionary did what he thought right.

During the sixties, however, a totally new theory and theology of mission were devised, largely in Geneva, but also in London, Berlin, and New York. This new view was propounded as the only correct, relevant, and adequate theory and theology of mission for our day. It is a very different kind of mission. Harvey Hoekstra calls it "new mission." Although it rises from theological roots very different from those of classical mission, it uses the same key words, systematically redefining them so that they mean something quite different.

"New mission" is now being impressed on all missions and denominations as the one correct mission for our day. Only this mission is relevant. Other views of mission are outmoded, unsuitable, dangerous, and contrary to the will of God. Section Four of the Findings of the Fifth Assembly of the World Council of Churches (Nairobi, 1975) was devoted to suggesting ways in which the educational tools of the denominations can be used to bring the whole Christian world into line with the concepts of new mission. Books, magazines, radio, curricula in theological training schools, themes of and speeches to great gatherings—all these and more are being, and are going to be, purposefully used to press all missionary efforts into this new mold. Professor Kim Sai Tan of Malaysia has written a book on this new program. He has titled it *The Great Digression.*

Believers in new mission who have passed through the training required and voice the new orthodoxy will be given posts of leadership and praised. Those who do not believe in new mission will be ignored, released, assigned to routine tasks, or returned to the pastorate where their opinions on missions will not count. Those who criticize new mission or declare it wrong will be accused of being narrow, divisive, and polemical. They are polarizing opinion. New mission must not be criticized. It is—one might say—the new inerrant revelation, fresh off Mount Sinai. Classical mission was and is inner-directed. New mission is outer-directed, from the top down.

Systematic reinterpretation of the basic concepts of mission is not a game. It is a heartfelt conviction of a large group, perhaps many thousands, which they intend to propagate throughout the entire church. Every branch of the church must be educated to carry on new mission. This reinterpretation is going on apace today and will continue for many years.

New mission can be impressed on Christians today because age-long injustices suddenly seem intolerable in the rapidly developing one world. The physical hunger of multitudes, famines which periodically ravage many regions, and oppression of the masses by the upper classes can be eliminated. Well-fed Christians in Europe and North America look at the poverty-stricken multitudes of so many countries of Asia, Africa, and Latin America and feel troubled. The constant teaching of Marxists, that the real cause of all this inequity is a class-ridden society, influences many Christians. It sounds reasonable. That poverty is caused in large part by the population explosion and by the continuing oppression of the weak in the Third World by the strong who live there is overlooked. Needy children, starving orphans, millions of refugees, drought-stricken areas in which people desperately need food—all these appear to Christians to be remediable problems. In this connection consider the titles of the articles appearing in a recent issue of a Christian magazine:

" 'Disappeared Persons' in Argentina Demand Action"

"1981 Is the International Year of the Child"

"Will Jesus Improve Conditions in Northeast Brazil?"

"Solidarity and Sharing with the Handicapped"

"Support and Political Action for the Poor"

"A Significant Victory for Victims of Famine"

"Hunger and Global Security"

"Organize for Christian Action in Bolivia"

Injustices which for many centuries have been considered irremovable are now being seen as removable. Christians are urged to remove them as the only correct Christian mission today. In too many cases, the gospel of eternal salvation is supplanted by the gospel of temporal improvements. New mission can be impressed on congregations and denominations everywhere, chiefly because the call for action seems so reasonable to such large numbers of Christians.

Imagine that we are seated on the moon, looking at Planet Earth, and that each missionary society in the world and each mission in each country (like the Southern Baptists in Korea, for example) is marked with a glowing light. As each country comes into view, we see it dotted with lights.

Now, further suppose that a green light marks each mission which determines its own theology and theory of mission in accord with the biblical injunctions to proclaim faith in Jesus Christ as the one way to eternal salvation and to disciple all peoples. As new mission comes to be accepted and implemented, the green light turns red.

As we sit on the moon watching the earth, we notice that most of the mainline missions in country after country have already turned red, and that the evangelical missions, one by one, here and there, are beginning to turn. A green light has just turned red, and over there is another. Those missions were inner-directed. They are now outer-directed. New mission has claimed another convert.

Major Emphases of New Mission

Nine main emphases of the systematic reinterpretation of mission deserve mention. They are not the only emphases, but they are prominent in the theory and theology of new mission.

1. *Recognize that a new world order is coming into being and that we can make it a just, peaceful world.* The old era, when countries were separated from each other by weeks, even months, of travel, is gone. All lands are within reach of all other lands. Our magazines and television screens

report affairs in far-off Iran, Namibia, or Argentina as if they were next door—as indeed they are. The empires of Europe have passed away. We live in a world of free and equal nations. But they are not really equal. The people of some nations are wealthy, comfortable, and well-fed. They have tremendous stores of grain and other foods. Very few go hungry. Other nations, to which we can talk instantaneously by telephone, have thousands or millions living in dire poverty. The masses, stimulated by the revolution of rising expectations, battle for their rights. Dictators rise to power. Governments fall. Guerillas wage war on the police. Communism comes to power in one land and is ejected from another.

Underneath the turmoil is a steady conviction that if men and women will but work at it, a just, peaceful, and righteous world can be brought into being. This conviction may be in error. Possibly turmoil is the lot of the human race. But the increasing chances that turmoil will trigger atomic war and render much of the globe uninhabitable lend urgency to the feeling that something must be done soon. The human race must work out a new world order or perish. This is one of the main emphases of the advocates of new mission. Conversion mission, they say, winning people from other religions or from no religion to ardent faith in Jesus Christ, is too slow and too other-worldly.

2. *Stress development, social action, and liberation.* Particular problems must be attacked and visible needs met. By development of a backward country its people can be helped to get more out of their land, manufacture, or trade. Advocates of social action say the lot of the people can be improved through changing social structures. Let us take away the land from the rich and give it to the poor. "The land belongs to whoever plows it" is a most welcome slogan to landless labor working the fields of the wealthy. Let us open our eyes and see that multitudes of men and women, children of God, are in bondage almost as demeaning as slavery. What is needed is not eternal life, but freedom from present ills. Do not talk about pie in the sky by and by. What we want is pie right now.

3. *Deemphasize reconciliation with God and push for reconciliation with other humans.* This principle is seldom stated so bluntly. Rather, it is maintained that since God cares for all humans, any real reconciliation with God will consist in reconciliation with them. If you bring an offering to the altar and there remember that your brother or sister has something against you, leave your offering there. Go and be reconciled. Then come and offer your gift.

Marx's teaching that all religions have been invented to keep the poor satisfied with their wretched lot has been a powerful factor in bringing about an uneasy conscience among well-to-do Christians. It is well to remember that the labors of generations of missionaries which induced millions of their supporters in the West to regard Africans and Asians as their brothers and sisters also reinforced the feeling that temporal improvements in the family of God are the really important task today.

4. *Talk little about liberation from sin and much about liberation from poverty, oppression, and the rule of foreigners.* Everything which demeans the human being must be opposed. Talk little about personal sin and much about corporate sin, particularly those corporate sins which the powerful and wealthy are likely to commit. Emphasize corporate rather than individual salvation.

"Salvation Today" was the main theme of the great Bangkok meeting of the World Council of Churches. It was given a biblical flavor by the simple device of quoting extensively from the Old Testament narratives which tell how God saved His people from hunger, the sword, and captivity. He gave them a tangible, visible, here-and-now salvation.

5. *Discontinue or scale down the program of sending missionaries to proclaim to the ends of the earth the Good News that through faith in Jesus Christ sins are forgiven and men and women become new creatures in Him.* Cease trying to win the world to Christ. Instead, in cooperation with men and women of good will from all religions and ideologies, inaugurate a great campaign to create a brave new world in which is no poverty, ignorance, or injustice.

In all the denominations which espoused new mission with enthusiasm, the sending of missionaries promptly declined. Many of the young churches entered a static period where their efforts were directed inward, to sectional strife, struggles for power, and learning how to manage themselves. There are some brilliant exceptions, but in general, the espousal of new mission by national denominations has not led to any notable surge of effective evangelism by missionaries to unreached segments of the world's population.

6. *Discontinue the program of multiplying churches among unbelievers in favor of creating just structures of society and improving existing Christians and congregations.* To date, the fruits of new mission have not been great new advances toward a righteous society, nor the establishment of thousands of new congregations where men and women gather around God's Word to learn how to make God's will done on earth as it is in heaven. Far from it. The fruits have been church politics, struggles for power, and constant leanings on Western churches for any ethical campaign. True, there has been a commendable sending of missionaries by African, Asian, and Latin American churches; however, this has happened not because of new mission, but in spite of it. The sending of sons and daughters of the young churches has not been an emphasis of new mission.

7. *Capture the apparatus and treasury of the missionary societies and use them not to proclaim the Good News and multiply churches, but to further revolution, and to express solidarity with groups and nations struggling against oppression.* When missionary societies are captured in this way, the number of mis-

sionaries sent promptly diminishes. A mission board which in 1950 sent out 1,600 missionaries sent out 349 in 1981. One which thirty years ago sent out 422 recently sent out 65. The missionaries sent overseas are not evangelists but specialists who work there for a few years and then come back. Their boards say that the day of sending missionaries is largely over. Developmental specialists, builders of new dwellings, administrators of famine and disaster relief, and technicians who will help in the revolutions which are bringing in the new world order—these are today's missionaries. Those who can organize labor unions to fight for a more equitable distribution of the profits of manufacture are the kind of missionaries needed in the modern world.

8. *Capture the theological seminaries and thus insure that those who are about to enter the ministry share the great goal of creating a new world order in which justice and peace prevail.* Train the leaders of Third World seminaries in Western seminaries which have caught the new vision and revised their curricula in line with the theory and theology of new mission. See that articles in seminary journals espouse new mission and the new world order whose coming is so patently urgent. Make funds available so there can be study and research on topics like development, human rights, and the classless society.

9. *Use the key words of classical mission but in a new sense.* The words *mission, evangelism, conversion, salvation, liberation, revelation,* and *church* form a major part of the advocacy for new mission; but they no longer mean what they have meant for the last nineteen hundred years. To a study of these words we now turn.

Redefinitions by New Mission

The advocates of new mission are redefining and using the key words of classical mission in unbiblical, humanistic, and Marxist ways. Each redefinition is carefully tied to the Bible by proof texts, most of which are taken from the Old Testament. This is to show that the new meanings are really biblical. And some texts do in fact support them, but they are not the mainstream of biblical teaching. As the key words have been reinterpreted, they form no part of Jesus' teaching or of the practice of the New Testament church. For example, "liberation" for our Lord and for Paul was not liberation from Roman rule, but liberation from self and sin. We shall briefly describe the new interpretation of each term and point out why it cannot be accepted.

1. *Mission.* Probably the greatest single change in the definition of missiological terms has come with the recent expansion of the word *mission* to include everything the church ought to do and everything that God wants done both inside and outside the church. The purpose of this

reinterpretation is simply to seize for social reconstruction the millions of dollars raised each year for discipling the nations. Given the new interpretation, all these millions become available for bringing in a new world. It is difficult to imagine a more effective way of ending efforts to carry out the Great Commission.

The classical meaning of mission is "evangelism and service across cultural barriers intended to bring men and women to a knowledge of the Savior and to persuade them to believe on Him and become His followers in the fellowship of the church."

Worship, caring for the needs of those who are already Christians, buying robes for the choir, supporting the work of reformers, and defending civil rights are all excellent activities; but they are not classical biblical mission. Contributing ten thousand dollars to the defense of Angela Davis is not mission. Fighting behind Che Guevara may be a fine thing to do, but it is neither what the mission apparatus was created to do, nor what it is funded to do.

2. *Evangelism.* Evangelism has been radically reinterpreted to mean the act of changing social structures. When you evangelize individuals, we are told, you make them Christians. When you evangelize social structures, you make them Christian—more just, more equitable, less oppressive, more brotherly, less racist. Note that in this case being "Christian" has ceased to involve personal belief in Christ; rather it implies an ethical way of life.

What shall we say in answer to this reinterpretation? The Christian maintains that all changing of social structures in the direction of equity is good. It is a foretaste of the kingdom of God. Some Christians may be called to such activity. If so, praise God. But to call this "evangelism," thereby denigrating classical biblical evangelism and church multiplication, and seeing people as suffering only from this-worldly deprivation (food, shelter, decent wages, health), is to paint a truncated and worldly picture. It accords neither with common sense nor with the Bible.

3. *Conversion.* The word *conversion* has classically and biblically meant "turning from other gods, self, and sin to belief in Christ as Lord and Savior and becoming a member of His body, the church." New mission goes into detailed investigation of the Hebrew and Greek words associated with "conversion" ("turning," "turning again," "repentance"). It finds out (wonder of wonders) that they mean simply turning from one thing to another. That is all. So new mission teaches that to be converted means to turn from low views of the human race to high views, from belief in Hitler to belief in democracy, from a class-ridden to a classless society. Conversion in the classical sense is seldom mentioned by new mission, which maintains that merely turning from the world to Christ is *not* the meaning of conversion.

What shall we say in answer to this reinterpretation? Christians should not accept this biased redefinition. It does not square with what conversion has always meant from the day of Pentecost onward. The basic meaning of biblical conversion is *conversion to Christ*. When the apostle Paul stood before Agrippa, he declared that the Lord Jesus had appeared to him and said, "I am Jesus. . . . I have appeared to you for a purpose. . . . I send you to open their [the Gentiles'] eyes and turn them from darkness to light . . . so that, by trust in me, they may obtain forgiveness of sins, and a place with those whom God has made his own" (Acts 26:16–18, NEB). Once they trust in Christ, the Bible is quite clear, men and women receive forgiveness of sins and power to live the ethical life, both on individual and corporate levels. They become better individuals, better citizens, abolitionists, liberators, prohibitionists, freedom fighters, and servants of the poor. Conversion is the root. The resulting good actions are the fruit.

4. *Salvation.* In the New Testament "salvation" means the conferring of a new eternal status on those who believe in Jesus Christ. At once, in the twinkling of an eye, they become the redeemed, new creations in Christ. Their burdens roll off at the foot of the cross. They walk light. They have been reborn. Their souls have been saved. Growth in grace follows. They are bit by bit conformed to the divine pattern.

According to new mission, which defends its position by liberal use of Old Testament texts, salvation means *salvation today* and consists of a series of this-worldly improvements. The human race is saved from poverty, oppression, ill health, poor eyesight, dehumanizing toil, racist scorn, illiteracy, hunger, and so on. New mission says little or nothing about the soul or eternal life.

Biblical missiologists cannot accept this misinterpretation. It substitutes fruit for root. It doubts that there is any immortal soul and hence centers attention on what is visible. Despite its claims, it is not holistic, for it leaves out the divine dimension, the soul. It abundantly quotes the Old Testament but seldom cites the New.

More must be said. In effect, new mission declares, "What is needed is *not* pie in the sky by and by. What is needed is pie right now." Biblical Christians object strongly to the word *not*. Biblical Christians affirm boldly (and will go to the stake affirming it), "There *is* pie in the sky by and by. That is God's truth." Biblical Christians go on to say, "Because eternal life is the inheritance of Christians, they can and will attack evil conditions here on earth more vigorously, purely, and effectively." Granting that the body is real and temporal improvements are desirable, biblical Christians nonetheless remember that the Lord Jesus Christ said: "What does it profit a man to gain the whole world and forfeit his soul? For what shall a man give in exchange for his soul?" (Mark 8:36–37, NASB). Good temporal improvements must not replace concern about eternal life.

5. *Liberation.* "Liberation" is a glorious biblical word. The Bible frequently speaks of liberty, freedom, and release: the year of release; the liberty of the sons of God; when the Lord liberates you, then you are truly free; the truth sets us free; God liberated the Hebrew slaves from Egyptian bondage.

In biblical thought, the human race is in bondage to sin and is liberated by belief in Jesus Christ. Paul was bound and in prison, but he never exhorted his disciples to liberate him. Nor did he advise the Jews to throw off the Roman yoke. Paul lived in days when, among Jews, liberating the homeland was the compelling national cause; but he never mentioned it. Neither did the Lord Jesus Christ.

Bruce J. Nicholls notes that "liberation theology has no place for the transcendent and the power of God to change human nature and create a new society . . . the kingdom comes when poverty is eliminated. The new man is the political humanist and the Kingdom of God becomes the kingdom of man." Nicholls attributes this indefensible stance in part to an erroneous hermeneutic. The modern-day social context is allowed to determine the interpretation of the ancient text. For example, in liberation theology the poor mentioned so often in the Gospels are interpreted to mean only

> the powerless and voiceless classes of society, the economic poor . . . the powers of exploitation are interpreted to mean the transnational corporation, governments, and the churches themselves and their missionary organizations where they have joined in exploitation and impoverishment. . . . Evangelicals . . . cannot equate this message of social justice with the Gospel itself. The Good News is first and foremost reconciliation with God and then compassion for the suffering and justice for the oppressed in society. . . . To those who put themselves under the authority of Scripture . . . the principle of Sola Scriptura continues to stand as the sole measuring rod of all theological systems and methodologies.[1]

6. *Revelation.* Christians believe that it has pleased almighty God to reveal Himself to the human race in and through the Bible. This is called special revelation to distinguish it from general revelation. God's self-disclosure is His sovereign prerogative. Why He chose to reveal Himself to an obscure people in a tiny country, Christians do not know. That He did so, they do not doubt.

New mission, arising on the *Shaken Foundations* which Peter Beyerhaus describes so well,[2] is most ambiguous about revelation. New mission quotes

1. Bruce J. Nicholls, "Theological Reflections on Melbourne" (1980), pp. 4–5.
2. Peter Beyerhaus, *Shaken Foundations: Theological Foundations for Missions* (Grand Rapids: Zondervan, 1972).

the Bible profusely when it suits its purpose to do so, but neglects totally those sections of Scripture which are damaging to new mission. Such a self-serving use indicates that new mission obviously does not accept Scripture as authority at all. For new mission, Scripture apparently is a compilation of contradictory voices out of many cultural conditions across ten centuries of time. God, new mission affirms, on occasion speaks above this compilation. When we read it devoutly we hear His voice. This is simply a way of saying that the Bible is a mine of useful quotations from which we can quarry whatever suits our need at any particular time.

Evangelical missiologists cannot accept this low view of Scripture and of revelation. It totally neglects the unity of Scripture and does not really accept that God is the Author. He has not, advocates of new mission hold, revealed Himself in an authoritative book. The Bible is simply what people in different cultural circumstances have perceived of God. Such a view falsifies the Bible.

7. *Church.* The final key term which is being radically reinterpreted is *church.* During the sixties the conciliar churches and the World Council of Churches repeatedly said that the church is a mere instrument used by God to bring in a better world. This is definitely not the classical understanding of the church. When the church is no longer regarded as the body of Christ, the unique and exclusive community of the people of God, reconciled to Him through faith in Jesus Christ, the covenant people and a royal priesthood, then the kingdom of God is considered merely the emergence of "a better world," and often a classless society. The church becomes one among many agents of change.

We all rejoice at the evidence that God does use many secular and religious powers and structures to bring about a more humane society. However, this is not to be identified with the forgiveness of sin and the gift of eternal salvation granted to those who believe on the Savior Jesus Christ. Nor must the somewhat more righteous social order toward which we move be identified with the true kingdom of God in which every citizen recognizes Jesus Christ as King. The world—even an ethical world—is not the church and never can be.

Reactions to New Mission

Any discussion of this massive reinterpretation, which has been so carefully planned and so deliberately carried out, will rouse reaction. Both those who advocate new mission and those who do not, on reading this chapter, will raise questions. We will evaluate six common reactions.

1. There are some people whose reaction will be disbelief. They are unaware of the process we have been describing. As they consider our picture of new mission, they are likely to exclaim that *no such clearly-*

thought-out theory and theology of mission can possibly have been framed. Let me speak to their difficulty. It was my own. I know it well. Until January 1968, while I read voluminously in missionary writings of many denominations and many councils, I was of the opinion that the many viewpoints being expressed amounted to minor differences on isolated issues. After all, mission is an enormous enterprise. Many viewpoints can be expected. Then in January 1968, as I read the preparatory documents for the Fourth Assembly of the World Council of Churches to be held at Uppsala, I suddenly realized that a whole new theory and theology of mission had been created and were being seriously advocated for worldwide adoption. The articles and books I had perused set forth not suggestions for a few isolated changes, but a whole new system which was cohesive and well thought out.

Let me assure the readers that new mission is a well-constructed creation. It is carefully crafted by able people who feel that their new theory and theology of mission are urgent needs of today. They expect to carry the churches along with them by using the key words *world evangelization,* but in the new sense of "world reconstruction."

2. There are some people whose reaction will be a spirit of conciliation and compromise. *Granting that there are two main tasks, let us not fight each other. There must be no polarization.* The task is essentially one. It is the great *Missio Dei,* the mission of God. *Both tasks, all tasks, must be done.* All are part of what God wills to happen here on earth.

This misses the point. "All" is exactly what new mission intends *not* to do. Mission from antiquity has been doing all. The budget of most missions has been used for development, service, education, medicine, agriculture, and evangelism; but the primary goal has always been propagating the gospel, spreading the Christian faith, and persuading men and women to become disciples of Christ. New mission speaks a great deal about holistic mission, but it intends very little conversion evangelism. By holistic mission it means changing the social structure. When it talks about "industrial evangelism," it means obtaining better working conditions and higher pay for factory laborers. This is the new "evangelism." As leaders switch to new mission, Christians and churches which have supported the evangelization of the world are giving millions less. They do not like this kind of "mission." Seeing the loss, new mission is now reluctantly building in a little conversion evangelism.

3. Another reaction to new mission is to call for adjustment in mission. *It is obvious that we face new conditions. We must adjust mission to meet them.* We dare not oppose progress. We do not want poverty. There is gross injustice in the world. The church must fight for justice, bring in a spirit of fellowship, and end oppressive structures of society.

No one doubts that we face a new world. The revolution of rising expectations is a patent fact constantly announced in the papers and shown on the television screen. We are acutely conscious of living in a world where Marxism keeps the attention of the masses focused on their rights and establishes dictatorships of the proletariat in as many countries as possible. Witness Angola, Ethiopia, Nicaragua, Yemen, and Afghanistan. Everyone knows that dehumanizing social structures are a common part of the world. All leaders of Christian mission know that new measures are urgent. Christians have been and are devising new measures right and left. The School of World Mission at Fuller Theological Seminary has been particularly bold in proposing innovative policies.

But what new mission is proposing is not the best way of bringing in a just society or of meeting new situations. New mission, in effect, denies the seriousness of personal sin, the urgent need for reconciliation with God, the absolute need of an infallible revelation from God, and the tremendous deprivations inherent in not knowing the gospel. New mission is strangely silent about eternal life. It says little or nothing about belief in Jesus Christ as the only way to obtain eternal life and the best way to obtain a more ethical society here on earth. New mission asks us to meet new conditions while paying little attention to the reconciliation of men and women with God. Classical evangelical mission, on the other hand, *is* meeting these new conditions while remaining focused on eternal life. New mission meets these new conditions while resolutely turning away from holistic mission. New mission is a new ball game, with new priorities, new and different theological emphases, and radically new interpretations of the key concepts of the missionary enterprise.

4. Another reaction is to accept new mission on the grounds that it furthers the work of classical mission. *Missions have always been heavily engaged in social service and social action. New mission simply extends the list. Why object?*

Missions have indeed been heavily engaged in social action and service, but never as a substitute for evangelism and church multiplication. Evangelicals have been active in true holistic mission—a sound combination of evangelism, social service, and social action, all aimed at discipling *panta ta ethne.* All these activities are carried out in the service of the long-range goal of multiplying soundly Christian churches.

Furthermore, what new mission proposes is not a more realistic approach, but a radically new and theologically different approach. The protest at Nairobi, which the architects of new mission did their best to silence, is abundant evidence that multitudes within the conciliar churches consider new mission theologically unsound.

5. Some people will regard new mission as the only safe and practical way in which to proceed. *In the world of newly independent nations, only this humanistic approach has any chance of succeeding.* Conversion missions are

part of the old imperialistic order and are impossible today. Evangelism by native citizens of a country is one thing; evangelism by missionaries from another country is an entirely different matter.

This reaction has some weight. At first thought, we tend to agree with it. Certainly, abrasive slogans and arrogant, aggressive campaigns to erase all other religions will run into trouble. The huge Muslim majorities in Bangladesh and Indonesia do not like American missionaries winning Muslims to Christ. It is easy for sovereign nations to deny visas to foreign missionaries, whether they come from Korea or Kansas.

On second thought, however, this reaction does not carry so much weight. Bangladesh and Indonesia can be reminded that religious freedom is one of the grounds on which the new world advances. Muslims are busy evangelizing in the United States. The Black Muslims build mosques in Detroit and Washington. Hindu rishis and maharishis convert thousands of Americans and take back to India millions of dollars. The new world coming into being will, above all else, be a world in which free interchange of ideas is encouraged. Persuasion and counterpersuasion are desirable characteristics of the good life everywhere. They are keys to progress.

That new mission is a better approach than classical mission because it is safer must be rejected on biblical grounds also. Our Lord did not command His followers to bear witness to Him as long as it is convenient and safe. Rather He said, "They will set upon you and persecute you. You will be . . . put in prison; you will be haled before kings and governors. . . . Even your parents and brothers, your relations and friends, will betray you. Some of you will be put to death; and all will hate you for your allegiance to me" (Luke 21:12–17, NEB). The spread of any new concept is seldom painless. The old yields reluctantly. Religious change, like any other change, is often painful. There is no way of bringing in the kingdom of God without sweat, toil, tears, and blood.

6. Finally, some people will assert that the dividing lines are not as clear-cut as we have claimed. *It is not true that the adherents of new mission (the villains) are all to be found in the conciliar churches and the adherents of classical mission (the heroes) are all in evangelical churches.* In conciliar churches and missions, many are distressed at new mission and protested it at Uppsala, Nairobi, and Melbourne. Furthermore, in evangelical churches and missions some are swinging over to the position that liberation and humanization are sufficient goals of mission.

It is true that many ecumenicals object to new mission, while some evangelicals carelessly espouse it. But the number of ecumenicals and evangelicals on each side of the question is not the issue. New mission substitutes ethical action (which in itself is good) for world evangelization. We hold that to replace discipling the peoples with any good thing (worship, Christian education, kindly relationships, just international dealings, the building of beautiful churches, or maintaining efficient social-service centers) is a mistaken policy. In its anxiety to achieve an excellent short-range goal, new mission neglects or omits the essential long-range goal. It minimizes the discipling of *panta ta ethne* for which the gospel itself was revealed by command of the eternal God (Rom. 16:26). Social engineering among unredeemed men and women of any race or nation yields only a thin trickle of advance. But carried on among households of God, social engineering yields a deep flood of advance. If we want a new humanity, a Christian social order, we must establish millions of soundly Christian churches, constantly engaged in winning their own children and others to conscious dedication to Christ. Otherwise our vaunted new world order, run by natural men and women whose hearts are full of selfish ambitions, jealousies, and hatreds, will greatly resemble the old world we know so well.

Systematic reinterpretation of the main concepts underlying Christian mission is an important part of our contemporary experience. In accordance with a worldwide plan this reinterpretation of mission is being implemented through the vast educational machinery of many denominations and their seminaries, conferences, councils, magazines, and books. Leaders of Christian missions must carefully evaluate this reinterpretation. Some of it they will welcome. Some of it is good. There are indeed new conditions we must face. Some of it they will reject. They will not deify the world. Scripture must continue to be the only ultimate authority. Short-term goals may change, but the long-term goal, the ultimate destination, must remain the same. The human being is both body and soul. Eternal life is the most basic need of mortals. Those who have through faith in Christ received eternal life are in the best position to strive for abundant life for their neighbors and their world. Reinterpretation there must be, but it must be done within the confines of the biblical revelation. God's message in Scripture must be taken seriously and as a whole.

4

The Current Conciliar Theology of Mission

Donald McGavran

$\mathbf{W}$e now turn to consider the conciliar theology of mission, that expressed and taught by the World Council of Churches and promoted and carried out by denominations affiliated with it.

"Theology" is a word of many meanings. Dictionaries define it in several ways. Theology may be "a study of God and His relationship to the human race." It may be "a disciplined reflection on the Word of God," "a rational interpretation of the Christian faith," or "a body of religious opinion distinguished by some characteristic emphasis." Systematic theology can fall under any one of the first three definitions. Specific theologies (e.g., a theology of pain, of work, or of mission) fall under the fourth definition. Theologies of mission, then, are not complete theological systems but are rather bodies of theological opinion distinguished by concern for mission.

Theologies of mission should be advanced on biblical rather than humanitarian grounds. The essential question in evaluating a theology of mission is: Is it truly biblical? Are its main emphases those of the whole Bible, that great revelation of God's will for the human race? Or does it take some one emphasis of Scripture and elevate it to a position of supreme importance? In short, is it true to the mainstream of biblical teaching on God's redemptive concern for persons and nations?

In its widest terms a theology of missions is then a body of theological reflection on Scripture distinguished by its concern for the work Christians do among nonmembers. Since what that work is has been defined differently by different camps within the total Christian movement, understandings of mission are strikingly diverse. As we have seen, for some Christian mission is world evangelization. For others it is helping to bring into being a more Christian world order. Each group maintains that what it conceives of as mission is pleasing to God and supports its position

62

by biblical quotations and theological affirmations, that is, by a theology of mission. Inevitably the theologies have marked differences.

In this chapter we shall consider the conciliar movement's understanding of mission as "the humanization of society." This body of theological opinion was set forth most explicitly by the Fourth Assembly of the World Council of Churches (Uppsala, 1968). The World Council feels that its missionary task is to work for a worldwide peaceful, just, and participatory society. It should be noted that we shall be discussing not the World Council's initial approach prior to Uppsala, but rather that body of contemporary theological opinion which maintains that God desires actions and programs designed to reform the structures of society along lines agreeable to Him.

The roots of this theology go back to the twenties and thirties but the current theology took definitive shape only in the mid-sixties. By 1965 it was beginning to be set forth as *the* theology of today's mission, the kind of mission which all Christians ought to carry out. During the late sixties and seventies this kind of mission and this kind of theology were preached in ten thousand pulpits and advocated in the leading magazines of many denominations. They became the official position of the conciliar camp. To proclaim this kind of mission, allocate budgets in accord with it, and train missionaries and leaders of younger churches who would carry it out were considered correct. To send such missionaries abroad (not many, but a few) was deemed intelligent, contemporary mission.

Although we disagree with this concept of mission, we shall attempt to be fair in portraying it. Every line of the portrait has been repeatedly checked across two decades against the documents available to all. We are reminded of the portrait of Winston Churchill which in the early sixties Parliament had commissioned a famous artist to paint. When the picture was hung in the House of Commons, a fury of protest was unleashed. It showed a haggard old man. Everyone was outraged but the artist maintained (correctly, we believe) that his was a portrait, not a caricature, of Churchill in his last years. We are going to present a portrait of the conciliar theology of mission. Many who have not studied the documents and followed the course of events closely will be surprised at the radical differences between new mission and classical mission.

It is essential to distinguish between a theology of mission and praiseworthy acts of the church. The great emphasis which the twentieth-century church has been laying on peace, fellowship, and justice is beyond question highly desirable. Christians praise God that conditions which for centuries have been considered the inescapable lot of the human race are now being seen as remediable, and are being remedied. Truly they must be abolished. For example, for thousands of years strong tribes and nations have conquered the weak and often exterminated them. All the land was owned by the king and his lords. Those who worked the land did not own it. They were landless peasants. Every region of the world was periodically ravaged by epidemics of smallpox, plague, cholera, malaria, and other diseases. The vast majority of people lay chained by illiteracy and had no rights. Famines swept whole populations and millions died. Poverty was the inescapable lot of most persons. Slavery was common. Wars were endemic. On every continent armies marched to and fro leaving rapine, death, and destruction in their wake.

Every one of these terrible curses of the human race is now seen to be remediable. Tremendous new ways of utilizing various sources of energy—fossil fuels, sun, wind, and atomic power—are being discovered. Medicine has eradicated smallpox and is being used to wipe out other diseases. A more equitable distribution of land, intelligent use of fertilizers, and advanced agricultural technologies give hope that poverty can be ended. Scientific utilization of the land and advanced modes of transportation make it possible to prevent famines. The population explosion (which the removal of these curses has made inevitable) can be ended by family planning. Wars of extermination—though still waged, as in Cambodia in 1978—are increasingly condemned by world opinion. Wars of conquest elicit tremendous opposition—see the outcry over the Soviet occupation of Afghanistan. Social structures which guarantee political power to all citizens (democracy) and which guarantee equal economic power to all (Communism) are being widely advocated and put into operation. The sinful and rapacious nature of the human race makes both democracy and Communism operate with marked inefficiency at times, but there is hope that these weaknesses can gradually be eliminated.

The curses under which men and women have so long labored must be removed. This chapter describes the theological justification of the many activities carried on by Christians and non-Christians to remove these curses, which is being set forth by conciliar churches as the only theology of mission acceptable today. It speaks to the contemporary agenda of the world. It is consonant with the signs of the times. We turn then to a consideration of the current conciliar theology of mission, which justifies activities that help remove the physical, social, economic, and political scourges no longer deemed to be unavoidable parts of human existence.

Abundant documentation is available. Conciliar leaders have written most extensively of their new approach to mission and have supported it with extensive theologizing. Anyone can read their descriptions of what mission is now supposed to be. More than fifteen years of publications are open to inspection. To what activities grants have been given, often in the face of opposition, is open to review. To what concerns conciliar leaders have given active support and to what they have given passive consent are easily discovered. What they have favored and to what they have been indifferent are not secrets. The material is so vast that in these interpretive chapters we will not make use of laborious line-by-line quotations, but rather of summaries of major trends. Back of each summary lie scores of typical statements.

The chief difficulty in portraying the conciliar theology of evangelism is the abundance of the material and the inclusiveness of official pronouncements. Sometimes strong pronouncements advocating two opposing points of view have been printed—and then only one side implemented. For instance, at Iberville in 1963, the World Council of Churches convened a Consultation on Church Growth, to which it invited representatives from all six continents. The Iberville Declaration on Church Growth is a powerful defense of evangelism and church growth. But after publishing it in the *Ecumenical Review*, those forming the conciliar theology of mission never once referred to it. What the World Council has implemented has been the diametrical opposite of church growth. One must, therefore, continually ask, "What is the mainstream of the conciliar theology of mission, and what are the peripheral concerns voiced now and then to satisfy fringe groups?" One must not ask, "What used to be true about the conciliar theology in the forties and fifties?" But rather, "What has been true in the late sixties, the seventies, and early eighties? How do conciliar leaders see mission priorities today?"

Different approaches to mission are continually being suggested. As a matter of fact, in early 1981, Emilio Castro printed in the *International Review of Mission* a plea for classical evangelism; but whether the conciliar camp ever ardently commits itself to it remains to be seen. We hope it will result in a shift in the conciliar theology of mission away from those axioms to which conciliar Christians appear fervently committed.

The Main Axioms of the Current Conciliar Theology of Mission

1. *Mission is everything God is seeking to do in the world.* God loves the world. He created it. He is distressed over its groaning in travail (Rom. 8:22) and desires ultimately to redeem and perfect every aspect of the whole world. The church's mission should reflect His concerns and actively relate itself to His sense of priorities. Christians must not suppose that God is concerned primarily with them—the church—and after that with the world. No. The right order is God–world–church. The church is to regard itself as only one of God's instruments for remaking the world. Indeed there are times when God deliberately gives higher place to secular liberation movements and political revolutions than to the church.

2. *God is at work among all peoples, in all lands, bringing in His reign of fellowship, justice, and peace.* He is removing oppression, breaking the chains

of racism, eradicating poverty, and rooting out diseases of all kinds. God is against everything which debases and demeans men and women.

God is smashing the selfish concepts which underlay former imperialisms and totalitarianisms. He is warring against all forms of injustice, particularly those imposed by the "have nations." These ruled the world formerly through the might of their armies and navies. Now they rule through the might of their economic systems, their finely tuned, computerized ways of production, and their clever manipulations of world trade. God is against all this and demands that His church speak and act strongly against it. Being prophetic in this sense and doing justice are the essence of the church's mission today.

3. *God is at work among men and women of all religions.* Modern mission therefore listens to adherents of other faiths to hear what God is saying to them and through them to us. The old idea that Christians are to proclaim to adherents of other religions the one way God revealed through Jesus Christ and the Bible must give place to the new idea that all religions have something to contribute to the wisdom of the world and to the salvation of the world. Christians will contribute what God has said to them, and others what God has said to them. All must listen as well as speak. God is saying something to Christians through Hindus, Muslims, and Marxists too.

God saves adherents of every religion, though Christians, knowing the way God has spoken to them and believing that it has universal applicability, will share what God has said and done in Christ. *Mission, therefore, is dialogue among equals.* Communication is a two-way street. Monologue is a poor system of communication. Respect for the integrity of the other person compels Christians to listen first and then tentatively and kindly to present the Christian way as the one they know.

God does not intend the church to incorporate the whole of the human race. It is to be but a small part of the world's population, illuminating the whole. Triumphalism, the belief that all will become Christians and other religions will be replaced, is wrong. The church is not sent out to conquer the world for Christ, but humbly to serve.

4. *Evangelism is that part of mission which is concerned with changing the evil structures of society so that the will of God for humankind may be done.* Evangelism is not leading slaves to become Christians, but rather, doing away with slavery. The purpose of evangelism is to help bring in God's kingdom of righteousness and peace. This is much more important than establishing new congregations amid the old, unjust structures of society. Emilio Castro, the executive secretary of the Division of World Mission and Evangelism, says, "Evangelization is essentially related to the struggle for social

justice in the world."[1] Does he mean that when Hindus or Marxists become Christians they have taken the longest single step toward a just society which it is possible to take? We fear he does not. The impression he gives is that correct biblical evangelization addresses itself directly to social structures and that becoming a Christian means smashing evil social structures. This seems to be his intent. In a paper prepared for the World Conference on Church and Society, he says, "We often hear the assertion: Change a man's heart and society will change. The fallacy of the argument is immediately apparent. No such thing as 'man's heart' exists apart from man's relations. . . . I exist . . . in a whole collection of relations. . . . To change my heart means, in some measure, to change those relations."[2]

The fact of the matter is, of course, that individual conversion and change of social structures are both used by God to effect improvement in earthly conditions. Individual conversion frequently leads to change of social structure. But change of social structures in and of itself seldom, if ever, leads to individual conversion. Beyond improvements in earthly conditions, and, according to Christ, vastly more important, is the question of eternal life. Evangelical Christians hold that evangelism must be holistic. It must be concerned with the total person—soul as well as body. Really it should be more concerned with soul than with body, because it is largely as the soul is saved, as one becomes obedient to Jesus Christ and filled with the Holy Spirit, that the body and society can be substantially improved.

5. *The church is one church everywhere and should help men and women transcend their sinful and selfish ethnic and personal hates, prejudices, and prides.* The church should therefore be emphasizing everywhere the things which unite the human race. Conversion from other religions to Christianity divides families and peoples, and should therefore be deemphasized. All kinds of activities for the common good unite the followers of varying faiths and thus form the proper employment for Christians. They are the essence of new mission.

Particularly vicious is that form of so-called evangelism which addresses itself to nominal Christians of another church. No matter how nominal they may be, if they are on the rolls or on the baptismal register of some church, then no other church should even attempt to convert them to Christ and incorporate them in its fellowship. Missionaries in particular must avoid conversion of Christians from one denomination to another.

6. *Salvation is salvation today.* Salvation is the essence of what mission

---

1. Emilio Castro, Editorial, *International Review of Mission* 64 (July 1975): 240.

2. *Drafts for Sections: Uppsala '68* (Geneva: International Review of Mission, 1968), p. 37.

is about. Though there is such a thing as eternal salvation, it must not be emphasized. What this day demands is that men and women forced to live under intolerable burdens—political, economic, educational, and social—should be freed to become fully human. They should be able to live abundant lives. They should be treated fairly and regarded as equal children of God, entitled to all the good things of life. Race, creed, color, and other such considerations should play no part in the degree of good life available to them. It is God's will that all men and women experience salvation today.

7. *Conversion is turning from all that limits life, all that is contrary to God's will for His people, to all that ennobles life.* This embraces clean air and water, freedom of thought and speech, full democratic control of the political machine, equal access to raw materials and to the processes of manufacture, an equal place in the sun and equal respect in the assembly of the nations.

Conversion should not be narrowly conceived as turning from Baal to Jehovah or from one system of beliefs concerning God's will in regard to moral and religious matters to some other system. Rather conversion is concerned with the things that really matter. Conversion must cease to be to a system of beliefs, such as God and eternal life, which can never be proved. Conversion should rather be to useful actions which truly liberate people.

8. *The supreme task of the church today is to liberate congregations and denominations from their egocentricity and mobilize them for new tasks in the world.* On the basis of the gospel, the church must make visible the outlines of a renewed, just, and righteous society. The church must act intelligently and responsibly in modern society. It must face the real world of today and take part in the interplay of forces which are actually shaping the contemporary generation.

Innumerable examples of how this axiom is actually being carried out can be given. The budget distributions of the World Council and its affiliates afford abundant illustrations. Social justice is an emphasis which good Christians believe is needed in the modern world. To work for this-worldly liberation is certainly one of the tasks of the church. But evangelicals doubt it is the supreme task. Conciliar leaders, on the other hand, state it again and again as the supreme task. Often it is the only task they mention. At Nairobi and Melbourne, when classical evangelism was mentioned, it was immediately linked to temporal improvements. It was held that unless the church works largely for this-worldly improvements, its call to God's eternal salvation will be neither credible nor honest.

We must be specific. Hence we call attention to Willem Visser 't Hooft's *Has the Ecumenical Movement a Future?* Visser 't Hooft has convictions on evangelization, but when he sums up eight great tasks of the church, he does not mention evangelization. He declares that the churches must engage in mutual aid, help those in need, create a responsible society, enhance the position of the laity and women in the church, demand the freedom of the churches vis-à-vis all ideologies, carry on development aid, champion human rights, and improve race relations.[3] *Eight great tasks the church ought to do—and never a word about evangelizing the three billion!*

Visser 't Hooft gives five reasons for church unity[4]—yet there is no mention of what our Lord in His high-priestly prayer specified as the basic reason for unity—that "the world may believe that thou hast sent me" (John 17:21). On the same page Visser 't Hooft mentions various tensions which have existed between churches and the World Council— caused by differing stands on capitalism and Communism, the Suez crisis, South Africa, racism, and the like; but not a word about the tension between the Geneva Secretariat and those many churches which believe that classical evangelism should constitute a chief and irreplaceable part of the work of the world church.

Visser 't Hooft goes on to say, "We need impatient people who call for boldness, imagination and forward looking hope in action."[5] Yet he gives us no reason to believe that he is thinking of advocates of evangelism and church growth, who on occasion have been markedly impatient in calling for bold action. He says the Council should "help the Churches crystalize soundly based conviction on great human issues," but he does not indicate that among these "great human issues" is the need of three billion souls to believe on Jesus Christ and be saved.

If this shortcoming is characteristic of Visser 't Hooft, who does have convictions about sinner-converting, church-multiplying evangelism, it is much more evident in the writings of Philip Potter, Emilio Castro, and other exponents of the conciliar theology of mission, which has dominated WCC-related denominations from 1966 to the present, and seems likely to continue influential. As we have said before, the leading advocates of the conciliar theology of mission are strangely silent in regard to eternal life, the Great Commission, conversion evangelism, winning souls to Christ, and multiplying churches on new ground. In 1973 at Bangkok, the general secretary of the World Council ruled out any discussion about the three billion—declaring it was "totally irrelevant."

John Stott (surely one of the most irenic and ecumenical of all evangelicals) said at Nairobi in a masterly understatement, "It seems to many of us that evangelism has now become eclipsed by the quest for social and

---

3. Willem A. Visser 't Hooft, *Has the Ecumenical Movement a Future?* (Atlanta: John Knox, 1976), p. 47.
    4. Ibid., p. 48.
    5. Ibid., p. 52.

political liberation. . . . We question whether the WCC has any longer a heartfelt commitment to world evangelization."

In 1975 Peter Wagner and I addressed an appeal to Philip Potter, general secretary of the World Council. Three paragraphs of that appeal read as follows:

> As we read the preparatory documents put out for the Fifth Assembly, your historic 1974 address to the Berlin meeting of the Central Committee,[6] and dozens of other important conciliar papers, we search for and do *not* find any WCC department which has been "unflinchingly active in meeting the human need" of salvation from eternal condemnation. We would like to see the Assembly "agonizing" over new programmes to bring a hundred million nominal Christians into living relationship to the Lord Jesus, or to bring the secular masses in Sao Paulo into joyous dependence on the Holy Spirit, or to lead twenty thousand Chokosis in eastern Ghana into baptized Bible-obeying discipleship to Christ, and on and on. We look in vain for some "new and imaginative programmes" having to do with multiplying churches among the 80 million landless Harijans in India of whom at least three million, searching for new life, have renounced Hinduism and converted to Buddhism in the last few years.
>
> You pen a few words about the reality of eternal salvation. For example, "God's justice manifests itself both in the justification of the sinner and in social and political justice." But that is the last we hear about the justification of the sinner! The WCC seemingly plans to spend no blood, sweat, toil and tears to help sinners realize their needs for justification. . . . You write, "We must seek under God's grace . . . to undertake the differentiated mission of God." But that part of the differentiated mission which has to do with the spread of the Christian Faith, the multiplication of Christian churches, the baptism of millions of penitent believers, is never mentioned.
>
> Many of our number roundly declare that the conciliar position is rational only on the grounds of a frank disbelief in the whole biblical affirmation of eternal salvation, a change of status achieved in the twinkling of an eye, through belief in Jesus Christ, and resulting in a gloriously more human life and an enormously tougher concern for our suffering brethren. We do not want to share this opinion, so we plead from you a new and unequivocal declaration of concern for the eternal salvation of the 2.7 billion unreached people of the world.

Despite these plain words and this courteous plea—to say nothing of the impact which the Lausanne Congress on World Evangelization had on the Christian world—the preparatory documents for the Fifth Assembly of the World Council of Churches were not modified in the least. Had it not been for the pressure of large numbers of delegates to Nairobi who insisted on classical biblical evangelism, Nairobi would not have mentioned it. In the end, Nairobi inserted into the record five small resolutions on evangelism—perhaps 1 percent of the total linage produced by that

---

6. Printed in the *Ecumenical Review,* October 1974, pp. 563ff.

great world conference. To date the World Council has not to our knowledge added one penny to any of its allocations for gospel-proclaiming, sinner-converting, church-multiplying evangelism, nor begged its affiliated churches to thrust workers into earth's many white harvest fields. We state this with regret, but fear it is true.

The conciliar theology of mission is voiced not only at the highest levels but in thousands of pulpits across the world. The pastor of a prominent church in California recently preached on the wrath of God. Noting that it is not in harmony with contemporary culture to think of God as an angry God, he asked:

> How can we live in God's world and claim to be God's people,
> and let half of His children starve . . .
> AND NOT ANGER GOD?
> How can we live in God's world and claim to be God's people,
> and let hundreds of millions remain illiterate . . .
> AND NOT ANGER GOD?
> How can we live in God's world and claim to be God's people,
> and observe hundreds of millions treated as inferiors . . .
> AND NOT ANGER GOD?

But he never asked,

> How can we live in God's world and claim to be God's people,
> and not tell three billion lost people about God's Son, our Savior . . .
> AND NOT ANGER GOD?

Though often unrecognized, the conciliar theology of Christian mission has become common in many congregations, and is contributing not a little to the decline of their concern for evangelism and to the decay of their mission structures also.

It is in this particular axiom of the conciliar theology of mission, which sees social justice as the supreme task of the church, that the difference between new mission and classical mission is most apparent. For thirty years before 1960, the Presbyterian Church in the United States of America declared that "the supreme and compelling purpose of the Christian mission to the world is to proclaim Jesus Christ as God and only Savior and to persuade men to become His disciples and responsible members of His church." The conciliar theology of mission, which took hold after 1960, declares that the supreme purpose is working for social justice and Christian unity. These are, it believes, the true goals of Christian mission. If before 1960 the major denominations had made out a list of eight great tasks of the church, they would certainly have placed world evangelization high on that list. But after 1960 the denominations associated with the World Council omit it entirely or add it as an afterthought.

When the intolerable burdens from which people suffer are cata-
logued, classical mission cannot but place inability to hear the gospel—to
become disciples of Jesus Christ—at the top of the list. Since 1960 the
conciliar theology of mission has passionately described all kinds of this-
worldly burdens, but has rarely included among them being a non-Christian, an idolater, atheist, secularist, or Marxist.

9. *Horizontal relationships are much more important than vertical.*

> We have lifted up humanization as the goal of mission because we believe
> that more than others it communicates in our period of history the mean-
> ing of the messianic goal. In another time the goal of God's redemptive
> work might best have been described in terms of man turning toward God.
> . . . The fundamental question was that of the true God and the Church
> responded to that question by pointing to Him. It was assuming that the
> purpose of mission was Christianization, bringing man to God through
> Christ and His Church. Today the fundamental question is much more
> that of true man and the dominant concern of the missionary congrega-
> tions must therefore be to point to the humanity in Christ as the goal of
> Mission.[7]

Among the hundreds of other writings and speeches stressing or assuming this axiom, we cite only Donald Shriver's 1977–1978 report as president of Union Theological Seminary (New York). His sole reference to
world mission is a brief comment about exploring "the most appropriate
ways for the seminary to relate to churches outside the USA." But focusing
merely on such horizontal relationships is at best severely truncated mission.

As a result of wholehearted acceptance of this axiom, the total corpus
of those biblical doctrines which require classical mission in every age
(from the days of the apostles till today) has either not been mentioned
by the proponents of new mission or has been radically reinterpreted to
mean reconciliation of human beings with each other rather than with
God. In other words, those doctrines have been bent to mean horizontal
reconciliation or have been ignored.

The conciliar theology of mission is a radically new theology which has
burst upon the scene. While it uses many of the key words of the classical
theology of mission, it uses them in a totally different way. The World
Council counts on its tremendous educational apparatus and its prestige
to bring the churches over to its new theology of mission. Sadly, the six-
teenth- and seventeenth-century Protestant confessions of faith are more
similar to the theological commitments of the Roman Catholic Church of
those times than the present conciliar theology of mission is to the way in
which classical mission has been understood and carried out by the churches
and missionary societies over the years.

7. *Drafts for Sections,* p. 34.

Lay Christians as well as church leaders, missiologists, and missionaries will have to judge whether they approve of these vast changes. It is their lives and the life of their world which are at stake. It is their money which is being spent. It is their children and their billions of neighbors who will be affected.

By emphasizing the totally different nature of the conciliar theology of mission, we do not in the least mean to imply that to act justly toward all people, to work for peace, to battle for human fellowship, to root out racism, and to labor for all kinds of temporal improvements are evil or unnecessary activities. Quite the contrary. We hold that they are good. We engage in them ourselves. But to substitute them for the basic doctrines, the main thrusts of Scripture, and to maintain that in these days the basic purpose of mission is not Christianization, not bringing men and women to Christ, but rather humanizing men and women everywhere with no regard to what they believe—all this, we maintain, is wrong. This is the great deviation of our day. It is our hope that the church will reject the erroneous reconceptualization, extracting from it what is good and attaching its worthwhile insights to the biblical position, which requires classical mission.

To substitute social action for evangelism is a capital error. The true and historic Christian teaching is that one must first turn to Christ and then will increasingly work at changing evil social structures. Once men and women have been won from the world and incorporated in the body, they can readily be aroused to work at curing the social, economic, and political diseases of the human race. They can be and are being aroused. But to call such arousal "evangelism," or to encourage people to take social action before telling them of Jesus Christ, is to put the cart before the horse. No, it is even worse than that. It is to "preach another gospel" (Gal. 1:7–9).

In 1975 Peter Wagner and I compared the theologies of classical and new mission. There is no reason to change any part of that assessment.

Two radically different systems of doctrine are battling for acceptance.

The one believes that the Bible is the inspired, authoritative, infallible Word. The other believes that the Bible is the words of men through which God speaks on occasion.

The one believes in eternal salvation, as well as temporal improvements. The other believes that temporal improvements are certain, but beyond them we are in the realm of speculative opinions.

The one believes that the Church is the Bride of Christ. The other, that the Church is one of God's many instrumentalities to bring about a juster social order.

The one believes that no man comes to the Father but by Jesus Christ as revealed in the Bible, and consequently proclaims Him as divine and only Saviour. The other believes that the Cosmic Christ has spoken and is speaking in all religions and consequently dialogue with other religions is the correct way of mission.

The one believes that the Kingdom of God will come only as God Himself destroys the enemies of mankind at the last day, and that until then only limited justice and righteousness are possible. The other believes that a new, just world order can be brought about by the cooperation of men of good will in all religions and ideologies.

The list of contrasts is much longer. A division as deep and lasting as that which took place in Europe in the sixteenth century may be imminent but we hope it can be avoided.[8]

10. *As regards evangelism and mission, the supreme authority in each country is the church of that land.* This axiom, which is aimed squarely at Western imperialism, has some strengths. Its anticolonial thrust is plain. Its concepts were framed in the thirty years immediately succeeding the breakup of European empires. It is quite true that contemporary mission can no longer be thought of as the Christian West carrying the gospel to the non-Christian East. The church, not the mission, is certainly the final authority in its own area. The axiom's emphasis on self-government is desirable and ought to encourage churches in every land to initiate their own missionary labors.

The axiom also has some grave weaknesses. It implies that mission is not to be carried out by Christians of one land to non-Christians of another. Paul ought not to have gone to Rome unless the church there had invited him. Also, in view of the many denominations which make up the church of today in almost every land, this axiom seems hopelessly simplistic. According to it, it would be impermissible for German Christians, let us say, to send missionaries to the United States, unless the missionaries were requested by the American church and agreed to work under its authority. One at once asks, Which denomination is to be regarded as the church in America? The Church of Rome is, of course, the largest denomination in America. Must, then, Lutherans in Germany who wish to send missionaries to a neglected pocket of Germans in Wisconsin ask permission of the Roman Catholic Church in the United States?

To use a germane illustration: in 1981 the Free Methodist Church in India was a denomination of fewer than 2,000 communicants in the eastern end of the state of Maharashtra. According to the axiom under consideration, the Free Methodists of the United States, a small but ardent denomination of 70,000 communicant members, ought not send missionaries to any section of vast India (700,000,000 souls) without the express permission of the Free Methodist Church of eastern Maharashtra. Once there, let us say in Himachal Pradesh, they would work under the authority of the tiny denomination of fewer than 2,000 members eight hundred miles to the south. And while the Indian Free Methodist Church ought—according to this axiom—to exercise authority over any American Free Methodist missionaries, it would have no authority at all over Roman Catholic or Baptist missionaries sent in from other nations.

More serious is the denial of religious liberty which this axiom entails. The modern world believes passionately that, when it comes to freedom of religion and freedom to propagate one's highest and best beliefs, no limitations are to be set. Neither the other religions nor one's own religion, neither the Roman Catholic Church nor the Protestant Church, ought to deny anyone the right to obey God by proclaiming Him in his or her own way. The erroneous doctrine of Sun Myung Moon, the Korean whose cult is spreading in the United States today, is a case in point. While his doctrine is obnoxious to Christians, they ought not, by force of law, keep him from proclaiming it and building up his church.

It is unthinkable for small denominations of a hundred thousand or a million to claim the right to exclude brother and sister Christians. They themselves would not exist, new denominations would never have been formed, if governments, churches, and missionary societies had not stood on the principle of freedom of religion.

Furthermore, while the conciliar theology of mission insists vigorously on this axiom, the conciliar forces during the last fifteen years have not been practicing it. On the contrary, they have used their international educational apparatus and their prestige to influence national denominations in all six continents in favor of new mission. They have vigorously propagated what Kim Sai Tan of Malaysia has called *The Great Digression.* The conciliar theology of mission has been piped into all channels of communication—magazines, broadcasts, seminary curricula, international gatherings—so effectively that it has rapidly become very widespread.

Section Four of the report of the Fifth Assembly of the World Council is devoted exclusively to suggesting ways in which the new theology can be taught to conciliar churches everywhere. When it comes to the new theology of mission, the supreme authority would appear to be not the national churches, but the official line laid down by Geneva and the mainline denominations in Europe and America. It seems as if the only correct theology for the last years of the twentieth century is not that determined by the national churches, but by the World Council. One wonders if this is not the latest form of imperialism.

Nonetheless, the axiom under consideration (like many of the others) has values. Foreign missionaries no doubt did in some ways exercise too much control on the denominations of Asia, Africa, and Latin America. To end foreign control over strong national churches is good, but removing foreign control must not mean chaining all sending churches and societies so that they cannot send missionaries to evangelize any portion of the three billion unless some local national church asks them to come and work under its control. Paul courteously tells the churches in Rome that he is coming. He does not ask their permission.

What must be said again and again is that the only authority in matters of faith and practice is the Bible, and the living Lord and the Holy Spirit understood in the light of the Bible. Neither London, nor New York, nor Seoul, nor Calcutta can be accepted as authority. Only the Holy Bible read by, debated by, understood by, and *agreed on by the church* can be accepted as authority. It is still the only rule of faith and practice.

"Agreed on by the church." What church? The answer to this must be, in the first instance, the church in every place. The interpreter of the Scriptures cannot be a foreign church. It must be a national church. Only a national or particular church can know enough of the local culture to make the right decisions. But these decisions must be defended, not by appeal to local culture or belief, but by appeal to the Bible. *The authority is the Bible,* in the light of sound interpretation throughout the ages.

A problem arises, however. The national decisions of some branch of the church may be in error. It is quite possible for some branch of the church (let us think of the Episcopal Church in the United States) to make a pronouncement about ordaining homosexuals as priests. The church universal in all six continents on biblical grounds regards this as quite wrong. So, in the second instance, decisions of national churches should be reviewed, and approved or condemned, as the case may be, by the universal church, on the basis of its understanding of the Bible.

It would be possible for some branch of the church in India (say the Church of South India), facing the problem of the caste system and the task of encouraging and perhaps enforcing fellowship among its members, to rule that it is necessary to condemn the practice of endogamy in the church as sin. "Christians," it might declare, "ought to marry across caste divisions. Christians of the Syrian ethnic unit ought to marry Christians of Naga or Shudra or Madiga background." Let us assume that this action in the first instance seemed correct to the Church of South India. But in the second instance, as this remarkable new departure was reviewed, let us assume that the world church, observing that no such regulation appears in the Bible, were to demur and say, "We believe you are in error. Fight all behavior which works against fellowship. You have abundant scriptural warrant for this. But to make the practice of endogamy a sin, punishable by excommunication, this, we believe, is not justified by the Bible. We urge you to reconsider." Such a procedure would be normal and in full accord with the historic function of the church universal vis-à-vis particular churches.

We conclude, then, that the axiom that each denomination in its own country is the supreme authority has values, but must be carefully circumscribed to protect freedom of conscience, to guarantee maximum proclamation of the gospel to non-Christians in all six continents, and to secure a faithfulness to the Bible which the Christian religion must practice if it is to remain the Christian religion. Each of the axioms we set forth previously might be similarly analyzed as to its strengths, its weaknesses, and the forms in which it might be useful to churches which count the Bible as the ultimate test of all such ideas and practices. Readers might very well carry out these three steps with each of the ten axioms of the conciliar theology of mission.

An Official View of the Conciliar Theology of Evangelism and Mission

As missiologists try to frame a biblical theology of mission and evangelism and to find their way around in the maze of opinions, half-truths, emotional reactions to today's oppressions, and philosophical meditations on the relationship of nations and religions, they will discover many different descriptions of the theology of mission held by conciliar leaders. Enormous confusion is part of the present-day thinking.

Our selection of ten axioms which in varying combinations are found in most formulations of the conciliar theology of mission ought to be regarded as but one attempt to describe the fluid, rapidly moving scene. The conciliar theology of mission will appear in one guise if voiced by a leading protagonist of the Faith and Order Movement. It will appear in a different guise if voiced by a missionary serving at the Geneva headquarters on the Commission on World Mission and Evangelism. If voiced by a Methodist leader, the conciliar theology of mission will have marked differences from what it would have if voiced by Bishop Paul Verghese of the Syrian Orthodox Church of Kerala. Nevertheless, we believe that the ten major axioms are a fairly accurate summary of the general tenets of the conciliar theology of mission.

It is fitting at this point to refer to an official description of the conciliar theology of mission, specifically an abridged version of a speech given by Philip Potter, general secretary of the World Council, to the Synod of Bishops of the Roman Catholic Church meeting at Rome on October 11, 1974. Speaking on "Evangelization in the Modern World," he summarized the conciliar theology of mission. Readers will observe that while Potter uses his own vocabulary and thought forms, the substance of what he says is similar to what we have set forth.

Potter devotes the opening of his address to the old theology of mission held by the Council. He quotes reports of the First Assembly in 1948, reports of the Second Assembly in 1954, and the minutes of the Central Committee in 1960, amply proving his point that "*the raison d'être of the church is evangelization.*"[9] Up until 1960, evangelization meant conversion evangelism, bringing men and women to faith in Christ and membership in His church. The quotations Potter cites prove beyond the shadow of doubt that before 1960 the World Council was strongly committed to that understanding of evangelization.

After discussing the old theology of mission, Potter develops what evangelization means *today*. He nowhere says, "The old concept of evangelization is now outmoded and we at Geneva have developed a brand new concept"; but that is what must be concluded. (It is possible that there may have been an explicit statement to that effect in the unabridged speech.)

Potter's major point, stated clearly three times, is that "the main focus of our concern . . . is to discover what the evangelistic task is in today's world." This is but a rhetorical device. Potter was speaking in 1974. Since 1966 he and the secretariat at Geneva had known perfectly well and in great detail what they had in mind whenever they spoke of "mission today" and what its supporting theology was.

The general secretary then emphasizes that Christian mission must be carried on in *today's* world. He describes various "signs of the times"— secularization, attempts to make life more humane, the discovery of a new asceticism in regard to the development and sharing of the world's resources, the creation of a just and classless society, and challenges by young people to the demonic structures of society. According to Potter, these and similar characteristics of contemporary society ought to determine what mission today should be. As humble servants and a minority in the world, the churches ought to read and act in accordance with these signs of the times. "It is possible to be sensitive to the natural traditional phenomena around us and yet be insensitive to the new and challenging issues of life and death significance for us." Clearly Potter believes that the whole church will someday see Christian mission as Geneva does, but at present there is a very human and natural time lag. "Give them time," he seems to say, "and they will see these very things, and define mission as we do."

Having noted that all the signs of the times constitute a preparation for "evangelism" and that humanity as a whole realizes that it cannot complete the task by itself,[10] Potter goes on to say that under these circumstances the *only* way forward is by means of costly dialogue, which takes others (including their peculiarities) with radical seriousness. He

---

9. Philip Potter, "Evangelization in the Modern World," *International Review of Mission* 64 (July 1975): 315.
10. Ibid., p. 317.

affirms that the gospel will take different shape as it arises in different cultures. Potter may be saying what most missionaries have been saying for a long time, namely, that the church in every culture, while remaining firmly within the authority of the biblical revelation, will have an individuality distinguishing it from the church in all other cultures. But, on the other hand, he may be saying that God is at work among adherents of all religions, and that some new synthesis of insight, to which Christian mission should be friendly, will develop from many religions and ideologies. "The only way forward is by dialogue." Dialogue is being substituted for proclamation and persuasion. Readers will remember axiom 3 (p. 66), which surfaces again and again in a thousand different costumes in conciliar writings.

Potter then stipulates that the evangelizing church should do two things. First, it should make its base of evangelization the local church. This apparently means no more missionaries evangelizing out beyond the local church. Thus, even if local congregations in Southern California are not adequately evangelizing the millions of Spanish-speaking Americans there, most of whom are either very marginal Christians or thoroughgoing materialists, it would be wrong for Mexican Christians to send in missionaries to do the job. Axiom 10 is clearly in Potter's mind. Even God ought not to send in anyone; only the congregations of Southern California should do that. Yet many of them are sleeping. If *they* do not awake and Potter's advice is followed, millions will not hear the gospel.

Second, the evangelization, which the church is to carry out in its own neighborhood and among people marked by its own particularities, must take into consideration the whole existence of the persons and the groups being addressed. In short, it must be holistic evangelism. Plainly put, it must work primarily to relieve poverty, racial discrimination, injustice, and oppression (axioms 2, 6, and 8).

Potter's concluding remarks voice an axiom which we have yet to describe. It plays an important part in the conciliar theology of mission. Let us call it axiom 11. Evangelization is credible only if those evangelizing live as flaming Christians. Since it is now the whole church evangelizing, *evangelization will be credible to those without faith only when all Christians are enormously concerned about removing the injustices and oppressions which exist in all countries in great measure.*

Conciliar writers repeat this axiom again and again. It is a refrain of the conciliar credo on mission. Let us consider its strengths, its weaknesses, and the form in which it can be useful to any biblical church.

An old proverb says, "Your acts shout so loudly that I cannot hear your words." Obviously, when the gospel is proclaimed by kindly, honest, industrious persons, full of the joy of the Lord and certain about eternal verities, it is more believable than when it is proclaimed by dishonest rascals and hypocrites who know nothing of the inner peace and joy which Christ gives to those who love Him. Christians (missionaries and others) who are deeply committed to God, know their neighbors well, live in harmony with the local culture, serve others, and have their welfare at heart, inevitably are more effective than those who do not manifest these qualities.

On the other hand, if uncritically accepted, axiom 11 has great dangers. It might render a church smugly content to do no evangelism. "We are not good enough yet," it might say. "Wait until we get renewed. Then we will become credible." The axiom thus can readily become an excuse for inaction. The fact of the matter is that the gospel is always proclaimed by fallible human beings, sinners on the way to Zion. They always make mistakes. Their churches are never free of quarrels and jealousies. They never have a completely adequate understanding of the Bible.

In this connection it is noteworthy that the early church experienced its first great growth while Ananias and Sapphira belonged to the body, and while all its members (including the apostles) believed that Gentiles should not hear the gospel. It was a monoracial church for many years and suffered from a certain chauvinism. The record says plainly that—despite the Samaritans and Cornelius—the early Christians spoke the Word to none but Jews (Acts 11:19). Yet they formed a true church and their numbers grew greatly. The secret lies in the fact that the Bible states explicitly that we are to proclaim not ourselves, but Christ. We are earthen vessels. We proclaim the Great Treasure.

Down through history, also, the great advances of the church have been brought about by small groups of warm-hearted, specially committed men and women. Their proclamation of the gospel was doubtless hindered by the sinful conduct of their fellow Christians; but they proclaimed Christ, and Christ shone through. The sinful conduct of their fellow Christians did not keep them from proclaiming the Good News. And when people believed, they were baptized and added to the church. On theological grounds, therefore, as well as practical, the axiom that the gospel is credible only when all Christians are enormously committed must be judged as error. Nevertheless, there is a modified form in which this axiom can be useful to churches which hold to the biblical concept of mission:

> There should be ceaseless efforts everywhere to fulfil the Great Commission—by the whole church, by societies of the warm-hearted, and by individual Christians led by the Holy Spirit, remembering always that where the conduct of the proclaimer and persuader is pleasing to God, the labor will appear more *credible* to those who listen, and God will bless it more abundantly.

The conciliar theology of mission has been formed in the midst of an enormous revolution, under the impact of several world-changing forces, any one of which by itself would have provoked a crisis. Inevitably those who have labored to hammer out a new germane theology of mission have made mistakes, overstated obvious truths, and indigenized so vigorously that the end results have damaged world evangelization and hindered carrying out the Great Commission.

We shall see, therefore, a gradual swinging back into more biblical orbits. The emotional nationalism of the Latfricasian churches and the guilt complexes of the Eurican churches and missionary societies will moderate. We shall think our way through to more reasonable and biblical positions. The three billion—shortly to become four billion—will be evangelized and the injustices and oppressions of the world will be combated. Christians will come to the highly defensible position that the more Christians there are and the more they believe the Bible and are indwelt by the Holy Spirit, the more likely it is that a just and peaceful society will, to some degree at least, be achieved.

Christians should thank God for the conciliar leaders' intelligent reflection on the Christian mission. The secretariat at Geneva has a great advantage in that it includes representatives of Latfricasian churches. Today the opinion of national churches from all six continents is highly valued. Every effort is being made to hold the whole together. A degree of insight impossible in former times is now possible.

However, Christians should also pray to God that the aberrations of the present conciliar theology of missions will be speedily corrected, that the evangelization of the world will receive at least half the time, attention, staff, and money which are provided by the affiliates of the World Council. Christians should pray that the conciliar theology of mission will take the Bible much more seriously than it has in regard to the lostness of men and women who have yet to believe in Christ and the sufficiency of His atonement. And that the churches of the world will press forward to a new degree of ardor and faithfulness in the discipling of the multitudinous unreached peoples of earth.

Till the ship returns to an even keel, evangelical Christians must do two things. First, they must constantly plead with their brothers and sisters in the conciliar ranks to take eternal salvation with biblical seriousness, and to develop a strategy which builds such seriousness into their *budget and staff allocations*. Second, they must withhold funds from conciliar organizations which do not sufficiently stress world evangelization. They will give these funds to those missionary societies, committees, and organizations which are multiplying churches of Christ around the world. The peoples of earth must be discipled. It is God's will.

5

Conciliar Perspectives

The Road to Reconceptualization

Arthur F. Glasser

Tracing the understanding of the Christian mission within the conciliar ecumenism poses some temptations to the unwary evangelical. The evangelical can easily underestimate the complexity of the task and make superficial or simplistic judgments. Evangelical writings, one often hears, reflect a "serious lack of direct and specific references to official ecumenical documents and representative writings . . . much of which flatly contradict the conservative charges." Or, "they have wrongly assumed that all advocates of ecumenism think alike, even on major issues."[1] Indeed, every so often a doctoral dissertation appears which exposes the inaccuracies, oversimplifications, and misconceptions found in evangelical writings on ecumenism.

We must respond to openness with openness, seeking to be both fair and irenic. Our opposite numbers who defend the new understanding of mission that has emerged within the World Council of Churches (WCC) have been willing to admit, in all fairness, that there are "acute defects and dangers in ecumenical thought and action."[2] They recognize that an evangelical critique cannot be expected to rely for evidence upon official pronouncements and representative writings alone. They admit ecumenism is an elusive target. Ambiguities are encountered again and again as one seeks to ascertain what the conciliar movement really stands for in regard to such issues as the nature of evangelism, the call to conversion, the values in non-Christian religions, the mission of the church, the role of mission agencies—in short, the successive issues that have dominated the ecumenical debate on world mission and evangelism over the years.

1. Harold Christian Andreas Frey, "Critiques of Conciliar Ecumenism by Conservative Evangelicals in the United States" (Ph.D. dissertation, Boston University, 1961), pp. 210, 212.
2. Ibid., p. 233.

In examining these basic issues as debated within conciliar gatherings, we trust that we shall exhibit a truly Christian spirit, chastened by our awareness that the issue is not between Christians and non-Christians. For Jesus Christ is freely confessed as Lord both within and without the conciliar movement.

Uneasy Orthodoxy—1910 to 1952

At the turn of the century, few Christian leaders seemed to challenge the bracing, evangelical simplicities of the Student Volunteer Movement (SVM), later reflected in the World Missionary Conference held at Edinburgh in 1910. We begin with the SVM because of what it represented. Its logic was that the gospel is true. It is true for all. To withhold the gospel from any segment of the human race is to regard that segment as inferior, its people as not worthy of being given an opportunity to enter the family of God. Through the SVM's promotion of the regimen of daily prayer, Bible meditation, and deliberate reflection on the spiritual needs of the many peoples making up the non-Christian world, it became the "senior department"—almost an elite presence—within the various interdenominational Student Christian Movements (SCM) of the World Student Christian Federation (WSCF). SVM members were not satisfied with the call, "Give your hearts to the Lord Jesus." Their concern was to press Christian students to take the further step of giving their lives to His service. Intercessory prayer for the spread of the gospel dominated SVM gatherings. By 1905 the WSCF claimed 100,000 members in forty countries;[3] its very worldwideness was uncritically regarded as a demonstration of the universal validity of the Christian faith. The WSCF was dominated by the ardent traveling secretaries of the SVM with their challenging watchword: "The evangelization of the world in this generation."

Many have commented on the virtual impossibility of overestimating the importance of this vigorous student movement in terms of its influence on a whole generation of church and mission leaders. Its organization, spirituality, and theology remain "extremely significant for an understanding of the processes of evangelism in the twentieth century"[4]—particularly within the conciliar movement, which has been greatly influenced by these student organizations. And yet, "the watchword" was a dead letter by 1919. The SVM disappeared in the 1930s and the SCM today is little more than a publishing house. How are we to interpret what appears to

---

3. Eleanor M. Jackson, *Red Tape and the Gospel: A Study of the Significance of the Ecumenical Missionary Struggle of William Paton (1886–1943)* (Birmingham: Phlogiston Publishing/The Selly Oak Colleges, 1980), p. 38.

4. Ibid., p. 19.

us as a terrible erosion of commitment to the basic components of biblical Christianity?

On this point Eric J. Sharpe and many others warn us against being captured by stereotypes as we seek to understand the shifts in the conciliar movement's theology of mission from 1910 to the present.[5] It is ever so easy to simplistically identify a distinctive of each successive conference of the conciliar movement's missionary arm, the International Missionary Council (IMC, formed in 1921), as contributing in some way to undermining the commitment of the church to mission as biblically understood and historically practiced (by Protestants). One has but to read carefully the conference reports and their subsequent official expositions to see how complex were the debates and how broad were the differences within each grouping of participants, whether evangelical or liberal, neo-orthodox or neoliberal. True, certain themes tended to dominate each conference, but the pressure of external considerations as well as the variety of theological positions held by the participants all served to contribute to the development of whatever consensus emerged from each separate conference. Indeed, the perusal of this vast literature gives one considerable pause and often prompts the question, "What would I have said had I been there?"

One can make a case for the thesis that from 1910 to the Korean War and the IMC gathering at Willingen, West Germany (in 1952), the great majority of Protestant missionaries were committed to the essential task of preaching the redemptive gospel, making disciples, and planting churches. Indeed, as late as 1960 Lesslie Newbigin, then secretary of the WCC Commission on World Mission and Evangelism (CWME), could affirm without fear of contradiction:

> When we speak of the mission of the Church we mean . . . preaching the Gospel, healing the sick, caring for the poor, teaching the children, improving international and interracial relations and attacking injustice—all of this and more can rightly be included in the phrase "The Mission of the Church." But within this totality there is a narrower concern which we normally speak of as missions . . . the concern that in the places where there are no Christians there should be Christians. . . . Foreign missions is the concern that Jesus should be acknowledged as Lord by the whole earth.[6]

However, despite this affirmation—with which evangelicals would heartily agree—there was even then a great deal of restlessness beneath

5. Eric J. Sharpe, "New Directions in the Theology of Mission," *Evangelical Quarterly* 46.1 (1974): 10.

6. Lesslie Newbigin, "Mission and Missions," *Christianity Today*, 1 August 1960, p. 23.

the surface in most mission agencies. The reasons for this are not hard to identify. They involved both external and internal factors.

External Factors

Three external factors are important. First, two world wars had ruthlessly demonstrated the moral bankruptcy of the West. Gone forever was the myth of the superiority of the so-called Christian nations. Their racial pride, their toleration of social injustice and economic deprivation, their widespread spiritual poverty had a negative influence on the missionary movement. How could it have been otherwise? Western missionaries were themselves conscious of the economic and social distress in their homelands. Many became increasingly pessimistic about the drift of the world, especially when they realized that it was the folly of their national leaders that had largely caused all this worldwide suffering, disruption, and malaise. And they became increasingly aware of the failures of their churches too. Significantly, William Paton, a key IMC leader, felt that from 1918 to 1936 his main role in India seemed to be "going around encouraging disheartened missionaries."[7]

Second, the peoples being evangelized were beginning to acquire a new awareness of their national identity and pride. They no longer felt themselves inferior to the West. Indeed, they knew only "rising expectations" as their leaders increasingly called for the sort of political activity that would eventually enable them to throw off the yoke of Western domination. In his extensive review of the IMC gathering at Jerusalem in 1928, Jerald Gort writes:

> The colonial legacy **of rac**ist domination was now beginning to give birth to bitter voicings of **frus**tration, to mordant denunciations, rebellion and demands for justice and self-determination—in society at large but also in church and mission. Leaders of the so-called younger churches were very much in the vanguard of this struggle. And it was these same leaders . . . who were taking part in such goodly numbers, relatively speaking, in the 1928 IMC gatherings.[8]

And, we would add, these leaders in increasing numbers would take part in all subsequent conciliar gatherings!

This points up the third external factor that caused uneasiness within the churches and their missions. Not only were Western Christians sensing their loss of face throughout the world. Not only was nationalism a growing worldwide phenomenon. Not only was this nationalism becoming

7. Jackson, *Red Tape*, p. 84.
8. Jerald D. Gort, "Jerusalem 1928: Mission, Kingdom and Church," *International Review of Mission* 67 (July 1978): 275.

increasingly wedded to the resurgence of non-Christian religions so that a good Thai was a good Buddhist and a good Indian a Hindu who had not broken caste by joining the Christian church. There was also an enormous growth in understanding of these non-Christian religions on the part of the missionaries themselves. With understanding came the desire to be more sympathetic to and appreciative of the moral, social, and even religious value of these religions. The word went out: all should be on the lookout for ways whereby the supremacy of the revelation of God in Christ might be conveyed through the use of redemptive analogies drawn from these indigenous faiths. The apostle Paul's example at Mars Hill (Acts 17:22–34) was often cited in justification of the thesis that missionaries should begin with the ideas of God which a people already have and should then use those ideas to point to the true God whom they are groping after in ignorance.

It needs to be pointed out that at the various IMC conferences some of the delegates occasionally made extravagant suggestions that repudiated the uniqueness, finality, and superiority of the Christian revelation. One recalls how John R. Mott and William Paton became uneasy over the syncretistic trend in some of the preliminary papers for the Jerusalem conference of 1928. In defense of the Christian faith they stood against Rufus Jones and William Hocking and, with Julius Richter, endorsed a declaration that included the ringing affirmation: "Evangelical missions are based on the great and absolutely unique acts of God for the redemption of mankind, particularly the sending of his only begotten Son, his death on the cross for the atonement of the world, his resurrection as the beginning of a new God-given life for the redeemed race."[9]

When later Hocking and Jones sponsored the Laymen's Foreign Mission Inquiry (1932), they did so independently of the mission boards, and conjured up a radicalism which could discuss Christianity without mentioning Christ and which was unable to define the concept *church* even in terms of Christian fellowship. It is significant that the findings of this inquiry were largely dismissed as "the product of amateurs," unrelated to the IMC. Actually, IMC leaders were embarrassed by it, and its recommendations were rejected by all missions with the sole exception of agencies of the Methodist Episcopal Church. Even so, some evangelical missions used it as an excuse to withdraw from the IMC.[10]

Subsequent conferences at Madras (1938) and Whitby (1947) devoted much time to discussing evangelism in New Testament terms and were

9. In *The Christian Life and Message in Relation to Non-Christian Systems of Thought and Life,* vol. 1 in *Jerusalem Meeting I.M.C. 1928* (New York and London: International Missionary Council, 1928), p. 288.

10. Jackson, *Red Tape,* pp. 114–21.

forthright in defending the uniqueness and finality of the gospel in relation to non-Christian religions. At Madras, Hendrik Kraemer was resolute in his opposition to theological liberalism and the possibility of continuity between the Christian faith and any other religion. He denied that there is divine revelation in any non-Christian system of thought and life. And a representative from Mexico, Professor G. Baez Camargo, appraised the IMC's repudiation of the liberal inclinations of the Jerusalem conference as follows:

> Certainly the idea so popular only one or two decades ago, of late has been steadily on the decline, namely, that Christianity was merely one among several good religions in the world, and that it should not claim any uniqueness or even superiority, but should simply go to others and share with them, in a give-and-take way, whatever of good it had. When, however, a conference as representative as Madras expresses a forthright rejection of this compromise and eclectic view, it undoubtedly marks a veritable turning point in the thought and life of the church, and particularly of its missions.[11]

Most delegates to the Whitby conference were as committed as ever to evangelism. Although some "social gospel" liberals were present, along with those who reflected the Barthian renaissance in European theology, not a few evangelicals were also present—so much so that some confidently believed missionary thought was returning to the evangelical pattern of the Edinburgh conference of 1910 with its stress on individual conversion. It is significant that at Whitby the delegates evidenced almost no concern over the problem of syncretism although the Indian delegation, while calling for more insight into how to combat the thoroughgoing syncretism of Hindu philosophers, felt there should be a measure of conservation of India's religious heritage. Their spokesman wistfully hoped "the Cross will still tower over the edifice of the Church in India, for the Cross is what India never had, but at its foot the Indian lotus and the lighted lamp will have their place."[12]

Internal Factors

Within the churches the factors that generated uncertainty as to the future of the missionary movement were both theological and ecclesiastical.

First, the theological situation in the homelands during this period became increasingly caught up in the polarization between "social gospel"

11. Quoted in William John Schmidt, "Ecumenicity and Syncretism: The Confrontation of the Ecumenical Movement with Syncretism in Special Reference to the International Missionary Council of the World Council of Churches" (Ph.D. dissertation, Columbia University, 1966), p. 149.

12. Ibid., p. 167.

liberals and the fundamentalists. Between the wars this tension was increasingly dominated by the mediating Barthian revolt along with the enthusiasts for either "realized eschatology" or a "theology of crisis." An additional reconciling presence was the growing vigor of the neoevangelicals with their capacity for appreciating those elements in Barthianism that represented a genuine return to Reformation theology.

Although it is somewhat difficult to measure the impact of these theological fluctuations on the missionary community during those years, one can detect a growing uncertainty about the essentiality of conversion. Questions were asked: Should missions deliberately work for the conversion of non-Christians, so that they might in turn be incorporated into churches? Is it not more "Christian" and more respectful of human personality to engage people in dialogic interchange than to confront them with the claims of Christ? Evangelicals did not entertain much doubt on these issues. Gospel proclamation, conversion to Christ, service in the church, witness in the world "by word and deed"—this is what mission is all about. But some were beginning to wonder whether this rigid sequence is valid. Could not people be recruited for service on behalf of others, or drawn into the corporate life of the church, with the expectation that in God's time this might—or might not—lead to conversion to Christ?

At the time of the Edinburgh conference (1910) the sequence was traditional: "The chief aim must ever be to persuade human hearts everywhere that Jesus Christ is their Savior, standing ready in an attitude of love, compassion and power, to realize to them, upon condition of repentance and faith, all that the Gospel promises to do for a soul that receives it."[13] By the time of the Whitby conference (1947), however, the subtle shift noted above had gained official sanction. Conversion was expected to occur within the Christian community, not in the course of preaching in the bazaar. People were encouraged to join the church "wherever you are in your journey of faith." Sharpe notes that The Christian Message to the Hindu, a book by A. G. Hogg which was popular at that time, contains a chapter entitled simply, "Come, Join My Church." And he comments, "He would indeed be a brave man who would write such a chapter today."[14] Not the traditional concept of a personal conversion to Christ followed by incorporation by baptism into the local congregation, but rather the sense of being drawn to the "Christ ideal" of service and enabled thereby to enter a "concerned community" whose dominant characteristic may be humanitarian service.

13. "Report of Commission 1: Carrying the Gospel to All the Non-Christian World," in World Missionary Conference, 1910 (New York: Revell, 1910), vol. 1, p. 312.
14. Eric J. Sharpe, "The Problem of Conversion in Recent Missionary Thought," Evangelical Quarterly 41 (1969): 224.

The second internal factor that contributed to the unease within the mission community was the growing widespread tendency in non-Christian lands to downplay Western mission agencies and regard them as anachronisms—vestiges of the dying colonial era. The younger churches were alone seen as having an abiding relevance. Although the subject of Western missions and Western missionaries had been discussed at Whitby and genuine appreciation was expressed for their contribution along with the expectation that they would still be welcomed by national churches, the major emphasis was that the "sending" Western and "receiving" younger churches were about to enter a new era of "partnership in obedience" characterized by "expectant evangelism." Indeed, the younger churches were seen as primarily responsible for the direction and accomplishment of Christian mission and the evangelistic task in the countries where they were located.

Whereas evangelicals rejoiced greatly over the deep commitment of Whitby's delegates to mission as traditionally understood, some wondered whether this focus on national churches would not diminish Western interest in missions because of its implicit postulate that frontier missionary evangelism was the wave of the past, and not of the future. Would not this overarching stress on interchurch partnership inhibit realization of the objective stated by the Edinburgh conference—"the speediest possible occupation of all unoccupied areas"? What if the younger churches did what the churches often do, and turned inward to become preoccupied with their own life and worship to the neglect of the regions beyond? Would Stephen Neill's dark judgment not then be repeatedly confirmed?

Some small younger churches are, in theory, "the Church" of a very wide area, which they may have neither the strength nor the inclination to evangelize. They may feel disinclined to invite missionaries from other lands to undertake that which is beyond their strength. Indeed, where ancient resentments are still smouldering, younger church leaders sometimes give the impression that they would rather that their fellow-countrymen died as heathen than that they should be brought to the knowledge of Christ by Christians from the West. If such a situation is reached, there is nothing for it but for the older churches to rebel. A dictatorship of the younger churches is no better than a dictatorship of the missionary societies. "Partnership" is not a human alliance for mutual convenience, it is partnership in obedience to the command of Christ to preach the Gospel to every creature. If this obedience is lacking on the one side or the other, the partnership would seem to lack a valid foundation. The world situation is changing so rapidly that opportunities are being lost every day. If an older church seems to hear a clear call to evangelize, it may be necessary that it should go forward, leaving the younger church to follow when it is sufficiently awake itself to hear the call.[15]

15. Stephen Neill, *The Unfinished Task* (London: Morrison and Gibb, 1957), p. 165.

To summarize: during the years 1910 to 1952 the missionary movement was largely characterized by an uneasy orthodoxy. Two world wars shattered forever the Western illusion of progress. The disintegration of Western colonialism and the rapid extension of Marxist power, particularly throughout eastern Europe and China, along with the great difficulty the Western powers encountered in containing the assaults of the North Koreans—all this contributed to setting the stage for the conference at Willingen (1952) at which the first steps were taken to create a distinctly ecumenical theology of mission. One delegate, Paul L. Lehmann, wrote: "At the conference itself, the long shadow of China spread an ominous cast over the present and future of missionary witness and policy in every corner of the earth."[16]

The new theology of mission which began to take form at Willingen would drastically polarize the missionary community. In no time at all evangelicals would be castigated for their nineteenth-century mentality, their spiritual imperialism, their reduction of evangelism to proselytism, their "suffocating and obscurantist pietism," and their inability to produce well-led churches capable of genuine spiritual independence.[17]

Willingen and MISSIO DEI

In 1948, shortly after the World Council of Churches was launched in Amsterdam, some leaders of the IMC convened a private meeting in Oegstgeest, the Netherlands, to discharge some essential business. While there they made a momentous decision. They called upon the research secretary of the IMC to initiate correspondence and studies on the theological basis of missions. This arose out of an awareness that the contemporary theological debate had yet to impact on the church's understanding of its missionary obligation. They looked for "the re-formulation of a theology of missions."[18]

At Willingen, the delegates reviewed the firstfruits of this research and sought to pursue its implications. It needs to be remembered that these preconference studies reflected the Barthian "biblical theology" renaissance that had increasingly triumphed over remnants of the embattled "social gospel" movement of the twenties and thirties and at the same time buttressed the confessional orthodoxy within the older churches. At any

16. Paul L. Lehmann, "Willingen and Lund: The Church on the Way to Unity," *Theology Today* 9 (January 1953): 434.

17. Lesslie Newbigin, "Call to Mission—A Call to Unity?" in *The Church Crossing Frontiers,* ed. P. Beyerhaus and K. Hallencreutz (Uppsala: Gleerup, 1969), pp. 255, 264.

18. Norman Goodall, ed., *Missions Under the Cross* (London: Edinburgh House, 1953), p. 11.

event, these studies largely reiterated what had earlier been affirmed at the Whitby conference; namely, that the eternal gospel of Jesus Christ is the unvarying gracious response of God to the continuing, unchanging, and persistent needs of the human race. And more, that the whole church, younger and older together, is under obligation to Him in an "accomplished mutuality" to "outline a single program for doing no less than carrying the Gospel to the whole world."[19] However, these concepts had yet to be developed within a theological framework which would trace the missionary purpose to its source in the Triune God and relate it to the inauguration of the kingdom by Jesus Christ.

However, not all of the preliminary papers were in this vein. Several of the authors, notably Johannes Hoekendijk, had taken very seriously the "new directions and stimuli" articulated by the research secretary of the IMC. More or less as a postscript (1950) to the earlier mandate (1948) to "restate the universal missionary obligation of the church as grounded in the eternal Gospel," they asked that this restatement be related to "the present historical situation."[20] These younger authors were not interested in any mere theologizing of the Christian mission in terms of the trinitarian nature of God. Indeed, they were drawn neither to the Christ-centered confession of the Jerusalem conference ("our message is Jesus Christ") nor to the church-centered approach of the Whitby conference. They were concerned to discover whether or not "the message and strategy of the Christian mission has a cutting historical edge." Whether there is any relation between the "salvation history" that theologians talk about and the history of the world outside the church. Whether there is any relation between "the Christian hope" and the nations. Whether there is "any direct line between evangelism and politics." At Willingen these issues were debated, and a report was drafted embracing them. However, it was "torpedoed by the Anglo-Catholics and the German Lutherans."[21]

What Willingen finally produced was a trinitarian approach to the theology of mission. And this was heralded as its great achievement. Subsequent expositions introduced the old classical term *Missio Dei* to represent the biblical basis of mission. The initiative for mission belongs to God. Each and every aspect of the total enterprise is under His direction. Evangelicals have derived much benefit from pondering the new literature on the subject.[22] It seeks largely "to say old things in a new way, to restore a

19. Kenneth Scott Latourette and William Richey Hogg, *Tomorrow Is Here* (New York: Friendship, 1948), p. 107.

20. Norman Goodall, "First Principles," *International Review of Missions* 39 (July 1950): 257.

21. Lehmann, "Willingen and Lund," pp. 434f.

22. Georg F. Vicedom, *Mission of God* (St. Louis: Concordia, 1965).

worn-out word [mission] to its original power, to revive it and to give it a new function."[23]

However, the young radicals were persistent. After Willingen they capitalized on the rather loose way in which "God's mission" and "God's action" were made virtually synonymous in the subsequent writings of Willingen's delegates (e.g., Walter Freytag, Lesslie Newbigin, John Mackay, Max Warren).[24] In the years that followed, *Missio Dei* became a neologism that blurred God's providential governance over the nations with the church's mission. Radical formulations came to the fore until *Missio Dei* was so reinterpreted and modified that it came to mean the action of God in carrying out His judgments and His ameliorating work among the nations in the revolutionary movements of our day. It became "the Trojan horse through which the (unassimilated) 'American' vision (the 'direct line between evangelism and politics') was fetched into the well-guarded walls of the ecumenical theology of mission."[25] Reading the sections on *Missio Dei* in the WCC studies *The Church for Others* and *The Church for the World* (1968), one will find statements such as the following:

> Partnership in God's mission is therefore entering into partnership with God in history, because our knowledge of God in Christ compels us to affirm that God is working out his purpose in the midst of the world and its historic processes.
>
> God walks among men . . . is active in the world . . . moves in history . . . the *Missio Dei* is at work beyond the churches (and various missions). . . . It embraces both church and world. . . . The churches serve the *Missio Dei* in the world when . . . they point to God at work in world history.
>
> We find ourselves becoming participants in the search for the ways and places where God is calling us to join him in his missionary work in the world.
>
> The church does not have a separate mission of its own.
>
> [The church] is to participate in his mission. . . . We have lifted up humanization as the goal of mission.
>
> Our focus on mission as God's mission leads us to understand history as God's "affair" with man, as the divine invitation to man to share the world with God.[26]

Among those who popularized the shift in emphasis "from the church to the world" in the years following Willingen, none had a more significant

23. H. H. Rosin, *Missio Dei* (Leiden: Interuniversity Institute for Missiological and Ecumenical Research, 1972), p. 20.

24. Ibid., pp. 18–26.

25. Ibid., p. 26.

26. *The Church for Others* and *The Church for the World* (Geneva: World Council of Churches, 1968), pp. 14, 16, 58–59, 75, 78, 94.

following than Hoekendijk. He was almost savage in his denunciation of
the illegitimacy of a church-centered approach to the missionary task. "In
no respect can the church regard itself either as the subject of the mission
or as its sole (and exclusive) institutionalized form."[27] And he deliberately
sought to swing the students of the WSCF to accept this secularization of
the missionary task of the church. At a very important WSCF "teaching
conference" (Strasbourg, 1960) to which all the big names were invited
(Daniel T. Niles, Lesslie Newbigin, Karl Barth, and Willem Visser 't Hooft),
it was Hoekendijk who dominated the center of the stage. The others
were shouted down, and the students could not hear too much of such
extravagant nonsense as: "Are there no revolutionaries here? People who
do not want to improve or to modify the structures and institutions of our
Christian life but who are ready to break out of these prisons? . . . Is there
any chance for you to avoid one of the major ecumenical sins, that is to
be churchly?"[28]

In time, the major implications of this reconceptualization of *Missio Dei*
began to filter down to the churches. In all too many circles they came
as heady wine. There was no longer any reason for the church to confront
the world with a message whose first word was "Repent!" There was no
essential difference between Christians and non-Christians. The significant activity of God was to be found in all those movements leading to
the humanization of individuals and society. Working for the conversion
of non-Christians was passé. Indeed, in G. H. Anderson's collection of
essays *The Theology of the Christian Mission*[29] one finds only two incidental
references to conversion (in 341 pages!). Christ now speaks to us through
the devotees of other religions as well as through the Scriptures. Hence
our Christian obligation to non-Christians is no longer to be subsumed
under the rubric of "witness." The new obligation is "dialogue" of the sort
that stops short of gospel proclamation and the essentiality of the call to
conversion. Although John 3:16 is quoted in the documents of the Third
Assembly of the WCC (New Delhi, 1961), one looks in vain for the words
"that whoever believes in him should not perish." They were left out. In
addition, the apostle Paul's words in 2 Corinthians 5:19 ("God was in
Christ reconciling the world to himself") are not related to Paul's call to
conversion in the following verse ("We beseech you on behalf of Christ,
be reconciled to God"). Indeed, within the churches one detected a grow-

27. Thomas Wieser, ed., *Planning for Mission* (New York: U.S. Conference for the
World Council of Churches, 1966), p. 44.
28. Quoted in David C. Edwards, "Signs of Radicalism in the Ecumenical Movement,"
in *Ecumenical Advance: A History of the Ecumenical Movement*, vol. 2: *1948–1968*, ed. Harold E. Fey (Philadelphia: Westminster, 1970), p. 406.
29. G. H. Anderson, *The Theology of the Christian Mission* (New York: McGraw-Hill,
1961).

ing silence concerning the coming judgment of God and much uncritical acceptance of the thesis that men and women have it within themselves to perfect human society.[30] John V. Taylor uttered a cautionary word concerning all this ferment: "There is a real danger lest the blanket phrase *Missio Dei,* which is meant to establish the divine initiative, is worded so vaguely that it includes the whole action of God throughout time and space, as though, if he chose, God might have accomplished the renewal of man without Jesus Christ."[31]

It goes without saying that the theological issues involved in the contemporary debate on mission are most complex. The New Testament clearly places the mission of the church within the larger context of God's purpose to renew the whole creation (Rom. 8:18–25). God is not indifferent to nor uninvolved in the contemporary struggles for justice, for the political liberation of peoples, for the development of the nations. There is a biblical validity to participating in the name of Christ

> in the struggle for a genuine human existence, for deliverance of the suffering, for the elevation of the underdeveloped, for redemption of the captives, for the settlement of race and class differences, for opposition to chaos, crime, suffering, sickness, and ignorance—in short, in the struggle for what we call progress—an activity that is taking place throughout the world to the honor of Christ.[32]

When the conviction began to grow, however, that mission must increasingly be interpreted in terms of "what God is doing in the world," in accordance with the secularized understanding of *Missio Dei,* a momentum for change began to express itself in a series of strikingly new movements. Since these had theological implications, we must discuss them.

The Feeble Offspring of MISSIO DEI

The Structural Revolt

Organizational changes gained impetus from theological reflection on the essence of the church. Does its apostolicity refer only to its being "built upon the foundation of the apostles and prophets" (Eph. 2:20)? Is there not also the obligation to serve as a company of God's envoys to the world after the apostolic model? And if so, is it ideal that missionary societies

30. David J. Bosch, "Crosscurrents in Modern Mission," *Missionalia* 4 (August 1976): 59–63.

31. John V. Taylor, *The Uppsala Report 1968* (Geneva: World Council of Churches, 1968), p. 23.

32. Hendrikus Berkhof, *Christ, the Meaning of History* (Richmond: John Knox, 1966), p. 173.

working alongside the churches dominate this activity? Is not the real missionary the church in its totality?

What the leaders of the IMC saw as impeccable theology pressed them to seek integration with the WCC; this was consummated at the Third Assembly of the WCC (New Delhi, 1961). This integration was heralded with much fanfare. The WCC immediately created a Division of World Mission and Evangelism (DWME) and gave it the mandate to bring the missionary dimension into the midst of the life and service of the churches. The delegates even spelled out "mission" in traditional terms—"to further the proclamation to the whole world of the gospel of Jesus Christ to the end that all men may believe in him and be saved."

This decision was surrounded by extravagant notions. Mission societies were seen as no longer needed. Enthusiasts coined a new slogan: "The church is mission!" And they ecstatically exclaimed, "All future growth will issue from the witnessing congregation and from an anonymous *laos!*" This dismissal of parachurch agencies as irrelevant reflected abysmal indifference to two thousand years of church history with its long record of the fruitful organized labors of specific missionary vocations. Without them Christianity would never have become a worldwide movement. It is only because of their discipling activity that the empirical church keeps penetrating new areas and peoples. Whereas the church needs to "put into practice the new insights given by the theological re-discovery of the Christian Laos . . . [missiologists] maintain that the Laos very seldom will proceed to action unless it is organized, inspired and supported by a specific ministry 'given for the equipment of the saints . . . for building up the Body of Christ' (Eph. 4:12)."[33]

The integration of the IMC with the WCC enjoyed only limited success. Because of the basic changes in the understanding of mission precipitated by the reconceptualization of *Missio Dei*, the missionary involvement of churches within the conciliar movement went almost immediately into sharp decline, and today their total commitment in career missionaries numbers less than one-tenth of all Protestant missionaries.

The Proclamation Revolt

Another offspring of the reconceptualization of *Missio Dei* involved the repudiation of traditional missionary preaching. This was precipitated by the General Committee of the WSCF. In July 1964, a few years after New Delhi, this committee came to the settled conclusion that words like "evangelization," "witness," and "mission" all suggest "a Christian behaviour of

33. Peter Beyerhaus, "The Ministry of Crossing Frontiers," in *The Church Crossing Frontiers,* ed. P. Beyerhaus and K. Hallencreutz (Uppsala: Gleerup, 1969), p. 41; also Paul Loffler, *The Layman Abroad in the Mission of the Church* (London: Edinburgh House, 1962).

speaking before listening, of calling people away from their natural communities into a Christian grouping, and of a preoccupation with the soul
at the expense of the whole of life ... [they also suggest] a certainty of
faith and purpose and an ability to conceptualize faith in terms which
create difficulty for many people."[34] Actually, as Sharpe comments, "These
words implied nothing of the sort; but to a new generation they suggested
these things."[35]

What to do? The General Committee had an answer and a "new pass-
word" was coined: "presence." Their understanding of *Missio Dei* led them
to conclude that as far as future mission was concerned "presence" was
the name of the game. In contrast to the older words with their precise
biblical connotations, they defined "presence" as "the adventure of being
there in the name of Christ, often anonymously, listening before we speak,
hoping that men will recognize Jesus for what he is and stay where they
are, involved in the fierce fight against all that dehumanizes, ready to act
against demonic powers, to identify with the outcast, merciless in ridi-
culing modern idols and new myths."[36]

Actually, the "presence" fever burnt itself out quickly with the rapid
decline of the WSCF. But it produced a series of books edited by Max
Warren that revived dimensions in the encounter of the Christian message
with non-Christian faiths and ideologies that evangelicals thought had
been laid to rest years before by such stalwarts as Robert E. Speer, Samuel M. Zwemer, Hendrik Kraemer, and others. Once again, the call was
sounded for Christians to remember that in their encounter with non-
Christians they should confess, "God was here before our arrival." They
were to avoid making judgments "outside the religious situation" of these
people; they were to "try to sit where they sit ... in a word, to be 'present'
with them."[37] There was to be little thought of "making disciples" and no
thought of planting congregations. That would be religious imperialism!

Inevitably, this vague theologizing did not escape evangelical scrutiny.
A good biblical case can be made for "presence" as a prelude to witness.
And dialogue is essential to understanding in religious encounter. But "if
God is present in the non-Christian religious situation, if that situation
were a point of holiness—in what sense is he present, and in what sense
is he more present in the Christian community?"[38] Once again, it is
apparent that the popularization of *Missio Dei* in its secularized form had

34. "The Christian Community in the Academic World," *Student World* (WSCF) 3 (1965):
233.
35. Sharpe, "New Directions," p. 16.
36. "Christian Community in the Academic World," p. 234.
37. Kenneth Cragg, *Sandals at the Mosque: Christian Presence amid Islam* (New York:
Oxford University, 1959), p. 9.
38. Sharpe, "New Directions," p. 17.

produced the sort of offspring that could hardly be expected to generate a renewal of missionary concern within the churches of the WCC.

The Hermeneutical Revolt

The WCC has never launched any attacks against the creedal affirmations of its member churches. Indeed, its Toronto Declaration of 1950 ("The Church, the Churches and the World Council of Churches") included the promise that it had no intention either of becoming a superchurch (III.1) or of tampering with any of the specific doctrinal commitments of its member churches ("no Church need fear that by entering into the World Council it is in danger of denying its heritage," p. 15). It regarded itself merely as a council for churches that possess "the common recognition that Christ is the Divine Head of the Body" (IV.1). Moreover, the WCC freely admitted that the Bible was a uniting factor in ecumenical encounter since all member churches appealed to it as their unique source of knowledge of Jesus Christ. Indeed, at New Delhi, when the WCC "basis" was enlarged to include the Trinity (several Orthodox Churches in joining the WCC had made this stipulation), the Norwegian churches requested a reference to the Scriptures. This was granted. Merger-conscious IMC leaders rejoiced, for this reinforced their preoccupation with the trinitarian approach to mission. While the revised basis was "less than a confession" it was "more than a mere formula or agreement."[39] It read: "The World Council of Churches is a fellowship of Churches which confess the Lord Jesus Christ as God and Saviour according to the Scriptures and therefore seek to fulfil together their common calling to the glory of the one God, Father, Son and Holy Spirit."

In 1949, twelve years prior to New Delhi, a gathering of biblical scholars from many confessions had met at Oxford under WCC auspices to define "guiding principles for the interpretation of the Bible." They agreed that "*the* biblical message" is its faithful and uncorrupted witness to salvation history and that Christ is *the* key to its interpretation ("in the Bible we confront the living Word"). They also affirmed that the Bible is authoritative and it can "guide us in the knowledge of God's will in every situation facing the church today." At that time the influence of the Continental Barthians was strong. Visser 't Hooft could even remark that "without this common biblical theology the ecumenical movement would have had no backbone."[40]

39. Hanfried Krüger, "The Life and Activities of the World Council of Churches," in *Ecumenical Advance: A History of the Ecumenical Movement*, vol. 2: *1948–1968*, ed. Harold E. Fey (Philadelphia: Westminster, 1970), pp. 34–36.

40. Willem A. Visser 't Hooft, "The General Ecumenical Development Since 1948," in *Ecumenical Advance: A History of the Ecumenical Movement*, vol. 2: *1948–1968*, ed. Harold E. Fey (Philadelphia: Westminster, 1970), p. 6.

In the conferences that followed, however, it became apparent that the Barthian Word-centered influence was beginning to wane. First, Bultmannian and then post-Bultmannian theses became increasingly popular. One has but to study the statements issued at Montreal (1963), Bristol (1967), Louvain (1971), and Loccum (1977) to note the way in which the radical perspectives inherent in the reconceptualized *Missio Dei* came to be justified exegetically through the use of a "new hermeneutic." The Montreal conference witnessed the big debate between Ernst Käsemann and Edward Schweitzer on one side and Raymond Brown on the other over the "diversity of ecclesiologies" in the New Testament.

From that conference onward the WCC no longer spoke of "*the* biblical message" or "*the* biblical doctrine" with respect to any particular issue. Moreover, it tragically overstated the thesis that the various churches today use different hermeneutical keys in interpreting the Bible and concluded with finality: "A mere reiteration of the words of Holy Scripture would be a betrayal of the gospel." The interpretative rules for biblical exegesis defined at Oxford in 1949 were no longer adequate. Indeed, the Bristol conference warned against having theological presuppositions when approaching the Bible since it is "but a collection of human writings." The word was popularized that one may be compelled to decide for *or against* any particular biblical concept. The great problem was seen to be the bridging of (or even whether one should bridge) the great historical gulf between the biblical writings and today.[41]

The Louvain conference grappled with the issue of the authority of the Bible and concluded that it should be seen as "a force capable of leading people to faith, but not as a fixed quality." Delegates were agreed there is no one center to the Bible; different sets of statements and different biblical writings have different decisive centers. The Loccum conference concluded that "no text is directly applicable to any present-day dogmatic or ethical question." From this we can only conclude that the new *Missio Dei* perspective had triumphed. Whereas the WCC still claims to operate "according to the Scriptures," one views the WCC claim with suspicion in light of the observation of its executive secretary that "to appeal to what the Bible says has become out of date."[42]

Much could be added to this discussion. In the sixties and seventies new words were added to the ecumenical glossary. There was the "Sal-

41. See Ellen Flesseman–van Leer, ed., *The Bible: Its Authority and Interpretation in the Ecumenical Movement,* Faith and Order Paper 99 (Geneva: World Council of Churches, 1980); Richard C. Rowe, *Bible Study in the World Council of Churches,* Research Pamphlet 16 (Geneva: World Council of Churches, 1969); Michael Sadgrove, "The Bible from New Delhi to Nairobi"—a private collection from Balliol College, Oxford (1975).

42. See Paul G. Schrotenboer, "The Bible in the World Council of Churches," *Calvin Theological Journal* 12 (1977): 144–63.

vation Today" focus (1973) that promoted the testimony of a Chinese "saved by Mao" alongside that of an American "saved by Jesus." There was the "Jesus Frees and Unites" slogan (1975) that overlooked the solemnizing fact that His truth divides men. Latterly, the emphasis has been "Your Kingdom Come" (1980). But these successive emphases have not led in any new directions in the development of an ecumenical theology of mission. Whereas evangelicals contend that a biblically vital church can be recognized by a burning desire—a yearning—to extend its joy, love, and fellowship to as many persons, peoples, cultures, and nations as possible, this concern appears to be increasingly muted in WCC-member churches in our day.[43]

43. Charles E. Van Engen, *The Growth of the True Church* (Amsterdam: Rodolphi, 1981), p. 497.

6

Contemporary Evangelical Theology of Mission

Donald McGavran

$\rm T$o portray the evangelical theology of mission is easier than to portray the conciliar theology of mission. The evangelical theology is definite and unambiguous. It neither disguises its purpose nor indulges in vague inclusive terminology. It says what it means. It is consistent with classical theology. According to the evangelical theology of mission, God has revealed truth in the Bible in intelligible form.

All the leaders of classical mission, William Carey, Adoniram Judson, Hudson Taylor, Robert E. Speer, John R. Mott, and a thousand others, defined and defended mission on what we today would call evangelical grounds. The great Wheaton Declaration (1966) and the magnificent Frankfurt Declaration (1970) are evangelical documents. A review of their historical antecedents makes abundantly clear that the evangelical theology of mission is no recent construction. Rather it is classical and deeply biblical theology which is not likely to be substantially changed as the world passes through various phases of development and—it is hoped—improvement.

Our portrayal of the evangelical theology of mission will not exactly suit all the many branches of the Christian church. Lutheran evangelicals will, in this chapter, miss some distinctive Lutheran stresses. Methodist evangelicals will miss some of the wordings they treasure. Calvinists would have phrased some of these doctrines differently. Indeed the phrasings we have used have been chosen, not because they represent our exact thought on the subject, but rather because we believe they represent common evangelical theological positions. Every evangelical church has its own wordings designed to fit both its understanding of the central teachings of the Bible and those contemporary issues of particular importance in its place of labor. We hope the following wordings of the main doctrines of the evangelical theology of mission will be accepted by evangelicals as substantially the truth set forth in the Bible.

It is to be remembered that this chapter presents a theology of world evangelization, that is, of mission. Were we setting forth theologies of work, Christian education, or worship, somewhat different groups of doctrines would be presented. This is not a systematic theology. Therefore we do not describe all the doctrines which undergird the Christian faith. However, we do attempt to portray those doctrines *which are essential for mission,* that is, a theology of the purpose of God in bringing unbelieving men and women into the life He intended for them, the life of conscious dedication to the Lord Jesus Christ as depicted in the Scriptures and of responsible membership in His body, the church.

Where some of our readers might prefer a slightly different phrasing, we would encourage them to make a substitution. When they express the doctrine in question, let them put it in words consistent with the position of their particular church. Let them also make sure that the words they use are faithful to the biblical revelation, and do thrust Christians out to the discipling of all the peoples, castes, and tribes of Planet Earth. In wording the doctrines underlying the evangelical theology of mission they should be acutely conscious of the fact that today more than three billion of the world's population have yet to believe on Jesus Christ. Unless Christian mission becomes much more effective, by the year 2000 nearly five billion will still be living worldly lives, alienated from God. Any true theology of mission must be framed facing that tragic fact.

We will present the doctrines underlying the contemporary evangelical theology of mission in two parts. First come the unchanging, eternally true doctrines. These we list under the heading *The Main Doctrines or Axioms.* Then come *Doctrines Speaking to Current Issues.* To be sure, all doctrines speak to contemporary issues. Sin is ever present. God rules over all areas and all peoples. Nevertheless, some issues to which a theology of mission must speak were unknown in their present form before 1900. For example, the Marxist heresy must be dealt with by any contemporary theology of mission. In short, our theology must speak to individuals and peoples where they are today.

The Main Doctrines or Axioms[1]

1. *The Absolute Inspiration and Authority of the Bible.* God has not left men and women to wonder and speculate concerning the eternal verities about

---

1. This heading might read "Foundational Commitments" and the following heading, "Contemporary Commitments." However, since we have used the word *doctrines* in the previous chapters, we shall use it here also.

Himself, humankind, sin, salvation, eternal lostness, eternal life, ethical conduct, freedom of will, the worship of idols, and the deification of human ideals, whether of power, sex, or money. On all these and other matters of enormous interest to human beings, God has given a clear revelation of His will. This is called special revelation. It is contained in the Bible, which is God's Word, His deliberate disclosure of His holy will through inspired writers.

God has revealed Himself to be the true and living God, the only God there is, Creator of the universe, perfect in love and righteousness in all His ways, existing eternally in the three persons of the Trinity—Father, Son, and Holy Spirit. God has spoken in intelligible words, in mighty acts, and in the person of Jesus Christ His Son. The Creator of the universe has disclosed His holy will in the exact form He desires. We can know the truth God has chosen to reveal. Jesus Christ is the same yesterday, today, and forever. Consequently the truth about God does not change from age to age or from people to people or from culture to culture. The applications of this truth certainly do change in accordance with the particular situation, but the truth itself remains the same.

It has pleased God to reveal Himself in intelligible language to the human race through His prophets, apostles, and the Eternal Word made flesh, as recorded in the Holy Bible, which is a trustworthy record of His divine self-disclosure. All the books of the Old and New Testaments, given by inspiration, are the written Word of God, the only infallible rule of faith and practice for all peoples in all ages. The Bible, whose books were written by different individuals in different ages, displays a marvelous unity, being the revelation of the one true God. The Bible is to be translated into all languages so that each person in each *ethnos* may read or hear God's Word in his or her own tongue and thus come to an accurate knowledge of the truth.

2. *The Doctrine of the Soul and of Eternal Life.* Each individual is an immortal soul in a physical body. When one believes on Jesus Christ, one's sins are forgiven. Now saved the individual has become a new creation and entered on eternal life. He or she starts to live as a member of God's household, part of the body of Christ. After the death of the physical body, both body and soul, in God's good time, are raised to eternal life. 1 Corinthians 15:52 says, "The dead will be raised imperishable and we shall be changed." The whole passage, verses 50 to 56, is a clear statement of this doctrine.

A corollary of this doctrine is that God bestows upon His people two gifts: abundant life now and eternal life in the world to come. Of the two, the second is incomparably greater than the first. The two cannot, however, be rigorously separated. The abundant life of the Christian is already part of eternal life. Eternal life bears fruit in current righteousness, peace, justice, fellowship, industry, humility, and courage. It is both future life with God and present life with God.

3. *The Doctrine of the Lostness of the Human Race and of Eternal Salvation.* God, by His Word and His glory, freely created the world out of nothing. He made Adam and Eve in His own image as the crown of creation, that they might have fellowship with Him. Tempted by Satan they rebelled against God. They were estranged from their Maker, yet responsible to Him. Therefore, apart from grace, we humans are incapable of returning to God. We are fallen beings. Unless we turn in faith to the Redeemer, we are lost. Through faith in Jesus Christ and His atoning death, we are justified by God, our sins are forgiven, we receive eternal life. We become part of the chosen race, the royal priesthood. This is eternal salvation. Eternal salvation is not gained by living a moral life or accepting one of the humanly devised ideologies or religions. It comes only through faith in Jesus Christ and His redemptive work for us. The evangelical theology of mission rejects universalism—the teaching that all will be saved—on the grounds that it is not part of the biblical revelation.

4. *The Doctrine of Christ, the Only Mediator.* The only Mediator between God and the human race is Christ Jesus our Lord, God's eternal Son, who, being conceived by the Holy Spirit, was born of the virgin Mary. He fully shared and fulfilled our humanity by His life of perfect obedience. By His death in our stead, He revealed the divine love and upheld divine justice, removing our guilt and reconciling us to God. There is therefore no way to be reconciled to God other than by believing and trusting in the atonement He has wrought by Christ. Since Jesus Christ is the only Mediator, it is by Him alone that we can come to God. There is no other name by which we can be saved. Only as people of every race, culture, language, condition, and economic status believe on Jesus Christ is it possible for them to be reconciled to God.

Evangelicals are well aware of the problem which this doctrine raises concerning those many millions who through no fault of their own do not know the gospel of Christ or are not in touch with His church. Yet evangelicals cannot believe that God will save such men and women, counting their belief in Baal, Ashtaroth, modern civilization, Rama, Krishna, Gautama, Marx, or money as sufficient to win them salvation. Rather evangelicals believe that, according to the teaching of the Bible, those who do not believe in Christ are lost. Evangelicals also believe that God is sovereign. Should He so choose, He can bring those who know nothing of Jesus Christ back into fellowship with Himself. But the means by which He might do this (and whether in point of fact He ever does do it) remains hidden. God has not chosen to reveal this in Scripture.

In consequence of this doctrine, an inescapable responsibility rests on Christians to proclaim the gospel and tell men and women everywhere of the only Mediator between God and them, and the only way of salvation, the cross of Christ.

5. *The Doctrine of the Church as Christ's Body, the Household of God.* God by His Word and Spirit creates the one holy universal and apostolic church, calling sinners of the whole human race into the fellowship of Christ's body. By the same Word and Spirit, He guides and preserves for eternity that new redeemed humanity, the church of Jesus Christ, which (no matter what their tribe, caste, clan, class, culture, or economic condition) is spiritually one with the people of God in all ages and constitutes the church of Christ on earth.

This church exists in discrete congregations and clusters of congregations called conferences, synods, dioceses, denominations, and churches. It is God's clear command that all *ethne* (peoples) are to be discipled— baptized, added to the church, and taught to observe all things commanded by the Lord. The missionary movement consists of all those who are engaged in multiplying these churches among every segment of the world's population. In some segments the work is seed sowing. In others it is harvesting, but all goes forward toward the one glorious end that before our Lord returns there be a congregation of the redeemed in every community everywhere.

Evangelicals before 1920 universally held that membership in Christ's church was the normal fulfilment of conversion. Converts confessed Christ and were incorporated into Christian congregations. After 1920, as evangelicals felt the need to stress the great issues which separated them from liberals, they emphasized instead some of the other main doctrines we have been discussing. Many of them were evangelizing on new ground and were seeing few new converts. Their task seemed to be proclaiming the gospel rather than bringing sheaves into the Master's barn. The Church Growth Movement, which has spread greatly among evangelicals, has largely reversed that temporary stand. Any truly evangelical theology of mission must set forth a high doctrine of the church, Christ's body. For by its presence, witness, and growth, the church is a central component in God's redemptive plan.

6. *Evangelization and the End Time.* The Bible repeatedly tells us of the last day, the day of judgment, the end of this world and the beginning of God's perfect rule in a new heaven and a new earth.[2] The twenty-fourth chapter of Matthew is only one of several passages which portray the ingathering of God's people from among the Gentile nations as prepar-

2. There are several schools of thought among evangelicals concerning the last day. Emphasizing different strands of Scripture, these schools consequently hold somewhat different theologies of the end time, the day of judgment. We present our own viewpoint, while regarding the others with respect.

atory to the end of the age. The present world will pass away. The signs of the last day are the beginnings of the birth pangs of the new world— the perfect kingdom of God. It is coming. Nothing can stop it. Before it comes, however, the world must be evangelized. "This gospel of the kingdom will be preached in the whole world as a testimony to all nations, and *then* the end will come" (Matt. 24:14, NIV, emphasis added).

In the tenth chapter of Matthew, where the end time is called "the day of judgment" (v. 15), Christ instructs His followers to witness amid the trials and tribulations which precede that day. Without fear Christians are to witness to everyone about Christ the King, the Judge, and Savior. "Every one . . . who shall confess Me before men, I will also confess him before My Father who is in heaven. But whoever shall deny Me before men, I will also deny him before My Father who is in heaven" (vv. 32–33, NASB).

Therefore, for evangelicals a major doctrine of world mission is: The day of the Lord is certainly coming. It will usher in a new heaven and a new earth. God's present rule, so flawed by human rebellion and sin, will then—after sin and death have been abolished—come to glorious fulfillment. But God will delay that day, when the gleaming holy city is to come down out of heaven, till the gospel has been preached to all and all have had a chance to confess Christ before others. Hence, in the economy of God, the discipling of all the peoples of earth is an essential first step in the advent of God's perfect rule, when every tear shall be wiped away and there shall no longer be any mourning, crying, pain, or death. The first things will have passed away, only because the evangelization of the world will have been completed.

7. *The Primary Mission of the Church.* God has given the church many tasks to perform. The church must evangelize the world and assemble Christians for worship, adoration of God, and systematic instruction in His Word. The church must rear its children in the fear and admonition of the Lord, and apply Christ's teaching on individual and corporate levels, so that all areas of life, whether the family, neighborhood, city, state, or world, will gradually be transformed till God's will rules them all. Jesus came preaching this kingdom of God.

Among these various tasks, the primary mission of the church is to tell everyone everywhere of God's provision for salvation and to enroll in the ark of salvation—the church of Jesus Christ—as many as believe. The church is both the body of Christ (and thus has eternal value in and of itself) and God's instrument for the propagation of the gospel and the spread of His kingdom. Evangelicals reject the false doctrine that the only valid goal is a Christian social order, and that the church is only a temporary expedient, an instrument toward this end. To be sure, the church is God's instrument. Our great Head does use His body toward His ends.

But the church is also the bride of Christ and has an absolute value completely separate from the achievement of a transformed society or an evangelized world.

Thus the primary task of the church is to call men and women *from death* (the present state of the unredeemed who believe in gods of their own manufacture, merely human wisdom, or pseudosaviors) *to life* (the state of baptized and obedient believers, redeemed children of God, members of the household of God). This foundational change of status of the immortal soul granted by God antedates all ethical acts of the Christian and gives the believer power to do whatever God wishes. The growth of the church is not therefore a retreat from ethical actions, but an enabling for them; not a retreat from the world, but an equipping of all the saints to worship the King and be the salt and light of the world according to His will. The church is thus the most powerful instrument known for ushering in a more peaceful, just, and harmonious society. The kingdom of God is found where Christ's will is done.

The primary mission of the church—world evangelization and church growth—involves both cross-cultural and monocultural evangelism. Those who do not believe in Christ are often far away in other lands. They are also often near at hand in lands where the church has long existed. Furthermore, since every denomination and almost every congregation has in it at least some (and often many) nominal Christians who lack real saving faith in Jesus Christ, Christian mission is often working at winning nominal Christians to genuine faith in Christ. Hence the church must constantly preach the gospel to its members for thereby nominal Christians can be brought to newness of life. This is technically described as E–0 evangelism. Reaching non-Christians in the same culture but outside the church is E–1 evangelism. E–2 and E–3 evangelism require special effort for they involve, respectively, evangelizing at a limited distance or at a great cultural distance. E–1, E–2, and E–3 are always Christian mission. E–0 is sometimes mission and sometimes shepherding. In either case, it has a high priority.

8. *The Doctrine of the Holy Spirit.* The Holy Spirit, the third person of the Trinity, who empowers believers to lead holy and righteous lives, also impels them to fervent, intelligent evangelism of *panta ta ethne.* Evangelism, whether of nominal Christians in the neighborhood or of persons in nearby and faraway lands who have never heard, is carried out under the direction of the Holy Spirit. Evangelism is not initiated by humans. We would never evangelize on our own. The nominal fringe of the church has no interest in winning others to life in Christ. The whole missionary movement is inspired, guided, directed, and brought to fruition by the Holy Spirit.

At Antioch the Holy Spirit said, "Set apart for me Barnabas and Saul for the work to which I have called them" (Acts 13:2). The church did this. Then we read, "So, being sent out by the Holy Spirit, . . . they sailed to Cyprus." They tried to go into Bithynia, but "the Spirit of Jesus did not allow them" (Acts 16:7). The Holy Spirit thrusts the church out into world evangelization and guides its efforts to perform this demanding task.

No wonder Vatican II in its decree on the mission activity of the church declared: "What was once preached by the Lord or what was once wrought in Him for the saving of the human race must be proclaimed and spread abroad to the ends of the earth. . . . To accomplish this goal Christ sent the Holy Spirit from the Father. The Spirit was to carry out His saving work inwardly and to impel the Church toward her proper expansion."[3] And no wonder the evangelicals assembled at Wheaton said in their historic declaration: "We acknowledge our utter dependence upon the Holy Spirit in every aspect of our missionary calling. . . . God's primary method for evangelism and church planting is the ministry of Spirit-gifted and empowered men and women preaching and teaching the Word of God."[4]

Those engaged in world evangelization speak often of the factors which cause the growth and expansion of the church into new territories. But who creates those factors? Evangelicals believe that it is the Holy Spirit who brings about conditions which enable His household to multiply and ramify throughout the earth, bringing blessings and salvation to all who believe in the Savior.

Doctrines Speaking to Current Issues

We live in the midst of a tremendous revolution which affects all aspects of life. Vast technological changes have brought the once unimaginable within the ordinary experience of hundreds of millions. We have the internal combustion engine and electricity. The powers of fossil fuels, the wind, and the sun have been harnessed, with consequent rising expectations that the good life is within the reach of all. There are equally vast changes in literacy rates and forms of government. A sense that unbearable conditions which for millennia were accepted as the lot of the human race can now be ended is commonplace on every continent and in most countries. Races once hidden away behind unsailed oceans or trackless deserts have suddenly become next-door neighbors. Peasants have aspired to the rich life of the aristocrats of yesteryear.

Each of these changes demands a new application of biblical truth. The

3. *Ad gentes,* in Walter M. Abbott, ed., *The Documents of Vatican II* (New York: Herder and Herder, 1966), p. 587.

4. Harold Lindsell, *The Church's Worldwide Mission* (Waco, TX: Word, 1966), p. 233.

truth does not change. But what the truth means in this culture or that
situation does change. When disease and famine wiped out millions and
all anyone could do was to accept these disasters as acts of God, God's love
and human responsibility meant one thing. But now that disease and
famine can be averted, God's love and human responsibility mean something quite different. In this section we will examine doctrines which have
become part of the evangelical theology of mission because they apply
God's revelation either to conditions common in today's world or to current compromises of biblical truth.

   1. *Biblical Truth Applied to Non-Christian Religions.* The day when Christians and non-Christians were separated by vast distances and Christians
knew little or nothing of non-Christian religions has passed. Today, knowledge of non-Christian religions and ideologies is widely available. Courses
in Communism, Hinduism, Buddhism, humanism, and the like are taught
in every university. Many of the teachers of these courses believe that all
religions are merely what various people have thought about God, human
freedom, the soul, life after death, and similar subjects. Consequently one
system is just as likely as another to voice at least some truth. Relativism
pervades the intellectual climate of today. It holds that the Bible is not
especially revealed by God, but (like other religious books) is a compilation
of what humans have thought. Literary and historical criticism of the
Bible, when applied on the presupposition that it is merely a human
creation, encourages the growth of relativism.

   Let us see what the evangelical doctrine of revelation and the Bible has
to say to this modern condition. God has made evident to men and women
what is to be believed about Himself. His attributes, eternal power, and
divine nature have from the beginning been clearly seen. But men and
women, even though they knew God, did not honor Him as God, but
became futile in their speculations and exchanged the glory of the incor-
ruptible God for images in the form of corruptible humans, birds, beasts,
and crawling creatures. They exchanged the truth of God for a lie (Rom.
1:18–23). Some of the religious systems and ideologies formed by humans
are sublime, some reasonable, some fanciful, and some are gross distor-
tions of God and of the human race. As Christians study non-Christian
religions (whether these be Marxist, humanist, Hindu, Muslim, Buddhist,
or other), they rejoice in all true insights which human beings, using their
God-given reason, have been able to form; but Christians measure truth
always by the revealed Word of God. Evangelicals do not believe that men
and women by their own unaided wisdom can perceive and frame religious truths which are superior to those given by God through His prophets and His Son. Evangelicals, however, teach that by observing the excel-
lencies of some parts of non-Christian ideologies and systems, Christians

may be stimulated to a fresh study of the Bible and find there truths of which they have been insufficiently aware.

2. *Biblical Truth Applied to Dialogue.* With the collapse of European empires, many European Christians suddenly realized that if they met their former subjects at all, they would meet them as equals. Consequently the Europeans asked, "How does one preach Christ to one's equals?" Certainly not, they thought, by proclaiming the truth. That would alienate the non-Christian. It is far better to talk as equals. To listen as well as speak. Respectfully to lay before the other what one believes to be the truth. Monologue—a superior telling an inferior of truth the latter does not know—must give place to dialogue or a joint search for truth.

What biblical truth does the evangelical apply to this demand for dialogue? God has commanded that the gospel be proclaimed to the ends of the earth, and that Christians bear witness to Jesus Christ everywhere and disciple all the *ethne* in the world. An essential part of this doctrine is that men and women are saved as they hear the gospel and believe on Jesus Christ. The Christian is an ambassador beseeching all to be reconciled to God through belief in Christ. Proclamation may be by word or deed, and must be unabashedly intentional. Of course, some aspects of Christian life are so winsome that without intentional proclamation outsiders may be attracted to the gospel, but the Christian who does not intend proclamation cannot lay claim to fulfilling God's command. Intentional witness and intentional proclamation are the duty of Christians and churches.

Dialogue with people of other faiths (and of no faith), listening to them and engaging them in discourse about ethics, religions, rites, ceremonies, and sacred books, and, in the process, telling them of Christ, is obviously one method by which the Christian discharges the Lord's command to spread the gospel. In dialogue, one can proclaim. One can also proclaim the gospel by distributing tracts, reading the Bible aloud, showing films, broadcasting by radio, teaching Scripture in schools, taking some sort of social action, treating patients in Christ's name, and many other ways. Dialogue is one of these. Christians may use dialogue as a method.

However, the Christian cannot use dialogue as philosophy. That is, in dialogue with a non-Christian one is not to agree in advance that what both of them believe are equally true. One cannot say, "Both of us have part of the truth. Let us pool what we know and come to a greater understanding of the truth." Such dialogue denies the authority of the Bible and is inadmissible in any sound theology of mission. The Bible tells us what God has revealed about Himself, the human race, eternal life, sin, salvation, and the like. No human knowledge, whether of Christians or non-Christians, can successfully contravene that authority. A Christian may properly engage in dialogue, provided he or she holds firmly to the final authority of the Bible.

Does this doctrine imply that the Christian speaks as a superior (usually European or North American) to inferiors of other races? Not at all. The Christian is simply an earthen vessel, like all other human beings. But the believer does have a golden treasure in that vessel. Those who do not trust in Jesus Christ as God and only Savior—be they Europeans, Africans, Asians, or Jews—do not yet have that treasure. Christians are simply beggars who, having found bread, tell other beggars where to find it. No superiority or pride is involved.

3. *Biblical Truth Applied to Holistic Evangelism.* We live in a world where Marxism has ridiculed all thought of the future life as "pie in the sky by and by." Communists have set out to give to peasants and factory laborers the food, comfort, health, education, and housing which formerly were available only to the wealthy. The northern fourth of the human race lives in affluence. The southern three-fourths live in poverty. Remembering our Lord's ministry to the poor and goaded by Marxist teachings and ridicule, some Christians are loudly proclaiming that any evangelism which so much as mentions eternal life is a detriment to the Christian cause. Instead, they say, we need an evangelism which spends all its effort fighting for temporal this-worldly improvements for the poor in every land. Facing today's conditions, this is "holistic evangelism."

What Christian truth does the evangelical bring to bear on this cry for holistic evangelism? Christians believe and the Scriptures teach that it is God's purpose in salvation that the whole individual be benefited. The Scriptures say, "Seek ye first the kingdom of God, and his righteousness," and clothes, food, and other material blessings will be added unto you (Matt. 6:33, KJV). Reconciled people live better in this world than do the unreconciled. The church, made up of saved sinners, is a community whose members obey God's laws and care for each other. Thus they, by God's grace, achieve a better life than do non-Christians. It is serious error to believe that becoming a Christian confers a benefit recognizable only after death. The salvation of Christ influences all aspects of human life, making them sweeter, more just, more harmonious, more peaceful, and more abundant. Eternal life is a reality and so is abundant temporal life.

In accordance with this doctrine, Christian missions through the ages have engaged in education, medicine, agriculture, development, and reconciliation of groups at enmity with each other. Many forms of social action and uplift have been carried on. A large part of the budget of most missionary societies has been spent on acts of humanization. Evangelicals repudiate the lie that they have neglected serving the present life of men and women. They point to whole populations delivered from disease, to famines alleviated, to school systems spread throughout entire nations, and to consciences pricked concerning the evils of untouchability in India, slavery in Africa, and other inhuman conditions in other lands. Christian mission, more than any other factor, has been responsible for the rise and spread of the movement to Christian unity. Holistic evangelism is—and has been—an essential part of Christian mission as revealed by the Bible.

However, in framing the doctrine of holistic evangelism we must take seriously our Lord's words in Mark 8:36, "What does it profit a man to gain the whole world, and forfeit his soul?" (NASB). When to these words we add those recorded in Mark 9:43–48, it becomes clear that no this-worldly good can compare with eternal salvation. Our Lord said, "If your eye causes you to stumble, cast it out; it is better for you to enter the kingdom of God with one eye, than having two eyes, to be cast into hell, where their worm does not die, and the fire is not quenched" (NASB).

Many other biblical passages make it clear that this-worldly improvements in and of themselves are in no sense salvation. They are the fruits of salvation. Moreover, on occasion they may be realized imperfectly or not at all without damaging eternal salvation. This was the case in the long ages before printing was invented and universal education became common. During those centuries, the widespread knowledge of God's Word now possible was impossible. Note also that when pestilence or famine sweeps a land, Christians die as frequently as non-Christians. They are fully saved, yet they too die in the great plague or the devastating drought. This truth excuses no Christian from sharing food, spreading health information, or removing unjust and oppressive structures of society. However, sharing food, spreading health information, or removing unjust structures of society cannot be understood as part of salvation. They are not the gospel. They are good acts enjoined upon the Christian by the Lord. Advocating them is not evangelizing. The kingdom of God is not the classless society or any other earthly utopia.

Evangelicals work at improving the social order. Evangelical missionaries train their converts and their churches to do the same. But they rigidly eschew interpreting their conduct as an expression of the doctrine of salvation by works. The gospel, as Paul makes very clear, is not a series of moral requirements. It is not a burden to be borne or good deeds to be done. It is Good News. It tells men and women that they can be saved by faith alone. Justification is by faith not by works. In their zeal to get Christians to work at social reconstruction of many kinds, some Christians today are forgetting that salvation is a free gift. The burden rolls off at the foot of the cross. The Good News is not, "Become a Christian and enter the army doing the Lord's will." The gospel is, "Believe on the Lord Jesus Christ, and thou shalt be saved" (Acts 16:31, KJV).

Evangelicals believe that good works are not required as a condition of becoming a Christian. Justification is by faith. Once saved, however, believers will do good works by the power of the Holy Spirit. The Bible warns Christians that they are not saved to sin. Though forgiveness of sins is free and salvation is by faith alone, they are not to accept salvation and then sin more greatly that grace may abound. Cheap grace is to be eschewed.

Many readers will be able to think of other doctrines to include in an evangelical theology of mission. It is impossible for a Christian in one piece of the mosaic of the human race to see the circumstances facing Christians in all the other pieces. The church in each piece must phrase its doctrines in the language and thought forms of that piece. The particular church must apply the doctrines to the precise conditions it faces. The World Council of Churches cannot do this for particular churches. Outsiders, even those who act with the best of intentions, cannot speak exactly to the real issues. Readers in various lands should regard the doctrines we have described and the applications we have made as models which seem good to us. We hope that these readers will make their own models. As long as the models accept the Bible as the infallible rule in faith and practice, God's revelation of His holy will for humankind, the final measuring rod for all religious and moral truth, they will be framing an evangelical theology of mission.

7

Evangelicals Find Each Other and Join the Debate

Arthur F. Glasser

"As usual, it began with the young people." Thus Willem Visser 't Hooft describes the Hoekendijk revolt at the well-planned WSCF Strasbourg gathering in 1960. "Karl Barth had had his day! We don't want high churchmanship; we want high worldmanship!" The church must turn towards the world and lose itself in it. The Christian must become "the man for others."[1]

Yes, students have usually generated the momentum for new mission epochs. The famous Mount Hermon conference of 1886, presided over by D. L. Moody, was transformed by participating students—with a very different agenda—into a stimulus for the Intercollegiate YMCA, the Inter-Seminary Missionary Alliance, and the Student Volunteer Movement for Foreign Missions (SVM). And it was the SVM that eventually made possible the Edinburgh Conference of 1910.

A later generation of evangelical students—far fewer in number—met at Asheville, North Carolina, in 1936 and took the first steps to call their fellow students to face the unfinished missionary task. They stand in sharpest contrast to the WSCF students of the Strasbourg gathering in 1960, because of their commitment to the authority of Scripture.

Actually, the time was not ripe for evangelical advance. The disastrous fundamentalist-modernist clash of the twenties had brought depressing consequences in its wake. The "separatist" withdrawal mentality caused many Bible-believing Christians to abandon their churches, retreat from culture, and forsake the arena of intellectual encounter. Whereas the redemptive gospel they sought to protect was actually a world-changing message, they "narrowed it to a world-resisting message. . . . Fundamen-

---

1. Willem A. Visser 't Hooft, *Has the Ecumenical Movement a Future?* (Atlanta: John Knox, 1976), pp. 24–26.

talism in revolting against the Social Gospel seemed also to revolt against the Christian social imperative."[2]

Liberalism was the orthodoxy of the day. In the mid-thirties the major denominations dominated university campuses with their professional representatives; they actively promoted the Oxford Peace Pledge, world disarmament, and square dances. No evangelical student movement of any significance existed. Indeed, was one needed? Committed Christians went to Bible schools or to the rare church-related college that had not capitulated to the humanism of the day.

However, despite the spiritual deadness in the university world, and the tragic, time-consuming preoccupation of evangelicals with the sterile theological controversies that had raged in earlier decades, missionary societies as a general rule gave the impression of health. Interdenominational "faith" missions were more vigorous than their denominational counterparts, possibly because of theological homogeneity and patterns of personalized support. They were free from uncertainty as to evangelistic and church-planting goals. And they did not experience to the same degree the anguish denomination-related agencies knew when budgets were cut, especially during the Great Depression. How often evangelistic programs were the first to be eliminated, especially when mission hospitals and schools were struggling to survive! Although not officially endorsed, the antievangelism mood of the Laymen's Foreign Missions Inquiry (1932) with its syncretistic overtones largely prevailed when the budgetary axe fell.

But this inquiry had no effect on evangelicals whatever. It was dismissed as hopelessly subbiblical—"the product of amateurs, more accustomed to the tangible results of business deals than the years of patient labor needed to establish the Christian Gospel in a hostile environment."[3] Actually, in those barren years, and despite the worldwide economic distress of the early thirties, one society, the China Inland Mission, issued an appeal for two hundred new workers within two years, and had the joy of seeing the target met—with all expenses paid! Evangelical lay people in many mainline churches supported this type of society because of its refusal to depart from the biblical gospel, and because of its sacrificial commitment to evangelism.

But there was no vigorous student missionary movement to replace the dying SVM, which by then had been completely captured by theological liberalism and by preoccupation with social and political issues. So the

2. Carl F. H. Henry, *The Uneasy Conscience of Modern Fundamentalism* (Grand Rapids: Eerdmans, 1947), pp. 30, 33.

3. Eleanor M. Jackson, *Red Tape and the Gospel: A Study of the Significance of the Ecumenical Missionary Struggle of William Paton (1886–1943)* (Birmingham: Phlogiston Publishing/The Selly Oak Colleges, 1980), p. 121.

small group of evangelical students we mentioned earlier launched the Student Foreign Missions Fellowship (SFMF) in 1936, and it grew steadily. Bible schools, Christian colleges, theological seminaries, and eventually the secular university world came within the range of its concern. In the years that followed, the few students who gave the SFMF birth became widely active, first as frontier evangelists and general missionaries, but later as mission executives, mission professors, and mission anthropologists.

During the war years (1941–1945) the SFMF had its struggles, but eventually it became the missionary arm of the Inter-Varsity Christian Fellowship—which by this time had come to North America from Great Britain. Soon a pattern of triennial missionary gatherings emerged—the Urbana conventions—and increasing numbers of students attended throughout the sixties and seventies and into the eighties with no let-up in sight. Indeed, the crowds have become so great (18,000 in 1979) that more frequent conventions have had to be scheduled, along with regional conferences. And the pattern has been repeated with similar success in Europe and in East Asia. This has even prompted such ethnic groups as the Chinese to convene their own Urbana-style conferences.

All this is cited because of the salutary impact successive "Urbanas" have had on the worldwide evangelical missionary movement.[4] Not only have they been used to stimulate reflection on the scriptural mandate calling the whole church to missionary obedience; not only have they challenged evangelical students to become "world Christians" in the old SVM pattern; but among other things, they have also provided the church with the men and women who are known as "Urbana speakers." In turn, these missionary speakers, coupled with the founders of the SFMF, contributed significantly to the development of a mood for evangelical ecumenism within the worldwide church in our day.

The Interdenominational Foreign Mission Association

During the earlier years of the Urbana conventions, interdenominational "faith" missions tended to be prominent. Prior to the formation of the IMC (at Lake Mohonk in 1921), these missions had organized (at Princeton in 1917) their own inter-mission structure: the Interdenominational Foreign Mission Association (IFMA). Their concern was that all faith missions be "in fellowship" with one another and express thereby the solidarity of the evangelical missionary movement. IFMA's focus for member missions was that all give "strict adherence to the evangelical

---

4. Rodger C. Bassham, *Mission Theology, 1948–1975: Years of Worldwide Creative Tension—Ecumenical, Evangelical and Roman Catholic* (Pasadena: William Carey Library, 1979), p. 186.

doctrines and the standards of historical Christianity and the burden to carry the Gospel to those regions where Christ has not been named." It was virtually this commitment that the SFMF adopted in 1936 for their new movement. However, whereas the students were vigorous in proclaiming their vision, the IFMA remained a rather passive body, somewhat lacking in the grace of self-criticism, and content to serve as an accrediting society for member missions. With the postwar dramatic increase in missionary interest among evangelicals, IFMA finally opened an office (in 1949), but it was not until 1956 that a full-time administrator was appointed. Its mood was one of benign interest in its member missions and its blind spot was the thesis that it would be unspiritual to evaluate critically their policies and field methodologies. Actually, the IFMA reflected the posture of the fundamentalism of the twenties. Its modified Calvinism made it critical of Arminianism. Its dispensationalism made it suspicious of Pentecostal and charismatic movements. Its eschatology made it eschew contact with anything "ecumenical," since "the WCC can easily adumbrate the Final Apostasy and the coming Antichrist." In IFMA's view the biblical warnings of the "falling away" in the last days (e.g., 2 Thess. 2:3–4) were not intended to deepen one's personal commitment to Christ but to enable the discerning to identify the churches that were "apostate" and withdraw from them. These churches were viewed as beyond the possibility of spiritual renewal regardless of everything the Bible and church history said to the contrary.

Despite these aberrations, which increasing numbers of evangelicals came to deplore, the evangelical understanding of the biblical basis of mission was impressive. This can be attributed to the writings of such earlier authors as John Nevius (1829–1893), Adoniram J. Gordon (1836–1895), Arthur T. Pierson (1837–1911), Robert E. Speer (1867–1947), Roland Allen (1868–1947), William O. Carver (1868–1954), and Hendrik Kraemer (1868–1965—particularly his 1938 book *The Christian Message in a Non-Christian World*). Mention should also be made of Robert H. Glover's widely used classroom text *The Bible Basis of Mission* (1946). This volume contained an enthusiastic introduction by Samuel M. Zwemer (1867–1952) of earlier SVM fame and a prolific writer on biblical themes and Islam. Then, too, one should not forget Johannes H. Bavinck's *Impact of Christianity on the Non-Christian World* (1949) with its plea for a trinitarian concept of mission, years before this was discussed in ecumenical circles (by Karl Hartenstein in 1952, Gerald H. Anderson in 1955, Lesslie Newbigin in 1963, and Georg Vicedom in 1965). Actually, in an extended study of *Missio Dei,* Robert Recker of Calvin Theological Seminary remarks that Samuel Volbeda of that faculty (1914–1952) was "ahead of this modern ferment in missiology . . . with his rejection of anthropocentric, ecclesiocentric, or soteriocentric missions, and affirmed that only theocentric missions are in accord with the genius of the Scripture. . . . It goes without saying that he rejected any humanitarian concept of mission . . . he simply contended for a trinitarian concept of mission."[5]

In many ways, the evangelical understanding of the theology of the Christian mission was no reflection of the parochial perspectives of the IFMA. Even so, the IFMA mentality dominated for a long time—despite the fact that, according to the Bible, the whole church is called to the missionary task and Christians with their varied traditions should seek to work peaceably alongside one another. Yet in many places field missionaries were beginning to shed IFMA's encapsulated mood and were finding that cooperative efforts with those outside its cautious conservatism were bringing personal enrichment and furthering the gospel, largely because of the spiritual oneness they discovered as they shared with one another. The Latin America Mission (LAM) was beginning (1959) its pattern of seeking the total mobilization of all Christians and the cooperation of all churches within a country for nationwide simultaneous evangelistic outreach. Those who participated found that their particular confessional loyalties were neither irrelevant nor restrictive, but rather became the means whereby they were able to contribute to the wholeness of the growing church in Hispanic America.

IFMA leaders were quite concerned over LAM's approach. And yet, they never were quite able to persuade LAM's leaders that Scripture endorses IFMA's posture of deliberate isolation from major segments of the church. Instead, they found themselves put on the spot. Tough questions were asked: Has God ever given a mandate that a Christian or church should, on the grounds of serious disagreements, separate from those who likewise confess His name? Does He not seek the renewal of His people? How can Christians become His instruments for renewal if they persist in withdrawing from those who need it most?

Despite this, within the IFMA parochialism triumphed over the biblical witness. The dénouement was a Congress on World Missions sponsored by the IFMA at Chicago in 1960. This was the last attempt of dispensationalist-separatists to dominate the American missionary movement. And it fell far short of being a success. The platform rhetoric soared to heights: the delegates were heralded as the missionaries most faithful to the tradition of the Edinburgh convention of 1910 and to the SVM watchword. Today, when one reads the plenary addresses and studies the transcripts of panel discussions, a sense of sadness grips the heart. Despite its warm evangelicalism, the Chicago convention was a curious mixture of triumphalism and pessimism. Its focus was on the IFMA-type Western society,

---

5. Robert Recker, "The Concept of the Missio Dei and Instruction in Mission at Calvin Seminary," *Calvin Theological Journal* 11 (1976): 192–93.

not on the national church—and only marginally on national Christians. Missionaries occupied the center of the stage and their perspectives were tragically flawed:

> The time ahead set for evangelizing Africa is 10 years . . . she needs people who can separate culture from conviction—so that religion is not carnal.

> Rome continues to corrupt the Gospel message. She may change her color, her reactions, but Rome never changes in her drive to unite Church and State in one governing power.

> A spirit of revolution has come over all the countries around the Caribbean; it is what the Bible calls the spirit of anti-Christ . . . causing unrest, and behind it is Communism which is always agitating among young people.[6]

Apart from the witness of two student leaders, and LAM's winsome Kenneth Strachan with his call for the total mobilization of national Christians (the beginnings of Evangelism-in-Depth), the platform was dominated by the old guard. No one would question either their commitment to Christ or their concern for world evangelization, but those who attended the Chicago convention could not be persuaded that this American effort was by any stretch of the imagination a "Congress on World Missions." It was a depressing scene, in such sharp contrast to the growing popularity of the Urbana gatherings. Only four church leaders were present from the Third World. And there was only one solitary non-IFMA speaker to represent all other Protestant missions. It was not without reason that a few months later the Wycliffe Bible Translators, under pressure to conform, withdrew from the IFMA.

Ferment Among Evangelicals

Actually, IFMA was not the sole evangelical inter-mission association in those days. This is what made the Chicago convention so tragic. Fifteen years before (1945) the Evangelical Foreign Missions Association (EFMA) had come into being to serve the mission boards of evangelical denominations, and to gather up those stray independent missions that could not in all conscience submit to the leadership of the IFMA. In no time at all, under very able leadership, the EFMA drew into its ranks a broad range of missions, from the Pentecostal to the Reformed. But its rapid growth and comparatively forward-looking vision were a sharp trial to the IFMA. Despite significant differences between IFMA and EFMA, these agen-

6. Jack O. Percy and Mary Bennett, *Facing the Unfinished Task* (Grand Rapids: Zondervan, 1961), pp. 26, 43, 63.

cies were both so avowedly evangelical that it seemed inevitable they would begin to draw gradually together and sponsor jointly the sort of marginal activities that could not possibly threaten either their separate theological integrity or structural autonomy. The Urbana speakers and others sought from time to time to suggest an outright merger, but with no success. To inject a personal note, I recall my own attempt to hoist a trial balloon at one of the IFMA annual meetings. It was in the form of a paper arguing for what I called the "H" plan. The suggestion was to find a convention center laid out roughly in the form of an "H"; that is, with two parallel wings connected at the middle with dining facilities and an auditorium. Hold simultaneous annual meetings in the two wings, but eat together and have the same speakers address joint plenary sessions. While few saluted the idea at the time, at present the two associations do hold joint meetings approximately every three years. All this began in 1966.

The year 1966 was truly crucial. Before it ended, a tremendous burst of dynamism had been released from within the evangelical wing of the church, and everything that had been tightly nailed seemed to come loose. The words of the psalmist came true: The Lord "turned again the captivity of Zion . . . [and] then was our mouth filled with laughter" (Ps. 126:1–2, KJV). New leaders came to the fore. Pent-up energies burst forth and the turbulent sixties ended with the evangelical missionary movement beginning to manifest an upsurge in character, size, and vigor.

It all began when the IFMA, under younger leadership, came to the realization that its missions represented but part of a much larger and variegated evangelical presence throughout the world. The sheer vitality of such EFMA-member missions as those belonging to the Pentecostal wing of the worldwide church could no longer be either dismissed or discounted. They represented a way of preaching the gospel that differed significantly from the somewhat cerebral and modified Calvinist form that characterized many of the IFMA groups. The heart and conscience were addressed in ways that made a more conceptual and somewhat polemic style suffer by contrast. The use of joyous song, vivid story, and even corporate dance conveyed biblical realities in ways that made these EFMA missions the envy of those whose preaching was heavily weighted with theology. More, these people unabashedly grappled with the complexity of the physical needs of those they sought to win for Christ. Healing services, coupled with friendly pastoral concern for those who were afflicted, were so "person-centered" and "health-centered" that more traditional medical outreach began increasingly to appear only as "bed-centered" and "cure-centered"—and hence somewhat sub-Christian.

Besides this, the Pentecostals were willing to tackle "the dark side of the soul" and challenge the growing phenomenon of occultism, Satan worship, and demon possession. Whereas IFMA people and other non-charismatic evangelicals (particularly the Baptists!) had found it relatively easy to expose the extravagance of the occasional charlatan, they were silenced in the presence of the Pentecostals' serious confrontation of the hard realities of the spirit world. Here was a spirituality which could not be ignored. Walter Hollenweger quotes the counsel of Dr. W. Schulte:

> It is not possible to give a diagnosis which distinguishes between sickness and possession . . . they represent two possible aspects of the same event. No discerning doctor will deny that the healing of a disease can only come about with the help of God. But this should not mean abandoning all medical activity in the sphere of psychological and mental illness and looking for help from a miracle of prayer.[7]

Alongside the growing influence of the Arminian-Pentecostal presence, the IFMA groups began to realize they could not discount the growing popularity and effectiveness of "crusade evangelism." As Billy Graham, Youth for Christ, Young Life, and Campus Crusade extended their labors beyond the church, it became increasingly unwise to ignore their efforts. Apparently, the recognized willingness of the Spirit of God to bless these activities in significant ways—both in the homelands and within the Third World—enlarged the vision of many a traditional evangelical laboring at the edge of gospel advance.

Still another factor was the way in which evangelicals within the conciliar camp began to reach out and contact their opposite numbers outside it. This resulted in what came to be known as the Malone Consultations. For almost a decade twenty to thirty leaders met for an isolated weekend each summer. They read papers and engaged in open discussions on the mission issues of the day. The reaction of those IFMA and EFMA executives who attended was mind-boggling, to put it mildly. Convinced evangelicals within the ecumenical movement? And loyal to the WCC?! No evangelical who attended a Malone weekend—and the list is long—could easily dismiss the WCC out of hand. All had to agree that its publications were worthy of the most careful scrutiny. The tragedy is that by the mid-sixties, when the secularized version of *Missio Dei* began to gain popularity, interest in the Malone Consultations suddenly evaporated. Judging that the world mission of the church was being undermined by the WCC, evangelicals were caught up in a new urgency: they must speak out, for the very integrity of the church was at stake.

But what particularly generated ferment within the nonconciliar evan-

---

7. Walter J. Hollenweger, "The Roots and Fruits of the Charismatic Renewal in the Third World: Implications for Mission," unpublished paper (University of Birmingham, 1979), p. 13.

gelical community, and made many missionaries both uneasy and excited, were the writings of a man who at first hardly knew that either the IFMA or the EFMA existed. His background was conciliar and his training liberal. However, after years of striving to serve the church in India as best he knew how, he came to a profound awareness of the bankruptcy of liberal Christianity and sought to return to the faith of his fathers (several generations of missionaries to India). In time he became a convinced evangelical and almost immediately began to explore the processes whereby people become Christians. He was Donald Anderson McGavran. His first book, *The Bridges of God* (1955), could not be ignored. Kenneth Scott Latourette described it as "one of the most important books on missionary methods that has appeared in many years." Many of those who read the book began to look at missionary practice as though they were seeing reality for the first time. They had to hear more of McGavran. What else had he written? To inject another personal note: Having never been given any instruction by senior missionaries as to the methodology I should use during my years in China, other than "just pray and trust God," I found myself strangely drawn to this man. Along with many others, I had to meet him and learn what mission was all about! His subsequent books on Church Growth were particularly gobbled up by the EFMA-member missions. And to think that his denomination was in the WCC!

Inevitably, Vatican II (1962–1965) also had its impact on evangelical missions all over the world. No one who heard the Roman Catholic system roundly criticized at the Chicago convention of 1960 rose in its defense. But the coming of John XXIII to the papal throne, and the *aggiornamento* he released—along with the manifest integrity of his Christian concerns, and the direction he gave to the council—all these made evangelicals very unsure of their dogmatic stereotypes of Rome. Again, the Latin America Mission was in the vanguard, calling other evangelical missions to catch the significance of the struggles of God within that ancient church. But what to do? Somehow, all felt the best minds among us should grapple with the implications of the coming end of the Italian domination of the Curia, and the tremendous theological pluralism within what the Chicago convention of 1960 had regarded as a rigid and oppressive monolith of religio-political power.

The Wheaton Declaration

Evangelicals must get together! The failure of the IMC to renew mission vision in conciliar churches pointed in only one direction: the eventual dismantling of the older mainline mission boards. The reconceptualization of *Missio Dei* and subsequent confusion over the theology of the Christian mission pointed in only one direction: the rapid erosion (within the churches) of biblical convictions about mission. The growing phenomenon of evangelical mission societies joining both the IFMA and EFMA pointed in only one direction: the possibility of a greater evangelical consensus being achieved on the urgency of the hour. If only IFMA and EFMA would together convene a conference to say something! All this made a jointly-sponsored congress—at Wheaton in 1966—not only a possibility but a necessity. And yet one recalls the dark note not infrequently sounded in the precongress debates. Supposing IFMA and EFMA acted jointly? Was there any guarantee of success? And if a "Wheaton consensus" were to develop, how could its essence be conveyed vividly to the widely scattered missionary force all over the world?

Those who were involved in the preliminary discussions, and in the piling up of pressures so that the leadership of IFMA and EFMA would face one another, declare a truce on promoting their distinctives, and issue a joint call for a congress on the church's worldwide mission, had no difficulty listing the issues that such a gathering would have to face. They were reasonably well acquainted with the writings of leaders within the WCC. So then, a list was drawn up:

1. Religious Syncretism, or how far should one go in a cultural adaption of the gospel?
2. Neo-universalism, or is there an eternal separation of the saved from the lost?
3. Proselytism, or do people have the right to change their religious allegiance?
4. Neo-Romanism, or to what extent is its new face God's call to evangelicals to revise their judgments of Rome?
5. Church Growth, or how responsible are missionaries to develop their methodologies in the light of the resistance/receptivity of peoples?
6. Foreign Missions, or is there a scriptural validity to a mission structure separate and distinct from the congregational structure?
7. Evangelical Unity, or how can the unity of the church be expressed when evangelicals are so fragmented in their organizational life?
8. Evaluating Methods, or what is the validity to harnessing the behavioral sciences to the heightening of effectiveness in the cross-cultural communication of the Christian gospel?
9. Social Concern, or how can the priority of evangelism be maintained when the Bible also stresses the obligation to labor for social justice and human welfare?
10. Hostile World, or how should evangelicals respond to persecution and opposition in the performance of their mission?

All were agreed: the congress should address these issues in depth. The delegates should participate in workshops which would give opportunity for all to bear witness to their separate concerns on each issue. And the congress should have plenary sessions calling evangelicals to reaffirm their commitment to the authority of Scripture, the essence of the gospel, the endowment of the Spirit, the nature of the church, the reality of the coming return of Christ, and His consummation of human history. The congress should also schedule "area reports" to provide one and all with an up-to-date picture of the advance of the gospel throughout the world.

Those were exciting days—preparing for Wheaton. One day while I was reading an article that sought to distinguish a creed ("I believe . . .") from a confession ("We confess . . ."), a new thought surfaced that immediately heightened my own sense of excitement. One uses creeds for worship, and thereby stresses the essentials of his or her faith. But confessions are addressed to one's contemporaries; they arise out of situations when truth needs to be defined and deviations need to be both enumerated and refuted. Did not the leaders of the "Confessing Church" in Germany take a stand against the pastors (90 percent of the total) who were taken in by the blandishments of Adolf Hitler? Did they not draft a declaration and send it to all the churches (the Barmen Declaration of 1934)? The confusion of the times demanded a "Wheaton Declaration"!

The idea caught on. Evangelicals as a united people were going to speak out and enter formally the complex debate on the nature of the mission of the church. This sent our minds soaring, and caused our eyes to shine! We studied the antecedents of Barmen and the manner in which at that time "the Church struggled against itself for itself."[8] We analyzed the structure of the document's *Erklärung* and decided it was too Teutonic. Furthermore, Karl Barth had hastily composed it "fortified by strong coffee and one or two Brazilian cigars" while most of the Barmen delegates were having a noon-hour siesta! No! We must seek a consensus document. All must be permitted to contribute, or no one would take seriously the claim of its being a collective evangelical confession of major significance. The assignment to attempt a precongress draft fell on me.

In no time at all, despite a heavy schedule of meetings, appointments, correspondence, and the like, spare moments were found to detail the questions that the delegates at Wheaton would have to answer. Why must we speak? What is our authority for doing so? Should we not begin with an extended public confession? But that is something self-assured evangelicals find difficult to do! And how should we address the many issues before us? Here is where I was greatly helped by the wise counsel and

8. Arthur C. Cochrane, *The Church's Confession Under Hitler* (Philadelphia: Westminster, 1962), p. 11.

indefatigable industry of Louis L. King, then the director of all overseas operations of the Christian and Missionary Alliance. I still vividly and gratefully recall spending a long evening (and much of the night!) sharing with him my text and its unresolved problems. Together we agreed that the declaration should affirm commitment to Christ and to the authority of Scripture. It should also demonstrate that the delegates sought to explore all sides of each issue, and to listen to the witness of relevant Scripture. In the end, they should not fail to declare in clear and unambiguous terms what they believe to be an evangelical response to each issue.

But how should the declaration end? Certainly there should be a renewal of commitment to the evangelization of this generation in the spirit of the Edinburgh conference of 1910. However, the precise wording eluded me. The solution came in a plane somewhere between Chattanooga and Philadelphia. In the seat pocket ahead of me was the airline's monthly magazine—and on the back cover the closing lines of the Declaration of Independence of 1776. This was just what I needed! History buffs will find something faintly familiar when they come to Wheaton's closing paragraph: "In the support of this Declaration we . . . do covenant together . . . so help us God."

The Wheaton congress somehow succeeded. Those were days of intense debate, the inevitable mixture of enthusiasm and overstatement, and long hours of seeking to be responsive to the insights of the delegates as they grappled with the herculean task of producing an evangelical consensus. But it was a high and holy moment when the 938 delegates from 71 countries representing 150 mission boards (50 non–IFMA/EFMA!) rose to their feet, and in unison read their pledge of support (à la 1776!). We then sang "A Mighty Fortress Is Our God," and "black, yellow and white children of God sat down at the undivided table of our Lord where together in true unity they ate the one bread and drank the one cup."[9]

The postmortems that followed the Wheaton congress were uniformly positive. Evangelicals had shown themselves capable of united witness in the face of the confusion precipitated in the worldwide church through the popularization of a secular approach to the missionary task. Arminians and Calvinists, Baptists and pedobaptists, denominationalists and independents, dispensationalists and charismatics—somehow, all these distinctives seemed peripheral to the chief task of making Jesus Christ known, loved, and served throughout the world. Friends in the ecumenical movement—who were present and warmly received—saw to it that the Wheaton Declaration was published in the *International Review of Mission* (October 1966).

9. Harold Lindsell, ed., *The Church's Worldwide Mission* (Waco, TX: Word, 1966), p. 16.

A few months later an even larger gathering of evangelicals took place in Berlin. The focus of its concern was the issue of evangelism. Under the rubric of "One Race, One Gospel, One Task," evangelical scholars as well as missionaries grappled with such important themes as the authority for evangelism and the basic theology of evangelism. The Berlin "Congress Statement" supplements what the Wheaton congress sought to say. And by 1974 evangelicals worldwide were caught up in preparing an even larger gathering to focus on world evangelization. This took place in Lausanne with over four thousand in attendance. The Lausanne congress marked a still further step forward in evangelical reflection on the missionary task. The "Lausanne Covenant," enriched and nurtured by both Wheaton and Berlin, has come to be virtually the rallying point of evangelicals worldwide. It provides them with direction as they move into the final years of the twentieth century. And the volumes of addresses from these three gatherings have become the foundation stones of a growing evangelical edifice of literary output that is rapidly exceeding in size, range, and quality the earlier writings of the SVM and the IMC. Evangelicals have at long last succeeded in establishing an identity within the Christian movement in our day.

8

Making Doctrines Missionarily Effective and Biblically Correct

Donald McGavran

A ny theology of mission is made up of many doctrines, each a statement of some aspect of biblical truth. These doctrines must be carefully expressed in ways that are true to the Bible *and* effectively forward the great task of discipling all the peoples of earth. They must reflect the fact that the gospel itself, by command of the eternal God, has been revealed precisely to bring *panta ta ethne* to faith and obedience (Rom. 16:25–26).

Unfortunately the doctrines of the church have usually been framed to correct errors and misunderstandings which were current at the time. They have not been framed to bring billions to faith and obedience. For example, the great theologians of the Reformation, whom we love and admire, to whom Christians owe an enormous debt of gratitude, were absorbed by the need to state doctrines biblically. The reason for this focus of the Reformers is clear. In the medieval church, the Bible had been available only in Latin, not in the languages of the common peoples. As a result many unbiblical views had been set forth as correct theology and ecclesiology for all time. When the Bible was translated into the vernacular and recognized as the authority (the traditions of the church had previously been so regarded), it became abundantly clear that many doctrines would have to be revised. This the Reformers did. But they did not frame the doctrines with a view to the vast non-Christian populations in Asia, Africa, and Latin America. Lesslie Newbigin calls this dramatically to our attention:

> For a thousand years when Christendom was sealed off by Islam from effective contact with the rest of the world, and was contracting, not expanding, it lived in almost total isolation from non-Christian cultures.
> In this situation the illusion that the age of missions was over became

almost an integral part of Christianity. The perpetuation of that illusion is revealed in our normal church life, in the forms of congregations and parishes, in our conception of the ministry and in the ordinary consciousness of churchmen.

Our theological curricula bear eloquent testimony to this illusion. *Our church history is normally taught not as the story of the triumphs of the Gospel, but as the story of the internal quarrels of the church; our systems of dogmatics are not directed toward the non-Christian faith.* The training of the ministry is not for a mission to the world but almost exclusively for the pastoral care of established Christian congregations.[1]

The Protestant theologians were concerned with establishing a biblically correct form of Christianity in Northern Europe, and later in North America. World evangelization did not enter into their doctrinal statements in any but the smallest measure. So until this day, the discipling of all the peoples of earth has remained peripheral to the main currents of Protestant thought.

Consider the following excerpt from a letter written by a graduate of the School of World Mission at Fuller Theological Seminary. He is writing from the campus of a famed seminary of a notable American denomination:

Neither in this seminary nor in any other seminary of our church is world evangelization taught as a required subject. The curriculum of the seminary includes many subjects—Greek, Hebrew, Old Testament, New Testament, Church History, Systematic Theology, Homiletics, and on and on, but there is no course on evangelism or Christian Mission. In a few of our seminaries, missions may be taken as an elective, if there happens to be a part-time adjunct professor handy.

However, when the missionary movement gained great strength in the twentieth century, a few seminaries here and there began to add missions to their curricula and appointed a professor of missions to their faculties. One thinks at once of Professor Kenneth Scott Latourette at Yale. Despite this, missions (the church's worldwide task) remains still a peripheral concern in the theological world. It gets only slight mention in the great creeds. In this chapter we are proposing that any *biblical* theological system, any well-constructed statement of faith which speaks to the crying needs of today, will contain a thoroughly biblical missionary dimension.

Any true biblical theology of mission must be constructed in view of the unswerving purpose of God to call out His church from among all the peoples of earth. This is the conviction which resounds throughout the whole Bible. We will cite only a few of many passages. Four times in the first book of the Bible (Gen. 12:3; 18:18; 22:18; 26:4) we read that

1. Lesslie Newbigin, "The Mission and Unity of the Church," Ainslee Memorial Lecture, Grahamstown, South Africa, 1955 (emphasis added).

in Abraham and his seed all peoples of the earth shall be blessed. This purpose of God is echoed again and again in the Psalms. For example, in Psalm 96:7–9 we read:

> Ascribe to the LORD, O families of the peoples,
>   ascribe to the LORD glory and strength!
> Ascribe to the LORD the glory due his name;
>   bring an offering, and come into his courts!
> Worship the LORD in holy array;
>   tremble before him, all the earth!

In Isaiah 49:6 God is represented as saying to the Servant of the Lord, the coming Messiah:

> It is too small a thing that You should be My Servant
> To raise up the tribes of Jacob, and to restore the preserved ones of Israel;
> I will also make You a light of the [peoples]
> So that My salvation may reach to the end of the earth. [NASB]

All the prophets spoke of God's purpose to redeem the peoples of earth. The English word *nation,* which has been used to render the Hebrew *'ammim* and *goyim,* was a correct translation back in 1600 A.D. Then "nation" meant tribe or people. But today the word means sovereign state. The correct translation of *'ammim, goyim,* and *ethne* today is *peoples* (tribes, castes, classes, and other segments of society).

God's unswerving purpose attested to throughout the Bible has been to save His people from among all the peoples of the earth. To be sure, as the apostle Paul so clearly says, this purpose was "hidden for long ages" (Rom. 16:25, NIV). But it was clearly seen by the Lord Jesus. His messianic consciousness rested on these "hidden" or neglected passages of Scripture. His own ministry, while it was confined to the Jews and to the one land of Palestine, constantly looked beyond to the peoples of earth. His was a universal message.

> *Every one* ... who shall confess Me before men, I will also confess him before My Father who is in heaven. [Matt. 10:32]

> Nor does anyone know the Father, except the Son, and *anyone* to whom the Son wishes to reveal Him. [Matt. 11:27]

> All authority has been given to Me in heaven and on earth. Go therefore and make disciples of [*panta ta ethne = all the peoples of Planet Earth*]. [Matt. 28:18–19]

> Repentance for forgiveness of sins should be proclaimed in His name to *all the* [*peoples*]. [Luke 24:47]

> *As many as received Him,* to them He gave the right to become children of God, even to those who believe in His name. [John 1:12][2]

2. NASB, emphasis added.

The point need not be labored. The early church carried out this unswerving purpose of God. Throughout the ages, when most filled with the Holy Spirit and most directed by the Holy Bible, the church has surged out in world evangelization to spread the light to the peoples yet in darkness.

The reader should now turn to the statement of faith used by his or her denomination and reframe each doctrine so that it is biblically true and missionarily effective. It should be remembered that in most cases these doctrines were framed in the past by people who were not flamingly mission-minded. They were correcting the doctrines of the Church of Rome, it may be, or of some other branch of the church. They were not looking intently at the three billion perishing in a famine of the Word of God (Amos 8:11–12). They were not asking themselves how the doctrines should be framed so that this appalling hunger might be met and people everywhere might feast on the Bread of Heaven.

Lest any think that this omission of the missionary dimension marked only ancient churches in the sixteenth and seventeenth centuries, let it be noted that serious revision of the creeds of the church to adequately reflect a biblical missionary dimension has yet to be done. When the United Presbyterians drew up their famed creedal statement of 1967, they made it strong in regard to Christianizing the structures of society, but very weak in regard to world evangelization. When in 1973 John Leith published his revised *Creeds of the Churches,* he included a creed on the relationship of the church to war—but not a word about its relationship to world evangelization. Other illustrations could be cited. We are simply proposing that what has been done for poverty, oppression, and war, now be done for spiritual destitution and death.

A Sample Revision

In order that we may think clearly about the situation, it will be helpful to illustrate what "making our doctrinal statements missionarily effective and biblically correct" means. Take the climactic doctrine in the Thirty-Nine Articles of the Anglican Church (1563), namely, "Of the One Oblation of Christ Finished upon the Cross." The atonement stands at the very center of the Christian faith and forms an essential part of all creeds. We will consider the Anglican formulation of this doctrine because most readers will be able to look at it objectively. It is not theirs. The Thirty-Nine Articles is, however, one of the great doctrinal landmarks of the Reformation and is still subscribed to by more than fifty million Christians. Article XXXI reads:

> *Of the One Oblation of Christ Finished upon the Cross*: The offering of Christ once made is that perfect redemption, propitiation, and satisfaction for all

the sins of the whole world, both original and actual; and there is none other satisfaction for sin but that alone. Wherefore the sacrifices of masses, in the which it was commonly said that the priest did offer Christ for the quick and the dead to have remission of pain or guilt, were blasphemous fables and dangerous deceits.[3]

This statement of the doctrine of the atonement was enormously effective for the growth of the Anglican Church since it had recently separated from the Church of Rome. Roman Catholic masses were labeled "blasphemous fables and dangerous deceits," while the essence of the biblical doctrine of the atonement was scrupulously preserved and exactly stated. However, once the separation from Rome had been completed, this statement of the doctrine had no power to thrust Anglicans out into worldwide mission. Although Article XXXI said that Christ's death was atonement "for all the sins of the whole world," it did not emphasize this, nor spell out its implication. It did not say that since the offering of Christ on the cross is the perfect redemption for all sins of the whole world, His purpose remains thwarted until Christians proclaim the gospel to one and all. This statement of the atonement was worded with attention fixed on the then prevalent misunderstanding of the atonement. Were it to be reframed with attention focused on the three billion who have yet to believe on Jesus Christ, it would be worded differently.

Were Article XXXI to be written today by theologians heavily burdened for the salvation of Marxists, secularists, Hindus, humanists, Buddhists, Jews, Muslims, and others, it would be stated differently. Consequently we set ourselves to the task of rewriting this article so that it is missionarily more effective and biblically more correct.

As we do this, we shall bypass the modern debate as to whether other theories of the atonement are not in fact the true biblical revelation. This debate has been mounted not in order to disciple the peoples of earth, but to make the doctrine of the atonement more palatable to a secular age. We shall assume that the substitutionary theory of the atonement, held by the framers of the Thirty-Nine Articles, correctly states the biblical teaching on the matter.

Furthermore, since our purpose is not to modernize the historic statement but solely to make it missionarily more effective and biblically more balanced, we shall retain as much of the classic phrasing as possible. How then will the reworded article read?

Of the One Oblation of Christ Finished upon the Cross: The offering of Christ on the cross is that perfect redemption, propitiation, and satisfaction for

3. "The Thirty-Nine Articles," in John H. Leith, ed., *Creeds of the Churches: A Reader in Christian Doctrine from the Bible to the Present*, rev. ed. (Atlanta: John Knox, 1973), p. 277.

all the sins, both original and actual, of all the thousands of peoples in all six continents and of all religions and ideologies. There is no other satisfaction for sin, but that alone. Therefore salvation is to be gained solely by believing on the finished work of Christ on the cross and becoming completely His follower. All human acts performed to secure forgiveness of sins and salvation are useless to achieve that end. Just and kindly acts, humanitarian labors, offerings at temples and shrines, blood sacrifices to propitiate gods and goddesses, and works of merit do not secure forgiveness of sins. All teachings leading men and women to practice such works of righteousness as means to redemption are blasphemous fables and dangerous deceits.

As we observe how Article XXXI has been reworded to bring it into line with God's purpose to redeem all the peoples of the world, we see that a new creed or new doctrines are not being proposed. Each denomination has its own creed or statement of faith. So do many seminaries, missionary societies, and parachurch organizations. Books are full of creedal statements which various groups of Christians have drawn up and which they treasure. Multitudes of wise theologians are expounding existing creeds or setting forth new ones.

We are simply asking that whatever their creed or statement of faith may be, readers now reframe each doctrine to reflect two specific emphases. First, let them reframe it to emphasize God's passion, expressed in the Old Testament and the New, to bring the multitudinous peoples of earth to obedience to the faith (Mark 16:15; Luke 24:47–48; Acts 1:8; Rom. 1:5; 10:10–15; 16:25–26; Phil. 2:10, etc.). Second, let them reframe each doctrine in such a way as to emphasize effectiveness in finding the winnable lost and discipling them. The goal is to make them responsible disciples, not sympathizers, church-attenders, or Sunday-school pupils—not even men and women who say they have received Christ but then do not become obedient parts of His body. Bands of committed practicing Christians is the goal of the Great Commission. This means that Christian creedal statements should include effectiveness as a test of faithfulness and obedience. When sent into a ripe field, the faithful Christian brings out many sheaves. In addition, church growth should be accepted as a test of good stewardship. If we are good stewards of the grace of God, we shall spread the light and multiply soundly Christian churches.

Reframing the doctrines of our creed in order to emphasize effectiveness in finding the lost means that we must not take shelter behind initial expressions of mission such as Christian presence, interreligious dialogue, cooperative service, and church unity. They are not ends in themselves. To be sure, the day is complex. We do face resurgent religions, state churches touchy about proselytization, hostile nations, and religious relativism. Nevertheless, good stewards must not emphasize forms of mission which give the three billion no chance to believe on Christ. The Great

Commission does not say, "Go everywhere and be careful never to tread on any toes." The United States did not fulfil the Great Commission when it passed the prohibition amendment. England did not fulfil the Great Commission when it outlawed the slave trade. Readers ought not to propose doctrinal statements which assume they did.

Objections to Reframing Doctrines

Before we rephrase another doctrine, we shall consider objections which may be raised to this whole procedure. First, some may question the necessity or propriety of making all doctrines missionarily more adequate. They may say, "Christians are commanded to do many things. The missionary must *not* consider one strand of God's purpose to be the sole concern of the church." We place this objection first, because it is very common. In reply, we point out that our proposal has a dual emphasis. The doctrine must be stated in missionarily effective terms and it must be stated in biblically correct terms. We believe that in order to be biblically correct, in order to maintain the emphasis that the Bible itself displays, doctrines must be framed with a view to the three billion who have yet to believe. *This missionary emphasis is biblically required.* It is not an illegitimate emphasis arising out of unbalanced missionary enthusiasm. It is simply faithfulness to God's revelation. It does not at all necessitate neglecting other tasks which Christians are called on to do.

We frequently have pointed out that every Christian is necessarily involved in many capacities. The believer worships God, repents of sin, studies the divine Word, rears children in the fear and admonition of the Lord, is a good neighbor and a good citizen. The Christian does good to all, especially those of the household of faith. The Christian gives cups of cold water in Christ's name, visits the sick, afflicted, prisoners, and the poor. This we never question. But as we look out on the actual life of the churches in country after country and continent after continent, what we see is that too many Christians stop after doing these things. They do not go on to spread the light, proclaim the gospel, carry out God's purpose so clearly revealed in the whole Bible to bring the multitudinous peoples of earth to glorious life-giving faith in Jesus Christ.

In this chapter we are proposing that the doctrines of the church now be inspected from the point of view of this unquestionable purpose of God, and the lamentably undiscipled condition of most men and women. Where the doctrines do not clearly reflect the missionary passion of our Lord, they should be reworded to make them mirror what the Bible clearly teaches.

The second objection might be phrased as follows: We seem to be saying that doctrinal statements which are damaging to the expansion of the church cannot be true theology, that is, true to the revelation given by God. How, then, do we evaluate Reformation theology—both Lutheran and Calvinist? It dealt the church a terrible blow. Was it therefore false theology? In reply we point out that one must distinguish between the "church" and the true church. Reformation theology did deal a corrupt church a terrible blow, but it also enabled the true church to flourish. Furthermore, Reformation theology has had an enormous effect on the Church of Rome. It sparked the Counter Reformation. It is still having an effect. To the extent that there is a true church within the husk of any church, true theology will enable it to grow and flourish.

A third objection sometimes raised is this: Would not a true statement of doctrine in many cases cut the church in half and purge it? Our reply is direct. If any denomination is asleep or corrupt, a true statement of doctrine will certainly purge it. But if the purged and cleansed half does not *then* grow, the doctrinal statement is imperfect and should be made truer.

A common objection is that since we are not commanded to be successful, but only to be faithful, we do not do well to emphasize that right doctrine will produce church growth. In reply we grant at once that when the servant is sent to sow a field, the Master does not expect the servant to come back the same day bearing sheaves. But when the servant is sent into a ripe harvest field, *faithfulness* means bringing out many sheaves.

A more weighty objection may be phrased thus: Since the human individual is free and fallen, how can we say that a missionarily adequate and biblically correct statement of doctrine should lead to church growth? May men and women not utterly reject Christ and His messengers? The answer to this is that they certainly may do just that. Nevertheless, two observations must be made. (1) God's purpose is that the gospel be accepted. He sends His servants out to beseech the lost to be reconciled to Him through faith in Jesus Christ. (2) Therefore God's obedient servant must do everything in his or her power to make sure that the message is heard, understood, and accepted. In the face of rejection, the servant holds fast to the fact that he or she has been sent to bring forth fruit, much fruit, and fruit that abides (John 15:1–8, 16).

Someone may say that God is absolute sovereign and the Holy Spirit acts freely in ways we cannot foresee. Therefore may not the proclamation of the most missionarily adequate and biblically correct doctrine actually harden hearts and turn them away from the church (Mark 4:12; 2 Cor. 2:14–16)? This objection has much evidence behind it. Humans do in fact frustrate God's will—at least temporarily.

Preaching the gospel is not a matter of mechanical effectiveness. Satan also is active and often thwarts the purposes of the most ardent Christians. It is quite evident that on hearing the truest word, spoken by the most loving servant of Christ, some turn from eternal life to eternal death. But that is not God's will. He does not will that any should perish (Isa. 55:1; John 3:16; 1 Tim. 2:4; 2 Peter 3:9). God's desire is that people believe the gospel and that churches multiply. That is why He sent His only Son, that whosoever believes in Him should not perish but have everlasting life.

A Formula for Reframing Doctrines

In this chapter we have been making three major emphases. First, most contemporary Christian doctrines have been framed with little if any intent to make them true to the missionary passion of God so clearly revealed in the Bible. Second, Christian mission (world evangelization) as a result remains peripheral to the main currents of life in the church and is being redefined to include every good thing the church ought to do. Instead of being a chief and irreplaceable function of the church, evangelism tends constantly to become something to be done, if at all, after other necessary tasks have been finished. Third, Christians ought to reword their doctrines while looking out on an unsaved world. The great doctrines of the church—if they are to be germane to the real situation today—should be reframed by Christians whose eyes are fixed on the unsaved billions who have yet to believe. If theologians cared tremendously for the salvation of their fellow human beings (Rom. 9:1–3), how would these doctrines be worded? Every leader of the church should, according to his or her best understanding of the Bible and with sensitivity to the leading of the Holy Spirit, work out a biblically correct theology of mission saturated with God's passion for the salvation of all.

We now summarize the proposal set forth in this chapter. Let each reader take the treasured doctrines he or she holds and, by carrying out the three steps below, make them truer to the Bible and more effective for world mission.

1. Write out each doctrine in the form in which it appears in some statement of faith or creed.
2. Describe the bearing of the doctrine *thus stated* on world evangelism—and in particular on the growth of your congregation or denomination. Under what conditions would the doctrine increase the church? Under what conditions would it incline Christians to evangelize their neighbors, minority groups in their communities, and the culturally and geographically distant peoples of their planet?
3. Rewrite the doctrine so that its very phrasing will thrust Christians and churches out into effective gospel-proclaiming, sinner-converting, and church-multiplying mission in the world of today and tomorrow.

We conclude this chapter by carrying out these three steps in regard to the doctrine of the Holy Spirit. This will illustrate the procedure recommended. Our illustration uses Article IV of the Methodist Articles of Religion of 1784.

1. *Write out the doctrine.*

IV. *Of the Holy Ghost*: The Holy Ghost, proceeding from the Father and the Son, is of one substance, majesty, and glory with the Father and the Son, very and eternal God.[4]

2. *Describe the bearing of the doctrine thus stated on world evangelism.* This statement of the doctrine is concerned exclusively with the nature of the Holy Spirit in relation to the other persons of the Trinity. It reflects the earthshaking debates in the early church and the errors then popular to the effect that the Holy Spirit is not one with the Father, and does not proceed from the Son. It says nothing about the function of the Holy Spirit to create in those He indwells holy and spirit-filled lives, although this function is often described in the Bible as an essential part of His being. Neither does this statement of the doctrine say anything about the Holy Spirit's thrusting Christians out into world evangelization. It was the Holy Spirit who said, "Set apart for me Barnabas and Saul." It was the Holy Spirit who sent them out on their mission. It was the Holy Spirit who directed their way.

When attention is focused exclusively on the *being* of the Holy Spirit and nothing is said as to His tremendous concern that evangelization be carried out at home and abroad, the church merely repeats the doctrine; it is not thrust out into mission.

The remarkable growth of the early Methodist church was no doubt due to the action of the Holy Spirit in the lives of its founders and first members, but when this first blazing fire grew dim, the doctrine of the Holy Spirit, as stated in a true, but limited way in Article IV, was of no help in producing, in the Methodist millions, a will to evangelize. Methodist denominations in America and around the world, which are merely holding even or actually declining, draw no stimulation to holiness or mission from that 1784 statement. What is needed is a more biblical wording of the doctrine which does much more justice to the biblical revelation and which focuses the attention of Christians on the unsaved multitudes who are the constant concern of the Holy Spirit.

3. *Rewrite the doctrine so that its very phrasing thrusts the church out into evangelism and church growth.*

4. "The Articles of Religion (1784)," in Leith, *Creeds*, p. 355.

The Holy Spirit proceeding from the Father and the Son is of one substance, majesty, and glory with the Father and the Son. The Holy Spirit through the proclamation of the gospel renews our hearts, persuading us to repent of our sins, and confess Jesus as Lord. By the same Spirit we are led to trust in divine mercy whereby we are forgiven all our sins, justified by faith alone through the merits of Jesus Christ our Savior, and granted the gift of eternal life.

The Holy Spirit, regarding compassionately all the peoples of the whole world who have not yet heard the gospel or believed on the Savior, constantly calls the church to seek and to find the lost. What was once preached by the Lord and wrought in Him for the saving of the human race must be proclaimed and spread abroad to the ends of the earth. To accomplish this goal, Christ sent the Holy Spirit from the Father. The Holy Spirit carries out His saving work and impels the church toward its proper expansion and the redemption of earth's multitudes.

It is our hope that in like manner all church doctrines will be rewritten with a view to the three billion who have yet to believe, who are now perishing in a famine of God's Word, billions for whom Christ died. These multitudes of our brothers and sisters could be evangelized in this generation. The existing churches have the resources to do that. Every man, woman, and child on earth is now reachable. None live behind uncrossable ranges or beyond unsailed seas. Our statements of faith and our creeds ought to be rewritten with a view to these present circumstances. Any contemporary theology of mission must be constructed with a view to today's world and take serious note of the fact that three out of every four human beings are now living without knowing of the Savior, without trusting in His atonement, without any promise of forgiveness of sins, and without receiving the gift of eternal life. As Christians and congregations confess their most holy faith, they ought to look directly at these current realities.

9

Particular Theologies and Theology of Mission

Donald McGavran

A ny germane and valid theology of mission must take serious account of the concept of particular churches and particular theologies. As world evangelization proceeds on its divinely ordained path, the church enters segment after segment of the human race. Each new church takes form in the womb of the mission, is born to a dependent existence, and speedily becomes a fully independent part of the body of Christ. It becomes a particular church and holds a particular theology. Each new particular church, that is, each new cluster of congregations in a particular segment of society where the church did not exist before (whether that be a class, clan, tribe, caste, or other homogeneous unit), is rooted in the racial, economic, and political order which obtains there. Its language and its customs are formed by the prevailing culture. It is seen by others in that segment as a genuine part of the society. At the same time, since it lives under the authority of the Word of God and is guided by the Holy Spirit, it is continually growing up into the fulness of Christ. It is an indigenous church—truly a part of its culture—and at the same time a part of the universal church whose Head is Christ Jesus, the Lord.

Particular churches, formed in great numbers in many nations, since they are authentic parts of the household of God, realize that God has established them and sent them precisely in order to present the gospel effectively to the multitudes living around them who have yet to believe. Particular churches become evangelists to the unevangelized sections of their own and neighboring societies. They also rear their best sons and daughters to become missionaries to the regions beyond.

We are told "the seed is the word of God" (Luke 8:11), and "the field is the world" (Matt. 13:38). There is one seed, the revealed *Word*; but the world is a vast mosaic crowded with different cultures. Some of these cultures are receptive, some resistant. When the seed falls into good ground (receptive populations) it sprouts, is watered by God's rain, and is transformed by the photosynthesis of God's blazing sun. From the ground the new sons and daughters of the kingdom, the new cells of Christ's body, draw nourishing cultural elements which are transformed into stalk, leaves, flower, and fruit. Thus the particular churches rooted in multitudinous human cultures *and in Christ* take to themselves, in a wonderful exchange, the riches of the nations. What the Word of God says so clearly, what God promises to His Son, comes to pass before our very eyes.

> Thou art My Son. . . .
> Ask of Me, and I will surely give the [peoples] as Thy inheritance
> And the very ends of the earth as Thy possession. [Ps. 2:7–8, NASB]

The Hindi Bible says, "Ask of me and I will give you the people of all the various castes." In Africa it would be tribes, in China clans, and in North America economic classes and minority communities. Consequently, into the church universal, from every nation and all tribes and peoples and tongues flow unbelievable riches—customs and mores, wisdom and insights, arts and achievements, learning and other sparkling gems. The multitude of particular churches will lay at the feet of Christ "all those things which can contribute to the glory of their Creator, the revelation of the Savior's grace, or the proper arrangement of Christian life."[1]

Any such acceptance and transformation of the cultural wealth of nations necessarily involve particular theologies. Often these particular theologies will guide thought and action at an unconscious level. Ordinary Christians and humble pastors reading the Word of God will debate within themselves whether such and such a component of their culture, now coming out of darkness into Christ's wonderful light, should be accepted as it is, or changed in part or in whole. To illustrate, in the early nineteenth century, the powerful Hindu culture of the southern tip of India ruled that women of the lower castes must wear no clothing above the waist. When some thousands of these humble women became Christians and the Holy Spirit and the Word became operative in their lives, they decided that that element of their culture was evil and had to be changed. They put on blouses. As a result they were manhandled in the village streets and marketplaces. Some were jailed. With the help of the missionaries, they appealed to the local courts but invariably lost. They then appealed higher, from court to court—and lost. Finally the highest court ruled that all Indian women could wear blouses. A particular theology (though it

---

1. *Ad gentes,* in Walter M. Abbott, ed., *The Documents of Vatican II* (New York: Herder and Herder, 1966), p. 612.

would never have called itself that) had transformed an evil component of an age-old culture in South India.

Often this particular theologizing will be carried on at a conscious level. Trained theologians will ask which of the components of their culture ought to come into the particular church unchanged, which must be slightly changed, and which must be radically transformed or abandoned. Cultural wealth from every homogeneous unit in every nation will flow into the church. To be sure, such of the wealth as is displeasing to God will be transformed or kept out of the life and practice of the new church. As the faith seeks to be better understood in each local culture, it will use local languages and world-views of hundreds of social units and also their innate wisdom and insights. By God's grace these will be purged and elevated and fulfilled as they flow into the church.

Contextualization

In this chapter we shall explore the extent to which particular theologies might differ from the general theologies which have been adopted by the church universal in its nineteen-centuries-long journey. Where they differ too greatly or deny some clear biblical truth, they must be deemed unacceptable. The goal, of course, is to frame acceptable particular theologies.

If theology is to be of any use to the people of a given culture, it must be framed in terms of their thought world. It must be understandable to them. This will usually mean that *they* will frame it. Christians in each *ethnos*, each homogeneous unit, each segment of humanity, will wrestle with the biblical revelation. They will not only translate the Bible into their own language, but will express its revelations in their own thought forms. A common word today to describe this process is *contextualization*.

Missionaries have been among the first to recognize the need for contextualization, and to do it. They have seen that the uneducated mind cannot comprehend the convoluted philosophical and theological formulations framed by scholars with many years' experience in universities. Illiterates cannot understand trigonometry and biochemistry either. Not because they are stupid. In their own worlds, they are highly intelligent. They cannot understand biochemical and theological formulations because these are the end products of years of particular kinds of learning. These formulas are the apex of pyramids which took decades to build. Without the years of learning, *no one* can understand sophisticated theological formulations. Missionaries see this. They have experienced it. They know their new Christian friends are highly intelligent. Given the opportunity, their national friends would do well in any university. But to speak to them, theological truth must be expressed in their language, in their thought forms, and as the apex of *their* pyramids.

A wise missionary in the early years of the twentieth century, finding that non-Christians were frequently asking scornfully, "Of what profit is it to become Christian?" framed in the local dialect a ten-point statement called "Ten Profits in Becoming Christian." This was memorized by all village congregations and became an effective sword. One of the ten great gains in becoming Christian was (those horrified by the population explosion, please take note) that Christians have more children than non-Christians. This was contextualization. Since all the peasants wanted children and since the loose sexual morality of the non-Christians made syphilis and gonorrhea common, causing high infant mortality, this advantage of Christianity was evident to everyone. That it was never mentioned in traditional theological statements of the profits of being Christian made no difference. For that particular church at that time, it was effective contextualization.

Acceptable and Unacceptable Ethnotheologies

Particular theologies, which may also be called ethnotheologies, are often much larger than the formulations which speak to small groups of new Christians established on new ground in Asia or Africa. For example, liberal Christian theology today among Western intellectuals has been framed over the last century to fit the secular scientific mind of modern times. It is an ethnotheology. Now every ethnotheology or particular theology, to be acceptable, must remain thoroughly biblical while adapting to a particular segment of society. Consider the case of a Methodist church in California which had declined in membership. The pastor became greatly concerned that the congregation recover its former great rate of growth. He assembled thirty lay leaders to study various books on church growth. His strategy, however, was not effective, because the church members were offended by the assumption underlying these books that those not in Christ are lost. The thrust of these books was unacceptable to the culture-based particular theology of those Christians. The pastor remarked that for his congregation ideas on church growth would have to be presented in theological terms which fit their generally liberal world-views. The human race is not fallen, but good. All religions are ways to God. No one is really lost. Such a congregation, the pastor thought, needed ideas on church growth which were framed in their own liberal ethnotheology. Here we see that if an ethnotheology, in adapting to a secular or polytheistic thought world, goes too far, it becomes nonbiblical and unacceptable.

In this chapter we explore the need of particular churches to hear each theological doctrine in their own language and cultural framework. Particular churches must draw up theologies of world evangelization which are both biblically true and congenial with their thought worlds.

As we do this, it will be clear that an acceptable particular theology must be true to the source of all theology—the Bible—and at the same time present its doctrines in the language and thought forms of the receptors. Often the two clash. Any presentation entirely in the thought forms of the receptors will be inadequate. It cannot satisfactorily state the truth. For example, there is no way to present the idea that 16 times 16 equals 256 in the thought forms of illiterate receptors, no matter how wise they may be. They do not have the thought forms needed to grasp that idea, and will not have those forms till they learn the multiplication tables. Once multiplication is mastered, however, the receptors can grasp the truth of the statement easily and use it effectively.

If men and women had already known the truths concerning God and the human race, there would have been no need for God to reveal these truths in the Bible and in Jesus Christ. So the task is not simply one of contextualization. It is rather that of contextualizing *revealed truth* in such a way that the truth is grasped, learned, and put into effect. A particular theology—an ethnotheology—ought to state biblical truth in a way congenial to a particular mind.

Information concerning Jesus Christ, the Holy Spirit, the human race, sin, salvation, justice, eternal life, and other truths which it has pleased God to disclose to us in the Bible is never fully grasped by Christians of any culture or of any degree of learning. New light is always breaking out of the Bible. Any theological formulation drawn up by any group is modified to some degree by the circumstances, special needs, and cultural compulsives of that group. The doctrinal statements of the Reformers were framed in response to the errors of the medieval church. They were framed by theologians who considered the Church of Rome the great enemy. The Reformers interpreted certain passages of Scripture in the light of what they saw as the notable errors of that day. When Christians today, in new circumstances, read those same passages and eagerly use them to defend their faith, they too modify them—slightly or greatly as the case may be—in the light of their own cultural compulsives and the errors of the different enemies who surround them.

If Christians modify any biblical truth too greatly, they warp it. The result is a false doctrine, a misrepresentation of biblical truth. We will present several illustrations of acceptable and unacceptable modification. They will help us see what is legitimate in the process of contextualization. We will then note that particular theologies qualify as part of a theology of mission only if they are effective in world evangelization.

Let us make a biblical statement as to the person of Christ. The Bible portrays Jesus in many places as fully human. He ate and drank. He walked and talked, He got tired and slept. He loved and served others, He taught and rebuked, exhorted and encouraged. But the Bible also portrays Jesus of Nazareth as the Word of God incarnate. "In the beginning was the Word, and the Word was with God, and the Word was God. . . . All things were made through him. . . . And the Word became flesh and dwelt among us, full of grace and truth" (John 1:1, 3, 14). "He who has seen me has seen the Father," said Jesus (John 14:9). He also said, "No one knows the Father except the Son and any one to whom the Son chooses to reveal him" (Matt. 11:27). In other words, Jesus the Messiah was fully God.

That Jesus was fully God and fully human has been the christological doctrine held by the overwhelming majority of Christians of all cultures since the earliest days. It has been held by Asians, Europeans, and Africans. It has been held in every century. It is a clear biblical doctrine and many books have been written proving it to be so. Now in the last hundred years, literary and historical criticism (based on the presupposition that the Bible is strictly the words of human authors) has led very large numbers of ministers and seminary professors to regard the Bible as a compilation of human opinions. Such scholars say, "Yes, those verses are truly to be found in the Gospel of John, but they were Greek reconstructions of the words of Jesus. He Himself never said anything like that." If the text in Matthew is cited, they reply, "This Johannine verse, so out of place in Matthew, must have been inserted by some early scribe. Matthew could not have written it." When these scholars form their doctrine of the person of Christ, they tend to frame it largely in Unitarian terms. Jesus was an extraordinarily good man, a religious genius, but not God incarnate, not the Word made flesh. When scholars form this christological doctrine, they are forming an ethnotheology. One which fits the intellectual framework of their secularized society and its convictions as to what is possible.

Any such contextualization is unacceptable. It is syncretism. In adjusting to the contemporary secular frame of mind, the contemporary culture, it has departed from the truth which the Bible clearly sets forth. It honors those verses which witness to the humanity of Jesus and cavalierly dismisses those that speak of His divinity. Such contextualization is a *mis*representation of the biblical doctrine. The doctrine has been so warped that as it is now stated it is no longer true.

Let us take this same doctrine and contextualize it acceptably. In the southeastern part of India, where watermelons are a common crop, a village pastor was explaining the Trinity to a large audience. God, he said, is like a watermelon. He exists in three parts which are all one, just like the watermelon. The watermelon is sweet pink flesh. That is like God the Father, who is everything. Then there are the seeds which will reproduce watermelons wherever they are planted. One watermelon becomes a hundred. The seeds, quite different from the pink flesh of the melon, are at the same time entirely one with the watermelon. In fact, without them, the watermelon would not be a watermelon. The seeds are like Jesus Christ, one with the Father and yet different. Third, there is the sweet juice which is in every part of the watermelon. The juice surrounds the seeds, and flows out of the melon when it is cut. That is the Holy Spirit. Now flesh, seeds, and juice are all melon. So Father, Son, and Holy Spirit are all one God. That was good contextualization for a particular church. The listeners understood perfectly. The pastor had used their thought forms. (Of course, this contextualization is not perfect, as readers will readily agree, for while the watermelon illustrates three in one, it is a thing, not a person.)

The matter is so important that we give an additional illustration. This time we shall state the biblical doctrine that God is a person. He acts, loves, judges, and rewards. He is a personal Spirit. The whole Bible is eloquent witness to the truth of this doctrine even though the personhood of the Godhead is a profound mystery which we see "through a glass darkly." God spoke to Moses and to all the prophets. God judged Ahab and Judas. Our Father God is a person, a God who acts.

But the dominant philosophical understanding of God in India is quite the opposite. The highest understanding of God is that It (not He) is an impersonal spirit or force that neither loves nor hates. "It" simply does not care about people. The primal force has many lesser emanations which take personal form. These are the great incarnations and the gods and goddesses that are worshiped in idols of wood or stone. But the real God, the high God, is unknowable, remote, and impersonal. Were Christian missionaries or evangelists to contextualize the biblical doctrine of the person of God into the thought forms of philosophic Hinduism, they might come up with something like this:

> God is an impersonal force so infinitely far above us that we cannot understand or comprehend It. We must not deceive ourselves into thinking we can please or displease It. It simply does not care about what happens here. Ten million die in a famine, a cyclone wipes out a thousand, and an epidemic of cholera kills hundreds of thousands. God neither knows nor cares. But a lesser emanation of God—Jesus Christ—is a person and does care.

Any such contextualization into a cultural form acceptable to Hindu philosophers is totally unacceptable to Christians.

This point will be even clearer if we contextualize the biblical doctrine of God the Father into Marxist thought forms:

There is no God, but there is an impersonal force, an "It" which drives human history forward in the dialectical sequence of thesis, antithesis, and synthesis: the combination of economics and the class struggle. We can "cooperate" with this force and work in the direction it appears to be going. Thus we can hasten the day when the classless society will come into being.

Any such contextualization of the biblical doctrine, of course, destroys the biblical concept.

In the Western world during the last thirty years, a new "Christian" theology called "process theology" has arisen. It understands God as "process." God grows and understands new conditions in somewhat the same way that humans do. Through the processes of evolution, change, and development, He is constantly making all things new. The loving, just Father God of the Bible, contextualized into process theology, might be defined as follows:

God is a principle of change and development which does not love or hate. He acts only through immutable laws into which good change has been programed. He has not revealed Himself in the Bible. What we read in the Bible is what its authors, moved on by the Spirit of change, believed they ought to say. Like all humans they were the captives of their world-views and their cultures.

Here again, the contextualization so falsifies the biblical revelation that Christians must refuse it. It is not acceptable. It is syncretism, a surrender to an erroneous and misleading understanding of God.

In these cases the ambassador of the King, wanting to be understood, mistakenly thinks, "The people of this land will never understand the message given me by the King. Therefore, I must change the message. Merely putting the strange message of my King into their language is not enough. They still will not understand it. I must put it into a form which they will understand and accept. It may not be exactly what my King told me to say, but it will be accepted. It will fit the culture of this land."

To be acceptable, ethnotheologies, while thoroughly cultural, must remain fully biblical. What the Bible says, they must say. But the words they use will be words understood by the receptors. Sometimes a fine line separates legitimate modification from illegitimate warping. Nonetheless, we can say that whenever an ethnotheology departs from the biblical revelation, it ceases to be a Christian ethnotheology and becomes a heresy. Let us illustrate this by stating two definitions of Christianity. The biblical definition might be phrased as follows:

Christianity is the embodiment of the truths which God has revealed through His prophets and His Son our Savior.

Now suppose that we were to adapt this statement to the contemporary world. We would note that this definition arose in Europe when that continent was Christian and there was little knowledge of the carefully-worked-out philosophies, cultures, and religions of the great civilizations of the non-Christian world. We would remember the profound thought of India and China, where people were civilized long before the savages of North Europe were able to read or write, long before they had any system of philosophy at all.

Today, we live in a different world. Eastern religions are being propagated in the West. Shaved-head Hare Krishna devotees dance down Pasadena's Colorado Boulevard in the Rose Parade. Hindu temples are built in Los Angeles. Buddhist temples appear in Asian residential areas of various cities of the United States. American men and women by the hundreds journey to India to be instructed by seers and sages teaching the Upanishads and the Vedas. In today's world, many hold that it is impossible for intelligent people to believe that God fully revealed Himself *only* in the religious writings of a small and unimportant tribe (the Jews) and in a rather extraordinary carpenter of Nazareth. To fit the multitudinous *ethne* of our present world, an ethnotheological redefinition of Christianity might be phrased as follows:

> Christianity, like all other religions, is human perceptions of God and speculations about His (or Its) intents and purposes. Teachings about the human race, society, values, and ultimate truths vary from religion to religion. All have some truth in them and must be respected. All have some error in them and must therefore not be taken too seriously.

To biblical Christians, this ethnotheological redefinition is unacceptable. In adjusting to the secular humanistic climate of thought which envelops so many of the intellectually elite of today, it has departed from the biblical revelation entirely.

While ethnotheology is permitted to adjust to the new thought forms *sufficiently to secure an understanding,* it must still set forth the plain teaching of the Bible. In regard to the relationship of the gospel to other religions, such a particular theology might run as follows:

> In all religions sages have meditated deeply on the ultimate nature of reality. Since the human being is a great discoverer, using God-given reason to think discriminatingly about important issues, these sages have been able to discover many true and beautiful things about God, the human race, creation, ethical values, sin, and righteousness. They founded many religions and wrote many scriptures. Christians appreciate all these good, true, and beautiful discoveries. (That puts this ethnotheology on the contemporary wavelength.) But many foolish, base, and erroneous propositions have also been discovered and stated as absolute truth. For example,

some people assign the creation of this marvelous, complex, and beautiful world to the Big Bang, or to an impersonal force zigzagging its way through time toward (wonder of wonders) a righteous society. Consequently God, Creator of this intricate universe, has been pleased to reveal all necessary ultimate truths about all matters of spiritual concern. God did this over a thousand years of history both in acts and words through inspired writers. His revelation culminated in His incarnation in Jesus Christ, the long-promised Messiah. All *human discoveries* are to be measured, weighed, and judged against *God's revelation* in the Bible and in Christ. *Christianity* is the religion which takes the Bible with utter seriousness. *Christianity* is an entirely reasonable religion. It has been held by simple believers and the most profound scholars alike. It is the fulfilment of all imperfect human systems and discoveries. It accepts the true, good, and beautiful discoveries of the founders of other religions wherever these discoveries measure up to God's revealed truth in the Bible.

Readers will recognize that this ethnotheology is similar to the one used by Paul on Mars Hill as he addressed the Greek philosophers. He got on their wavelength and then told them plainly that God has overlooked the days of ignorance and has now appointed a man through whom to judge the world (Acts 17:30–31). Most of his hearers laughed. But to a few the ethnotheology appealed.

As we pursue the matter of framing particular theologies which remain truly biblical and truly Christian, we must take account of a well-thought-out adaptation proposed by Robin Boyd, an Irish Presbyterian who taught in Gujerat, the westernmost state of India. Boyd set his ethnotheology forward in *India and the Latin Captivity of the Church,* published by Cambridge University Press in the early seventies. He maintained that contemporary Christian theology is built on a Latin and Greek base, and that the great teachings of the Bible can equally well be set forth on the Sanscrit base of Hindu philosophical systems. The teaching, he held, rides on the philosophical system as a man may ride on a horse. He can change horses and still remain entirely the same man.

For example, Boyd says that the triune nature of God was understood by the Greeks as being something like three personae or masks worn by the same actor in a drama. Now the actor appeared as one character, now as another. He remained, however, one person. So the one God could be understood as three: Father, Son, and Holy Spirit. In India, however, Dr. Boyd argues, ultimate reality is expressed in three Sanscrit words—*Sat, Chit, Anand.* These may be rendered roughly in English by the words *Reality, Intelligence,* and *Joy.* God is Ultimate Reality. He is Ultimate Intelligence. He is Ultimate Joy. If the Trinity, argues Boyd, were in India to ride on this steed, it would at once be understood by the philosophical Hindus, and would become more acceptable.

In a personal letter Boyd asserts that he takes the ultimate authority of the Bible most seriously. His proposal therefore must be understood as one intended to help non-Christians in India understand the Triune God portrayed in the Bible. This attractive contextualization is, however, vague in regard to definitions, and the idea of riding on the *Sat-Chit-Anand* steed is ambiguous. One must ask, then, if the following is an accurate representation of what Boyd is saying to the philosophical Hindus:

> The personal Spirit, Creator of the universe, Savior of the human race, who regards all people as His children and longs for their salvation, may, as your great philosophers have said, be regarded as Ultimate Reality. He is the only God there is, Maker of heaven and earth. He may also be regarded as Ultimate Intelligence, the Infinite Mind. Our reasoning powers are but a faint reflection of His omniscience. And also as Ultimate Joy. Thus the Triune God—Father, Son, and Holy Spirit—is the fulfilment of what the great Hindu philosophers almost saw as they said that God is *Sat, Chit, Anand.* God's self-revelation in Christ and the Bible is thus the crown of Hinduism, expressing the Trinity of *Sat, Chit, Anand* in the *truer* personal terms of Father, Son, and Holy Spirit.

If this is Boyd's particular theology, it is acceptable. It is valid and illuminating contextualization, while preserving the strict biblical trinitarian doctrine.

Suppose, however, that someone were to use the *Sat-Chit-Anand* formula in the following way:

> The Indian philosophers and sages probed the ultimate meanings of life more deeply than any other human beings ever did. They all agreed that the Ultimate Reality is also the Ultimate Mind and the Ultimate Joy. But this Atman or Spirit is so far removed from our human intelligence that we cannot understand It. Atman is utterly remote from and indifferent to us. But an emanation of Atman did become incarnate in human form in Jesus of Nazareth and taught that God is a triune force—Father, Son, and Holy Spirit. Thus the Eternal Trinity taught by Christianity is substantially the same as that taught by the Hindu sages. Take the Word of God, the Bible, and read what it says about *Sat, Chit, Anand.*

This ethnotheology is scarcely Christian. Rather it is a Hinduized form of Christianity—a heretical syncretism.

The Necessity of Effectiveness

Since we are discussing theologies of *mission* and are asking how effective such theologies are in world evangelization, we must note here that many acceptable particular theologies have had little missionary significance. In the Christian seminary in Gujerat Professor Boyd for many years promoted his contextualized understanding of Christianity. Alas, his effort did not lead to any ingathering at all from the Hindu philosophers of that state. Some missiologists, concentrating on the evangelization of Muslims and knowing of the objection many Muslims have to the concept of "the *Son* of God," declare that in working with Muslims the idea of Jesus as the Son of God must be rigorously avoided. The words of the Koran which speak of Jesus as the Spirit of God (*Ruh i Allah*) should be employed instead. This is reasonable contextualization. But reasonable though it is, its employment has not led many Muslims to Christ. Indeed in the only place in the world where over a hundred thousand Muslims have become followers of Christ (eastern and central Java) the Gospels which speak of the Lord Jesus as the Son of God are read with great pleasure by the new converts.

Many contextualizations and ethnotheologies fall under the heading of "things that ought to work but don't." They have only slight missiological significance. As theologies of mission they should be disregarded. Missiologists should concentrate on contextualizations which God has obviously blessed to the spread of the gospel.

Some contextualizations have had much missionary significance. They have been blessed of God to the discipling of many *ethne*. Consider, for example, a form of contextualization adopted in societies where important decisions are invariably multi-individual. In those societies, *until the group decides,* no one moves. The Christianizing process must be adapted to this cultural component. In such cases contextualization means making the decision to follow Christ a group decision, or better, *a multi-individual decision.* This form of contextualization has been enormously influential in the spread of the Christian faith. Whether indigenous tunes are used or not, whether incense is burned or not, whether people enter the place of worship barefoot or not, when the decision to follow Christ is undertaken in a multi-individual way, multitudes turn to the Lord.

Similarly, where an endogamous society hears the gospel, the process of becoming Christian must be seen as preserving endogamy. The resulting cluster of congregations must observe the old confines as strictly as did the pre-Christian society. Otherwise, the gospel is rejected. It is rejected not because the hearers dislike the gospel, but because they see it as bound to a repugnant concept that Christians will marry anyone, that the church is made up of mongrels who have no proper loyalty to their own people. The conglomerate church is anathema to any endogamous society.

As missiologists consider this particular form of contextualization (an endogamous church as opposed to a conglomerate church), they must ask, Does Scripture require either endogamy or mixed marriages? Or is the matter of marriage left by Scripture to the good judgment of the cluster of congregations concerned? The history of Christianity furnishes abundant proof that the spread of the gospel is greatly aided when a new church preserves the endogamous practice of its society. This has been true in Europe, Africa, and Asia.

A particular theology which emphasizes endogamy as entirely permissible in the church has much biblical evidence to commend it. One thinks at once of the strictures in Ezra and Nehemiah against mixed marriages. Historical evidence also commends it. One remembers the four hundred years during which the Mennonites comprised an endogamous society. Surveying the spread of the church around the world, one sees again and again tribes, clans, castes, and other segments of society becoming Christian and continuing to marry very largely within the same social unit. The careless mixed marriages of an atomized, fragmented society, such as that of North America, must not be taken as the universal biblical model.

In summary one may state the principle that, to be classed as part of a theology of mission, a particular theology must have as its intent obedience to Christ's command (Matt. 28:19). It must be effective. It must play a major role in bringing men and women to commitment and baptism. And this holds true for all theologies of mission—liberal, conciliar, evangelical, Roman Catholic, or other.

A theology of mission must be biblically true and *missionarily effective*. Otherwise, it is not a theology of mission. It is of no importance in world evangelization. The missionary is not interested in preserving the old culture or in changing it. He is interested in making such cultural adjustments as enable the King's message to be heard, understood, and accepted.

We have already asked whether the conciliar and evangelical theologies of mission are biblically true. Let us now ask whether each of them makes disciples. Does it disciple *panta ta ethne*? If not, it may be good for some purposes, but it is not a theology of mission.

We have asked these questions to improve the doctrinal statements of the theologies drawn up in the past centuries. Let us now ask the same questions regarding all adaptations and contextualizations intended to make Christian beliefs and practices more understandable to particular cultures. Is this ethnotheology biblically true? Does it *in fact* bring men and women to Christ and multiply churches? These are crucial questions.

10

Liberation Theology Bursts on the Scene

Arthur F. Glasser

Since midcentury, the church has been bombarded by new "ologies" and "isms." Everything old has been suspect. Fortunately, many of the most loudly-trumpeted new perspectives have been short-lived. But one relatively new "ology"—it surfaced in 1968—appears destined to be with us for a long time. Because of our conviction that "liberation theology" is in a class by itself, we must diligently seek to understand its roots, its concerns, and its serious efforts to contribute to the current debate on the theology of mission.

Antecedents

In the years immediately following World War II the nations—both the victorious and the vanquished—rebuilt their shattered cities and rejuvenated their depleted economies. The stronger helped the weaker; massive aid programs such as the Marshall Plan put nation after nation back on its feet within a decade. Meanwhile, expressions of social concern were rather mild. When the World Council of Churches was formed at Amsterdam in 1948, the dominant social concern was that the leaders of each nation bend their energies to produce "the responsible society." This meant not only "economic justice" for all citizens but also that they be given "freedom to control, to criticize and to change their governments, [and] that power be made responsible by law and tradition, and be distributed as widely as possible through the whole community."[1] This concern was very much needed, but in those busy days of frantic reconstruction few national leaders appeared interested in anything other than

1. Paul Bock, *In Search of a Responsible World Society: The Social Teachings of the World Council of Churches* (Philadelphia: Westminster, 1974), p. 69.

restoring the political and social conditions which had prevailed before the war. In the northern tier of nations, this was largely what the people wanted: a humanized reproduction of yesterday.

However, in the southern tier of nations—what Sukarno of Indonesia dubbed "the Third World" because of their resistance to any entrapment in the East-West struggle of the Cold War—postwar reconstruction did not have the same élan and success. Actually, it followed an unexpected pattern. The war had so adversely influenced the social fabric of these nations, shattering their traditional patterns without providing economic growth, that they could only look with envy at what was happening in the northern tier. They heard of the emergence of the welfare state but could only watch its development from afar. They could only dream of some distant future when all political and economic energy would be devoted to meeting the material and social needs of their people from the cradle to the grave. They marveled that Adam Smith's "iron law of wages" could be so easily set aside (keep the workers hungry to keep them working) and replaced with a state-subsidized "full employment" approach.[2] The citizenry of the southern tier knew only the growing presence in their midst of the transnational corporations with financial power, technological skill, many wares (to sell!), and an insatiable hunger for the raw materials their countries could supply. And these same people knew via the media that their opposite numbers in the northern tier were beginning to enjoy unbelievable affluence. "Up there," everyone seemed to be luxuriating in the "good life."

Just about this time something started to surface that had been stirring deep within the Roman Catholic Church for some years. A good man with a great heart—Pope John XXIII (1958–1963)—began increasingly to experience a measure of disquiet. His earliest encyclical (1961) endorsed the movement of Western societies to make accessible "the goods and services for a better life to as many persons as possible . . . to eliminate or to keep within bounds the inequalities that exist . . . to ensure that the advantages of a more humane way of existence . . . [and] social security . . . [will enable all to look] to the future with tranquillity" (*Mater et magistra* 79, 105).

Whereas Pope John expressed gratitude to God that in the economically advanced nations of the northern tier the common people were enjoying "the conveniences of life . . . a sufficiency and abundance of everything," he was concerned that the economically underdeveloped nations were increasingly experiencing "dire poverty" (*Mater et magistra* 157). Although he noted "with pleasure that countries with advanced

---

2. Joseph Gremillion, *The Gospel of Peace and Justice: Catholic Social Teaching Since Pope John* (Maryknoll, NY: Orbis, 1976), p. 6.

productive systems [were] lending aid to less privileged countries, so that these latter may the more readily improve their condition" (160), he regarded as "the most pressing question" of the day the relationship between the northern and southern nations (157). His great fear was that the economically developed countries would fall prey to the temptation "to turn the prevailing political situation to their own advantage and seek to dominate [the underdeveloped nations]." In his judgment this clearly would be but a disguised form of colonialism reflecting an earlier but outdated dominion (171–72).

The sixties saw Pope John's fear fully realized. Multinational corporations with their rapacious self-interest found it a relatively easy matter to use economic aid and technical assistance to make the poorer nations dependent on them. More than fifty new nations in Africa and Asia, although politically liberated from Western domination after World War II, now began to awaken to the fact that neocolonial economic bonds had been quietly but inexorably forged on them by these multinationals. Their poverty gave them no alternative but to capitulate before glittering systems of economic aid and technical assistance. What else could they do? These multinationals had found that underdeveloped nations could be brought to dependence quickly and inexpensively—by catering to the ruling elites. Conveniently overlooked was the fact that their rule was often oppressive and almost totally lacking in concern for the aspirations of the majority of the people they governed. Development, Western-style, increasingly became an anathema in much of the world. But what could Third World nations do? Seek to play East against West in the superpower confrontation?

Within Latin America, however, the situation was somewhat different. These nations had a different historical background and a more enlightened spiritual heritage. They had known almost four hundred years of Iberian Catholicism—the sort that had brought all citizens into at least nominal relationship with a church dominated by European clergy. This church catered to the superstitions of the masses and was surprisingly indifferent to the Christopaganism that permeated religious life. And its hierarchy largely supported the small wealthy oligarchies that dominated the impoverished masses.

But the stirrings in Rome and the new themes being debated at Vatican II roused the hearts of many of the Latin American clergy. In the past the church had made a few attempts to ameliorate the condition of the poor. For example, some seventy years previously, a papal encyclical (*Rerum novarum,* 1891) had asserted that industrial workers have the right to organize their own unions in order to press the authorities to act justly on their behalf. This had been ignored in Latin America. Few were the reforms that were introduced as a result of papal pressure. But in the sixties new winds were blowing.

Pope John's second encyclical (*Pacem in terris,* 1963) concentrated on the rights of all people and "the proper development of life." And the great encyclical of Vatican II (*Gaudium et spes,* 1965) was the most comprehensive and detailed statement any church had ever issued on social justice. That it was the product of the council fathers rather than a single pope added weight to its authority, for all Latin American bishops had a part in the debates that brought it to birth. This "Pastoral Constitution on the Church in the Modern World" with its ninety-three separate sections was read widely at the same time that the implications of the multinational presence in Latin America were taking hold of the socially-minded. Figure 1 depicts the exploitation that was taking place.

Figure 1

"The System" Takes from the Poor
and Gives to the Rich

Developed Nations

Profits

Less Developed Nations

Commodities
and Raw
Materials

Large landowners, "middlemen"

Sharecroppers, small farmers,
wage laborers

From Waldron Scott, *Bring Forth Justice* (Grand Rapids: Eerdmans, 1980), p. 136. Used by permission.

No wonder that when Pope Paul VI issued his encyclical *Populorum progressio* (1967) on the "development of peoples" it was in Latin America that he evoked the greatest response:

29. We must make haste: too many are suffering, and the distance is growing that separates the progress of some and the stagnation, not to say the regression, of others.

30. Injustice cries to heaven. When whole populations destitute of necessities live in a state of dependence barring them from all initiative and responsibility, and all opportunity to advance culturally and share in social and political life, recourse to violence, as a means to right these wrongs to human dignity, is a grave temptation.

It was inevitable, then, that something would happen that would challenge the church to face up to the growing tensions between the rich and the poor, the comfortable and the frustrated, the oppressors and the oppressed, the selfish and the angry. As a study group said at the time: "It would be wrong for every North American child to have an electric toothbrush before every Latin American child has a daily bottle of milk."[3] The issue was now seen to be "international economic justice."

We should not overlook the fact that a comparable social awakening was taking place within mainline Protestantism and Orthodoxy during this same period, but it was more diffuse and hence less easy to document. Thus in Paul Bock's excellent review of the social teachings of the World Council of Churches (which was published as late as 1974), one looks in vain for any mention of either the theology or theologians of liberation.

Emergence

As we have seen, "development" (or economic growth) was the dominant concern of many in the fifties and early sixties. Throughout Latin America, much energy was devoted to expanding the technological base and stimulating industrial growth, served by what was hoped would be an efficient, corruption-free bureaucracy. The Catholic Church encouraged this with a supportive and sanctifying theology of development. But toward the end of this period it became apparent that Latin American development was really leading to dependence and underdevelopment. This was "the dark side of northern development."[4] Gustavo Gutierrez, a Peruvian priest, persuasively demonstrated that development had become "synonymous with reformism and modernization, that is to say, synonymous with timid measures."

> [These are] really ineffective in the long run and counterproductive to achieving a real transformation. Because development has been promoted by international organizations closely linked to groups and governments which controlled the world economy, the changes it advocated were within the formal structure of the existing institutions without challenging them. Great care was exercised, therefore, not to attack the interests of large international economic powers nor those of their natural allies, the ruling domestic interest groups. . . . The poor countries are becoming ever more clearly aware that their underdevelopment is only the by-product of the development of other countries, because of the kind of relationship which exists between the rich and the poor countries. Moreover, they are realizing that their own development will come about only with a struggle to break the domination of the rich countries.[5]

3. Bock, *In Search of a Responsible World Society*, p. 47.
4. Jose Míguez Bonino, *Doing Theology in a Revolutionary Situation* (Philadelphia: Fortress, 1975), p. 16.
5. Gustavo Gutierrez, *A Theology of Liberation*, trans. Caridad Inda and John Eagleson (Maryknoll, NY: Orbis, 1973), p. 26.

We should catch the significance of Gutierrez's final line: not development but liberation. He had presented this theme at a meeting of priests and laity in Peru in mid-1968 under the title "Toward a Theology of Liberation." He repeated it at the Second General Conference of Latin American Bishops (CELAM) in Medellin (Colombia) a few weeks later. When the bishops responded with an endorsement of his new and revolutionary way of approaching the social, economic, and political problems of Latin America, liberation theology was on its way!

What made the Medellin gathering significant was the presence of Pope Paul VI. In his opening address ("The Present-Day Transformation of Latin America") the pope defined the role of the church and praised the bishops for their growing desire to break with the past practice of buttressing the oligarchies and to assault "those systems and structures which cover up and favor grave and oppressive inequalities."[6] The CELAM gathering produced four documents, two of which ("Justice" and "Peace") "attacked the twofold oppression of dominant groups and privileged sectors within each country and external neocolonialism . . . [with their] international monopolies and international imperialism of money" (Medellin Document, "Peace," 1.8–9).

Medellin did something for Latin American Catholicism. In no time at all a veritable flood of writings appeared which reflected the tension that had been building up in the church—writings which called its leaders to identify with the oppressed, the poor, and the marginal elements of society. These writings tended to divide the church into the "popular" (for the people!) and the "official" (for neutrality in political matters) camps, a divisive tendency that the visit of Pope John Paul II to a subsequent CELAM gathering (Puebla, Mexico, 1979) failed to resolve. No one can predict what the eventual outcome will be.

All agree that the issues facing the church at this time are too far-reaching to be easily resolved. Furthermore, the theologizing that has continued unabated for more than a decade has had such an influence on the younger generation of Catholics that there is little likelihood of any Latin American country remaining unchanged throughout the eighties. The reasons for this will become apparent when we catch the full measure of what liberation theology is all about. True, there are those who argue that militarism is so well entrenched throughout Latin America (particularly in such major countries as Mexico, Venezuela, Brazil, and Argentina) that basic social changes will not take place. Notwithstanding, the theology of liberation will capture the minds of many. It will be extensively exported to all parts of the world, there to be adapted and refined until it becomes the driving strength behind social revolutions in many

6. Gremillion, *Gospel of Peace*, p. 18.

places. Of course, all this is conjecture, but there are signs among the nations today to caution us against believing that it has spent its force and is in the process of disintegration because of the varied and diverse elements in its makeup.

Presuppositions

Because the theology of liberation is still in the early years of its formation, one inevitably encounters much diversity of emphasis in its proliferating literature. This is undoubtedly due to the diverse backgrounds of those contributing to its development. As intimated above, its pioneers are Catholics: Gustavo Gutierrez, Juan Luis Segundo, Hugo Assmann, and Jose Porfirio Miranda. Protestant contributors include Rubem Alves, Jose Míguez Bonino, Julio de Santa Ana, and Emilio Castro. Despite their diversity, no small measure of agreement exists when it comes to their presuppositions.

1. *Theology is occurring in a new context: the dialectic of oppression/liberation.* Theologians of liberation are concerned with but one frame of reference. They look at all reality through the eyes of the poor and the oppressed. Their dominant concern is that the victims of exploitative and dehumanizing social structures be liberated. This dialectic of oppression/liberation stands in sharp contrast to earlier theologies in the long history of the church. Not mortality/immortality, reason/faith, law/grace, guilt/ forgiveness, but something distinctly new: a focus on one's neighbor rather than on oneself.

This being so, we would expect theologians of liberation to stress the importance of history. Catholics have long held that throughout the history of the church God's word of revelation continues to be heard. Hence, liberation theologians, though they accept the validity of "salvation history" as it is recorded in Scripture, will not tolerate any dualism between the Bible's "spiritual" history and the "time-conditioned" concrete historical situation in which they find themselves today: "History is one; there are not two histories, one profane and one sacred, 'juxtaposed' or 'closely linked.' Rather there is only one human destiny, irreversibly assumed by Christ, the Lord of history. His redemptive work embraces all the dimensions of existence and brings them to their fulness. . . . The history of salvation is the very heart of human history."[7] This means a repudiation of the classical conception of the relation between truth and practice: that absolute Christian truth and universally valid Christian principles are enshrined in Scripture, and in the pronouncements of the Catholic Church,

7. Gutierrez, *Theology of Liberation*, p. 153.

and that more or less imperfect applications of this truth have been made throughout the long history of the church.

Theologians of liberation reject any ideas that do not arise from "the *logos* of a *practice*." They find "no truth outside or beyond the concrete historical events in which men are involved as agents . . . no knowledge except in action itself, in the process of transforming the world through participation in history."[8] Whereas they underscore the importance of profane history they nonetheless argue that revelation history (the Bible) is normative. But the biblical witness must not only be heard in the historical context in which it was originally uttered. It must be heard in the context of today, and this poses the hermeneutical task of seeing that the contextualization process is not hindered by the spiritualizing tendency (Hellenization) reputedly so dear to the North Atlantic evangelical mind. Indeed, liberation theologians doubt the ability of any whose context is not one of oppression to understand what God is saying in the midst of the oppressed throughout the southern tier in our day.

2. *Classical theologies lack contemporary relevance and must therefore be repudiated.* The multifaceted emphasis which Latin American theologians place on practice, on involvement, on theologizing within the context of identification with oppressed peoples, inevitably causes these theologians, evangelicals included, to fault Anglo-Saxon theologizing—especially theology of mission. As a result they find the North American missionary presence in their midst an insufferable trial because of its preoccupation with evangelism, discipling, and church planting. They challenge the way evangelicals appeal to biblical sanctions to justify this activity. In their judgment this defense is based on outmoded hermeneutics. And these liberationists cannot but be impatient with all who would tacitly endorse the neocolonialism of the Western powers—the economic imperialism that impoverishes, dehumanizes, and enslaves their fellow Latins.[9] In their eyes "church growth" theology, among other Western theologies, has made evangelical missionaries an unconscious advance guard for American imperialism—the ideological allies of forces both *within* and *without* Latin America that are reducing its great peoples to dependence and slavery. In an "Open Letter to North American Christians" thirteen Latin Protestant leaders repeatedly charged that

> the oppressive power of America is turning Central and South America into one gigantic prison, and in some regions one vast cemetery. . . . Today, we Latin Americans are discovering that, apart from our own weaknesses and sins, not a few of our misfortunes, miseries and frustrations flow from

8. Míguez Bonino, *Doing Theology,* p. 88; Lesslie Newbigin, *The Open Secret* (Grand Rapids: Eerdmans, 1978), p. 107.

9. Míguez Bonino, *Doing Theology,* p. 18.

and are perpetuated within a system that produces substantial benefits for your country but goes on swallowing us more and more in oppression, in impotence, in death. In a few words: Your precious "American Way of Life"—the opulence of your magnates, your economic and military dominion—feeds in no small proportion on the blood that gushes, according to one of our most brilliant essayists, "from the open veins of Latin America."[10]

It should be noted that serious charges of this sort cannot be casually dismissed. They come from various segments of the Protestant church and from those whose evangelical integrity is well known. As a result they press all would-be missionaries to make sure that their theologizing on the Christian mission includes serious reflection on all impinging political, social, and economic realities. Theology must be contextualized, as well as biblical!

3. *The role of Scripture is supportive—not determinative.* Theology as traditionally understood has meant disciplined reflection on Holy Scriptures by the people of God with a view to discovering its application to the historical context in which they find themselves. In salvation history the focus was on the theocentric message of redemption—"God in Christ reconciling the world unto Himself." It was a theology of past historical events of great christological significance. Liberation theologians, however, have uniformly broken sharply with traditional Christianity by calling for a theology of history in the present—which means politics. The focus must now be on God's activities in the world "wherever the action is." All theology must become the servant of social change, and the church in response to its perspectives must function as God's partner in ushering in the kingdom of God.

In this ferment, basic questions are being asked. For instance, does God exist? The liberationist answer is: "We can be sure of His reality only in pondering the humanizing movements in the world today. We must make sure of His presence apart from and prior to any reference to the Bible. Only then can we turn to the Bible for theological perspectives—truths—that can authenticate our efforts to be God's partner." So then, the theology of liberation is built on social action (making human the structures of society); it starts not with the Bible text but with the existential situation. The prior commitment to concrete action on behalf of the oppressed, with full knowledge that this inescapably involves the risk of working alongside God for their liberation, means that Scripture's ethical norms dare not override the norms dictated by the existential situation.

10. Gerald H. Anderson and Thomas F. Stransky, eds., *Mission Trends No. 4: Liberation Theologies in North America and Europe* (Grand Rapids: Eerdmans, 1978; New York: Paulist Press, 1979), pp. 71, 73.

4. *The theologian must make use of Marxist analytical tools.* Because of the facile way in which Marxists attribute all dehumanization and exploitation to the class struggle, and because of the tragic way in which the ruling oligarchies in Latin America over the centuries have used the Catholic Church to help them maintain the status quo—as Marx predicted—most liberation theologians have uncritically adopted a Marxist approach to social analysis. But is it possible to commit oneself to a process of social analysis which elevates material (economic) production to a higher level than any other dimension of human existence, and not (albeit unconsciously) adopt the Marxist ideology at the same time? Will not Christian presuppositions eventually come to be regarded as so much idealistic lumber? Will one not come to believe, for instance, that bread is far more to be prized than freedom?

Will not someone who accepts the Marxist analysis of society, and as a result becomes convinced that participation in the struggle for social justice is the top priority, be irresistibly drawn to the Marxist solution of class warfare as the means whereby the dialectic of oppressor/oppressed reaches the synthesis toward which history—according to Marx—keeps inexorably moving? Will this not entail the essential tactic of so aggravating the tension between these opposites that the point of revolutionary transformation will be hastened? But will this not involve the accentuation of the hatred on the part of the oppressed in order to stimulate their revolutionary activities? As Gutierrez states: "The goal is not only better living conditions, a more radical change of structures, a social revolution; it is much more; the continuous creation, never ending, of a new way to be a man, a permanent cultural revolution."[11]

We do not mean to imply that Latin American theologians are uncritical in expressing their indebtedness to Marx and the Marxist approach to social analysis. Indeed, they almost uniformly contend that the conscience of the church in Latin America can be stimulated to contribute significantly to the revolutionary renewal of society—something Marx would vehemently deny. Yet, despite excoriating Marx for denying the possibility of the proletariat's "converting religion into their own weapon in the class struggle," Segundo freely admits, "Whether everything Marx said is accepted or not, and in whatever way one may conceive his 'essential' thinking, there can be no doubt that present-day social thought will be 'Marxist' to some extent, that is, profoundly indebted to Marx. In that sense Latin American theology is certainly Marxist."[12]

And what does this mean? Far more than an offhand expression of

11. Gutierrez, *Theology of Liberation*, p. 32.
12. Juan Luis Segundo, *The Liberation of Theology*, trans. John Drury (Maryknoll, NY: Orbis, 1976), pp. 16, 35 n. 10.

gratitude to Marx for pointing out that exploitation arises because of the class stratification of society. Marxist political action begins to make sense with its call for the violent overthrow of the oppressors by the proletariat. And it is here that Marxist revolutionary action seems practical and realistic—and is most readily adopted—despite its anti-Christian overtones.

Marxist revolutionary action will occur in a series of steps. First, the denunciation of the oppressors: this is "the first sign of the true believer." Second, the call to the oppressed to know the enemies and seek ways to thwart the extension of their exploitative activity. Third, the organizing of the oppressed to nullify the effectiveness of the coercive forces of the status quo and reach for political power. Only then will it be possible to remove the structures that have been used against the people and eliminate the class divisions in society. Admittedly most liberation theologians are sufficiently Christianized to shrink from using force to eliminate people. But once one looks for sin largely in "oppressive structures, in the exploitation of man by man, in the domination and slavery of peoples, races and social classes,"[13] one's view of reality begins to lack both depth and breadth, and ethical judgments become inevitably flawed. Rubem Alves even sees the use of evil to overcome evil. His justification: when any group of people is oppressed, their humanity is distorted; the violence of the oppressors robs them of any free relationship with either the world or their future. In sanctioning the evil committed by an individual, Alves adds: "The violence which this man was under became part of his own being. It created him in its own image. And now as he decides to take his future and destiny into his own hands, he cannot avoid the explosion of that violence which colonialism injected into his veins. He becomes violent in order to be returned to the normality of a free man."[14]

None of us would deny that the biblical gospel should bring liberation to the structural problems of injustice, racism, poverty, and inequality. But Carl Braaten's caveat regarding liberation theology is worth noting:

> Liberation theology is right in broadening the concept of sin to include the social dimension, but its view nevertheless remains rather shallow. Sin is basically a lack of original righteousness (carentia iustitiae originalis), a classical definition that points to a false relationship with God. Sin is concupiscence, the driving tendency of the human heart to curve in on itself manifested as rebellion against God. Some of the richest pictures of sin in the Bible and the classical tradition are blurred in liberation theology. Sin provokes the wrath of God; it is slavery to Satan; it is a state of spiritual death; it is a disease of the whole person—a sickness unto death. It is a state of corruption so profound that the elimination of poverty, oppres-

13. Gutierrez, *Theology of Liberation*, p. 175.
14. Rubem Alves, *A Theology of Human Hope* (New York: Corpus Books, 1968), p. 11.

sion, disease, racism, sexism, classism, capitalism, etc., does not alter the human condition of sinfulness in any fundamental way.[15]

It is rather significant that Robert McAfee Brown's keynote address at the Fifth Assembly of the World Council of Churches (Nairobi, 1975) identified the chief oppressions in the world today as "racism, sexism, classism and imperialism." This highly selective list provoked Kenneth Hamilton to wonder as to why Brown was silent "about nationalism, terrorism, anti-Semitism, . . . totalitarianism and the police state."[16] And what about the awful oppression of "sin in our members"—the universal affliction of the human race?

The Exodus Motif

The basic datum of the Old Testament, according to Miranda, is *mishpat*, or social justice, the salvation of the poor.[17] With this postulate he reviews salvation history and concludes that it clearly establishes the fact that the dominant activity of God in history is to achieve justice for the poor. At first glance this seems fully consonant with Jesus' preaching, for He repeatedly identified the poor as those for whom the salvation of the kingdom is destined. But who are the poor? We have only to turn to Herman Ridderbos for his classical summation of the biblical witness on this point.

The "poor" or "poor in spirit" (meek) occur again and again in the Old Testament, particularly in the Psalms and in the prophets. They represent the socially oppressed, those who suffer from the power of injustice and are harassed by those who only consider their own advantage and influence. They are, however, at the same time those who remain faithful to God and expect their salvation from his kingdom alone. They do not answer evil with evil, nor oppose injustice with injustice. That is why in the midst of the ungodliness and worldly-mindedness of others, they form the true people of God. As such they are again and again comforted with the promise of the coming salvation of the Lord and the manifestation of his kingly redemption (cf. Ps. 22:27; 25:9; 34:3; 37:11; 72:12–13; 147:6; Isa. 11:4; 29:19, etc.).[18]

15. Carl E. Braaten, *The Flaming Center: A Theology of the Christian Mission* (Philadelphia: Fortress, 1977), pp. 154–55.

16. Kenneth Hamilton, "Liberation Theology: Lessons Positive and Negative," in *Evangelicals and Liberation,* ed. Carl E. Armerding (Nutley, NJ: Presbyterian and Reformed, 1977), p. 125.

17. Jose Miranda, *Marx and the Bible: A Critique of the Philosophy of Oppression,* trans. John Eagleson (Maryknoll, NY: Orbis, 1974), p. 109.

18. Herman Ridderbos, *The Coming of the Kingdom* (Nutley, NJ: Presbyterian and Reformed, 1976), pp. 188–89.

Despite this precise definition of "the poor" in Scripture, theologians of liberation rather arbitrarily confine its meaning to the economically and socially deprived and then relate this restricted definition to the basic salvation paradigm of the Old Testament: the exodus. Brown enthusiastically summarizes (and endorses!) the manner in which this epochal event is utilized:

> a) God is a God who takes sides, rather than remaining neutral and aloof; b) God sides with the poor, the dispossessed, the slaves, rather than with the Pharaohs, the powerful, the influential people in society; c) Those, therefore, who are the poor and the dispossessed can be confident that the alleviation of their misery is one of God's concerns; d) God calls on them to work with him in overcoming injustice; e) Since God is a living God, this means that what was true for the Israelites back then can become true for their modern counterparts today, i.e., their liberation from oppressive structures. Consequently, the story of the Exodus is a story of Good News today, the Good News that God is a liberating God. "Religion and politics don't mix?" On the contrary, they are mixed up all the way through the story.[19]

Any careful exegete of Scripture will protest this deliberate subordination of the Word of God to make it serve the human context. Whereas it is true that the exodus was a political event, it was also religious in that it was within the ongoing redemptive purpose of God as well. The Israelites were already the people of God: the Book of Genesis (12–50) records the covenant relationship God established with the line of Abraham, Isaac, and Jacob. But before they could enter into their destiny as a separate people in the midst of the nations, God so superintended their history that the Egyptian oppression overtook them. Prior to this they were devoid of an experienced cohesion. Brother sold brother; much conflict characterized their corporate life. God sent seventy of them into the Egyptian furnace, where through a protracted period of shared oppression and suffering, they came to a growing awareness of themselves as a people. When by miraculous means—not by the civil disobedience of the midwives or by the violence of Moses (Exod. 1:15–2:15)—God delivered them from Egypt, they came to a vivid awareness of themselves as a people set apart for a unique role in redemptive history. The point of the account of the controversy with the pharaoh is not that God wanted to make the Israelites His people because they were poor and oppressed. Moses' words to the pharaoh indicate they already were God's people:

19. Robert McAfee Brown, *Theology in a New Key: Responding to Liberation Themes* (Philadelphia: Westminster, 1978), pp. 88–90; "Liberation Theology and the Coming of the Kingdom," Ventnor Conference of Evangelical Mission Executives (April 20–21, 1979), p. 6.

"Thus says the LORD, 'Let my people go, that they may serve me' " (Exod. 8:1).

So then, we conclude our discussion of the exodus by underscoring the importance of a biblical hermeneutic that does not confine "captives" and "poor" to the political and economic dimensions of life. At the same time we reaffirm that the biblical theme of redemptive liberation should not be so spiritualized that God is regarded as indifferent to the political and economic needs of His people. However, the theologian of liberation who stresses political or military action on behalf of the oppressed, with only passing reference to God, is making a grave mistake. The Old Testament prophets denounced those who took their destiny into their own hands—who made political alliances and called for military uprisings, to the neglect of putting their sole confidence in God and calling on Him to act (Exod. 14:13–14; Isa. 30:15–18; 28:16).[20] And we should remember that

> Jesus' proclamation and inauguration of the liberating activity of God seems not to have focused on the plight of His people under Roman oppression. He certainly was aware of this plight . . . however, in the true prophetic tradition, He was aware of a much wider spiral of oppression— a spiral which extended well beyond, but certainly included politics, economics, culture and social life, and a spiral in which His own people were involved not only as oppressed but as oppressors—God's wider plan for human liberation.[21]

All this poses the basic question: what is the gospel? Good news about political and social liberation, about individual wholeness and personal fulfilment? Not exactly. "The gospel of God . . . [is] the gospel concerning his Son" (Rom. 1:1–3). When someone dislodges self from the center of his or her being and deliberately, by an act of faith, enthrones Jesus Christ there, and then turns to disciplined reflection on Scripture, there develops a new inner concern for liberation and wholeness and fulfilment. The individual discovers that to know God is to be concerned for the poor and the downtrodden—in short, to do justice (Jer. 22:13–16). Worship of God, to be acceptable, must be interwoven with expressions of justice (Isa. 58:6–7). And the liberation of the persecuted from all forms of oppression must engage the heart and life of all who call Jesus Lord (Luke 4:16–30).

Evangelicals should be grateful to the theologians of liberation for challenging them to a heightened sense of concern for more than ortho-

20. Ferdinand Deist, "The Exodus Motif in the Old Testament and the Theology of Liberation," *Missionalia* 5 (1977): 67.

21. Ephraim Mosothoane, "The Liberation of Peoples in the New Testament," *Missionalia* 5 (1977): 78–79.

doxy. There must also be orthopractice. To love our neighbor as ourself
. . . this entails a concern for the total range of our neighbor's needs. And
to do justice to the holistic import of the gospel, we should be diligent and
perceptive students of society. We should seek the assistance of the social
sciences to enable us to discern the oppressive dimensions of societal evils.
Furthermore, we should seek ways to rescue evangelical Christianity from
being so captured by the political and economic status quo that it unwit-
tingly contributes to the aggravation of the plight of the poor and the
downtrodden.

Liberation Theologies: Their Missiological Implications

We begin the final section of this chapter by speaking of liberation
theologies. This is necessary, since there is no one liberation theology.
Indeed, there has been a proliferation of liberation theologies throughout
the world in the years since the writings of Latin American theologians
began to be translated into other languages. Black theology, feminist theology, Amerindian theology, Chicano theology—the list keeps growing.

This ferment gained great impetus through the 1973 Bangkok meeting
of the WCC Commission on World Mission and Evangelism (CWME).
The theme was "Salvation Today." Two years later at the Fifth Assembly
of the WCC in Nairobi, the liberation theme again dominated ("Jesus
Frees and Unites"). The 1980 CWME gathering at Melbourne ("Your
Kingdom Come") was so deeply committed to listening to voices from
Latin America that great contemporary missiological issues were hardly
given serious attention. Few delegates raised a call for evangelism and for
response to the challenge of resurgent ethnic faiths (e.g., militant Islam,
sectarian Hinduism, secularized Buddhism). Few pondered the evangelistic implications of millions turning from animism and other millions
turning to occultism. None spoke of the decay of ideological Marxism-
Leninism-Maoism. Indeed, all these issues were deemed of only minor
importance to a gathering convened under the banner of "World Mission
and Evangelism."

There is only one valid test of any theology of mission: does it contribute to our Lord's command to make Jesus Christ known, loved, and
served throughout the world? Does it constrain the people of God to
carry out His final commands concerning the proclamation of the Good
News of the kingdom to the total human family, the issuance of the call
to conversion, and the planting of churches? Does it make possible everywhere the healing, liberating, serving presence of Christ? Evangelicals are
committed to this priority, and are tenaciously determined to devote to
this task their time, strength, and resources.

It is within this frame of reference that we probe Latin America's stimulation of what its theologians describe as "doing theology." How has this process moved the people of God to investigate and seek to remedy all that oppresses and exploits their neighbors? It is said that Latin America has left its mark on all theologies of liberation. If so, what is that mark?

In Latin America the great majority of the people are baptized Catholics. The church is not a small minority surrounded by vast Muslim, Hindu, Buddhist, or Shinto peoples. According to sacramental theology, all baptized Latins are Christians, although they might spend far more time appeasing the spirit world than practicing their faith. As a result, liberation theologies are only marginally involved in the evangelistic task and in encounter with the great ethnic religions. True, writers frequently refer to the three levels of liberation that Gutierrez identifies: the political, the cultural, and the spiritual.[22] But one rarely encounters any translation of "spiritual liberation" into evangelism and the call to the evangelistic task so that our generation might be liberated from idolatry, pantheism, polytheism, spiritism, atheism—and from sin, so that people might be brought into relationship and fellowship with the living God. This silence is inexcusable.

Whether deliberate or not, liberation theologies have given precise content to the secularized *Missio Dei* of the sixties with its questionable assertion that relating to anything one thinks God is doing in the world today is the church's "mission." Liberation theologies have transformed *Missio Dei* into politics. Some predict that the eighties will see the flowering of liberation theologies. The church is being told that its priority of priorities is to work for the sort of social change that will minimize the anguish of the human race: Christians must not only be socially compassionate, they must be socially creative as well. All the energies of Christians and churches must be devoted to this task. If so, what about evangelism?

There is another aspect of Latin American Christianity that is being stamped on liberation theologies: a myopia of missionary vision. In our day we are witnessing the emergence and growth of literally hundreds of mission societies in the Third World. Their missionaries number in the thousands (some say between fourteen and sixteen thousand). Asians and Africans are freely crossing cultural and linguistic barriers to share Jesus Christ with their generation. But not Latin Americans. *The Ten-Year Horizon* (1981–1990) of the Latin America Mission touched on this in the following fashion:

The Latin American Church has not spawned foreign mission agencies in the numbers and size seen in Asia, for example. It is strongly evangelistic within its own context, but lacks an inner imperative to cross-cultural com-

22. E.g., Newbigin, *Open Secret*, p. 111; Gutierrez, *Theology of Liberation*, pp. 176–77.

munication of the Gospel. This lack of missionary altruism (i.e., a concern for one's less privileged neighbor) has been attributed to many things—to a psychotic self-pity; to the fact that Latin American people have never been on the conquering end of colonial imperialism and have not had the same contact with the needy overseas; to a revulsion for their own ancestors who confused the cross and the sword; and to Spanish individualism. In general, the Latin American Church has not even fulfilled its clear obligation to evangelize the Indians in its midst, let alone to reach beyond its borders.[23]

This negative attitude toward cross-cultural missionary involvement appears to have rubbed off on liberation theologians. They are not interested in forming parachurch mission structures to go to other countries. Their concern is to arouse the consciences of Christians already within the churches in those areas where injustices need to be rectified. They also help finance valid liberation movements whether Christian-motivated or not. Whether they can transform churches into political weapons largely remains to be seen. Indeed, it is difficult to see how the theologies of liberation can escape the flaw of many ideologies, that is, how they can accomplish much more than raise expectations.

Whereas some might argue that the pressure of Catholic citizens and the Roman hierarchy on the government of Poland to grant Polish workers freedom to organize their own labor unions was due to the impact of liberation theology, few if any religious analysts have confirmed this. Taken by itself, liberation theology, which attempts to point the way toward a new understanding of mission, has yet to establish its validity in terms of actual achievement.

One does not want to be skeptical. God calls His people "to do justice, and to love kindness, and to walk humbly with [their] God" (Mic. 6:8). In that notable book, *Signs of Hope and Justice,* edited by Jether Perlira Ramalho,[24] one finds heartwarming descriptions of the pilgrimages of various churches of the poor as well as some of the latest official statements of the obligation of churches to be involved. But, again, little else. Nothing of what Vatican II called the unfinished missionary task: "Sent by Christ to reveal and to communicate the love of God to all men and nations, the Church is aware that there still remains a gigantic missionary task for her to accomplish. For the Gospel message has not yet been heard, or scarcely so, by two billion human beings. And their number is increasing daily."[25]

23. Clayton L. Berg and W. Dayton Roberts, *Ten-Year Horizon (1981–1990),* Background Briefing Paper 12 (1980), p. 2.

24. Jether Perlira Ramalho, ed., *Signs of Hope and Justice* (Geneva: World Council of Churches, 1980).

25. *Ad gentes,* in Walter M. Abbott, ed., *The Documents of Vatican II* (New York: Herder and Herder, 1966), pp. 596–97.

11

Papal Advocates

Catholic Mission Theory to Vatican II

Arthur F. Glasser

In 1906 the Protestant missiologist Gustav Warneck produced his magnum opus, *Evangelische Missionslehre,* a scientific investigation and theological statement of the principles and rules which should govern the labors of the church in spreading the Christian faith throughout the world. With dogmatic finality this encyclopedic and pontifical German work affirmed: "Roman Mission literature lacks even the slightest approach to a mission theory, whether in ancient or modern times. Not even the individual stones from which a mission theory could be constructed are in existence."[1] In his other famous work, *Outline of a History of Protestant Missions,* he rubbed in yet more salt:

> Although the Catholic missionary enterprise is much older than the Protestant, it has so far produced no scientific missionary system. Even works from the pen of individuals dealing with the theory of missions, such as abound in the protocols of Protestant missionary conferences and missionary periodicals, are as good as non-existent in Catholic missionary literature. Hence we can study their methods only as we see them in practice, which practice is guided chiefly by tradition.[2]

As we would expect, these uncharitable remarks could not be ignored. Joseph Schmidlin, the polemic Roman Catholic professor of missiology at the University of Münster, rose to the challenge. His *Catholic Mission Theory* begins with a thorough review of the history and literature of Roman Catholic mission theory to show Warneck's "ignorance of our Catholic mission literature of earlier times." Schmidlin then follows with a positive response to Warneck's criticism:

---

1. Quoted in Joseph Schmidlin, *Catholic Mission Theory* (Techny, IL: Missions Press, 1931), p. 5.
2. Gustav Warneck, *Outline of a History of Protestant Missions* (New York: Revell, 1906), p. 408.

167

Granted that Mission theory has seldom been systematically treated, the cause for this phenomenon must be attributed primarily to the fact that no need for such a work was felt. On the one hand, the official decrees of the Popes and propaganda, with the practical precepts of the mission superiors, seemed sufficient for immediate needs. On the other hand, the practice of the different missionary fields diverged so widely that the elaboration of a uniform mission theory seemed impossible.[3]

The sixteenth and seventeenth centuries marked unprecedented advances for the Roman Catholic Church in its missionary outreach. Gregory XV, in founding the Sacred Congregation for the Propagation of the Faith (the Congregation of the Propaganda) in 1622, confirmed that the spreading of the Word of God was the special concern of the vicar of Christ. In turn, the Propaganda founded (1627) and directed a missionary seminary, the Urban College of the Propaganda, which soon became deeply involved in writing and publishing in the field of missions (e.g., Lawrence Cardinal Brancati's famous *De procurande salute omnium gentium*, three centuries before the science of missiology was created). Later, Alexander VII in his famous *Instruction of 1659* on behalf of the native priests of Goa laid the foundations of pontifical missionary doctrine as it is understood today.

In the eighteenth century what Schmidlin called "grievous afflictions" shook his church, among them the Jansenist controversy, the suppression of the Jesuits, and the French Revolution. To these must be added the rapacious policies of Christopagan white colonials in the New World. Their pattern was either to destroy or enslave indigenous Indian peoples— and to round up baptized blacks in Africa to help them develop their plantations. The priests who protested were driven off. The question inevitably arises: Was the purpose of missions to domesticate savages so they could become slaves? Foreign missions began to recover from these afflictions only in the mid-nineteenth century.

It was in the twentieth century, however, that the Catholic Church began, once again, to define its mission policies systematically. This occurred chiefly because of the vision of four successive popes. Their encyclicals on the mission of the church brought about a revival of missionary passion and outreach that bodes well to make this its most glorious century for growth throughout the world. From 1920 to 1950 membership increased from 390 million to 460 million. By 1979 it had jumped to 739 million. In 1926 there were approximately 400 missions serving throughout the world. By 1951 their number had increased to almost 600; today they number over 700. This rapid growth is significant in that the church, following World War II, lost heavily in Eastern Europe, China, and the countries making up Indochina.

3. Schmidlin, *Catholic Mission Theory*, pp. 3, 5.

In this chapter we are concerned to explore the church's earlier understanding of its mission to the nations. This will enable us to appreciate Vatican II better, particularly its struggles for change and renewal. So then, we begin by reviewing the missionary encyclicals of the four missionary-minded popes of the twentieth century: Benedict XV (1914–1922), Pius XI (1922–1939), Pius XII (1939–1958), and John XXIII (1958–1963). The documents of Vatican II are studded with references to these encyclicals and seek wherever possible to reflect continuity with them.

Missionary Encyclicals of the Twentieth Century

> What is the aim of the missions if it is not to establish and implant the Church in these immense regions? . . . The prime reason for the existence of the Church is not the number of the present members but all mankind . . . the Church has no other reason for existing than evangelizing . . . throughout the world to make all men participate in God's saving redemption. [Pius XI—*Rerum ecclesiae*]

1. MAXIMUM ILLUD (Benedict XV —November 30, 1919)[4]

After an exhausting and inhuman world war that seemed to have destroyed forever the dream of universal harmony, Benedict XV drafted an "apostolic letter" which he entitled *On Spreading the Catholic Faith Throughout the World.* He began by reviewing the abiding mandate Christ gave His church to "preach the gospel to the whole creation" (Mark 16:15), and briefly sketched what had already been accomplished by God's grace. He rejoiced over the sacrificial obedience of missionaries, then abruptly added:

> 6. To anyone who weighs these facts, the realization must come as a shock that right now there still remain in the world immense multitudes of people who dwell in darkness and in the shadow of death. According to a recent estimate the number of non-believers in the world approximates one billion souls.

Benedict XV proceeded to reveal his purpose in writing:

> 7. The pitiable lot of this stupendous number of souls is for Us a source of great sorrow. From the days when We first took up the responsibilities of this apostolic office We have yearned to share with these unfortunates the divine blessings of the Redemption. So We are delighted to see that, under the inspiration of the Spirit of God, efforts to promote and develop the foreign missions have in many quarters of the world increased and intensified. It is Our duty to foster these enterprises and do all We can to

4. Thomas J. M. Burke, ed., *Catholic Missions: Four Great Missionary Encyclicals* (New York: Fordham University, 1957), pp. 9–23.

encourage them; and this duty coincides perfectly with Our own most profound desires.

The thrust of this encyclical is both clear and pointed. Benedict XV calls for continued advance. There must be no slackening of effort, no rest sought. More and better trained missionaries, more stations, more converts, more catechumens, more interaction on missiology among mission leaders, more recruitment and training of what were called "native clergy," more spirituality on the part of all who thus serve Jesus Christ. On and on. It is a moving document.

Doubtless due to follies of nationalism vividly displayed during World War I, Benedict XV interjected a warning to his missionary priests:

18. Carry the light to men who lie in the shadow of death and open the way to heaven for souls that are hurtling to destruction. Assure yourselves that God was speaking to you, to each one of you, when He said: "Forget your people and your father's house" (Psalm 44:11 [45:10]). Remember that your duty is not the extension of a human realm but of Christ's: and remember too that your goal is the acquisition of citizens for a heavenly fatherland, and not for an earthly one.

19. It would be a tragedy indeed if an apostolic man were to spend himself in attempts to increase and exalt the prestige of the native land he once left behind him.

This encyclical also marks the beginnings of the church's new emphasis on making its congregations indigenous to the culture of the people in which they are planted. At all costs, Benedict XV wants his missionaries to avoid giving the impression that the "Christian religion is the national religion of some foreign people" and that anyone converted to it is "abandoning his loyalty to his own people and submitting to the pretensions and domination of a foreign power" (par. 19). How can missionaries avoid giving this impression? Chiefly, Benedict XV says, through diligence to excel in "moral integrity . . . like their model, the Lord Jesus."

2. RERUM ECCLESIAE (Pius XI—February 28, 1926)[5]

The striking emphases of Pius XI's missionary encyclical are its intimate linkages with *Maximum illud* (which it quotes extensively), its overarching concern to foster missionary zeal, and its affirmation that the principal duty of the vicar of Christ will not be realized until the evangelization of the world is complete:

1. The Church was established precisely for this task, to spread the kingdom of Christ throughout the world and to afford all men a share in His

5. Ibid., pp. 26–38.

salutary Redemption. Thus, whoever functions as the earthly Vicar of Jesus Christ, the Chief Shepherd, cannot be content merely to guard the Lord's flock from danger. His special position demands that he make every effort to gather into Christ's fold those who still languish outside it. . . .

9. Ours is the primary responsibility for the spread of the faith, whereas each of you should unhesitantly share this burden with us . . . in this matter God will one day exact of us a strict accounting.

No Protestant mission leader has ever been more forceful in calling the whole church to intercede before the "Lord of the Harvest" that laborers be sent out and that mercy be shown to the "unfortunate . . . non-Christians" (par. 11). No Protestant mission leader was ever more forthright in stressing the need for indigenous churches served by national pastors.

24. From the fact that the Roman Pontiff has entrusted to you and your workers the apostolic task of preaching the truths of Christianity to non-Christians, you should not conclude that the role of the local clergy is merely to help the foreign missionaries in lesser matters or in some minor fashion to supplement their work.

25. Why should the local clergy be prevented from cultivating their own vineyard or from governing their own people?

Pius XI reminds his missionaries that the ever-present threat of war means the ever-present possibility of their being expelled from the countries to which they have been sent. He makes this the basis for a renewed call for the indigenization of the church: "What trials would the Church then suffer in those regions, unless throughout the land there were a veritable network of native priests to care for the Christian converts!" (par. 26).

Pius XI calls for regional seminaries to train local clergy. Are they not potentially "equal in knowledge and powers" with the missionaries? He stresses the organizational dimensions of this vast training task. Again and again he calls for advance. Every area must be completely penetrated. He reminds all that hearts can be won by deeds of practical charity. He does not want spectacular and expensive buildings. Humble chapels will do. And yet he does not want the local gentry overlooked: "We know from history and experience that when once the leaders of the people have been converted to Christianity, the ordinary people follow closely in their footsteps." The note of urgency suffuses the encyclical. Pius XI wants the missionary stage to end throughout the world as soon as possible so that local bishoprics can be created. Hence, he calls missionaries to remember that they have "not received their portion of the Lord's vineyard by a kind of private title in perpetuity. Rather, they hold it at the will of the Holy

See, whose right and duty it remains to provide for their proper development" (par. 39).

3. EVANGELII PRAECONES (Pius XII—June 2, 1951)[6]

Exactly twenty-five years after *Rerum ecclesiae*, and in honor of it, Pius XII issued an encyclical entitled *On the Development of the Missions*. He wanted to continue the missionary labors of his predecessors. He quotes their encyclicals with hearty approval. Whereas Pius XII rejoiced over the enormous gains achieved by the church in Africa and Asia, he wanted to move ahead even faster in the task of making Christ known throughout the world. Statistics are cited of previous achievements, and the human cost that made them possible. But the church must advance! The supranational character of its mission is reiterated. There is also a call to establish diplomatic relations with non-Catholic countries in order to interpret the church's supranational mission to their leaders, lest they be tempted to feel the church can be used to further political ends.

Evangelii praecones, however, is chiefly known for its enlarged emphasis on the importance of a national clergy. The missionary task is not so much to raise up new Christians, as it is to form a native clergy and prepare a local hierarchy "to extend the Church into new districts in such a way that she may enroot herself ever more deeply in them, and that after it has developed there it may be able, soon afterwards, to live and flourish without the aid of missionary works" (par. 34).

Since Pius XII is convinced the role of the laity is crucial to the success of the mission of the church, he devotes eleven paragraphs to a historical review of their service in earlier centuries. He wants the laity to be involved in the church's school system, in the development of its national press, and in its charitable institutions. And he looks beyond the church to the contemporary world. "Why should not the social order be renewed by the presence of the Church in its midst? Why should the strength of the Church not be placed in opposition to Communistic secularism? Why should national cultures not be respected?" He amplifies his directive that the church "preserve the natural culture of the pagans":

> 87. When the Gospel is accepted by diverse races, it does not crush or repress anything good and honorable and beautiful which they have achieved by their native genius and natural endowments. When the Church summons and guides a race to higher refinement and a more cultured way of life, under the inspiration of the Christian religion, she does not act like a woodsman who cuts, fells and dismembers a luxuriant forest indiscriminately. Rather, she acts like an orchardist who engrafts a cultivated shoot on a wild tree so that later on fruits of a more tasty and richer quality may issue forth and mature.

6. Ibid., pp. 40–61.

In this connection Pius XII quotes from his first published encyclical (*Summi pontificatus*), which dealt with adaptation: "Anything whatever that is not inextricably bound up with superstition and error, is at all times weighed sympathetically and, if possible, retained intact and unmarred" (par. 92). There is significance in this reference to an earlier encyclical. Indeed, Pius XII frequently spoke of the mission of the church. His definitions are illuminating. The church's task is "to propagate the reign of Christ, that is to say, to make the frontiers of the Kingdom of God coincide with those of the world." He was imbued with the desire to make catholicity the characteristic note and distinctive sign of the church: "Make the entire world a holy land and carry the reign of the risen Redeemer (His empire over hearts) across the continents to the most remote man in our planet."[7]

Pius XII interjected a note of urgency into his call for advance. He agreed with Pius XI's eagerness to see an end to the work of missions achieved, when the living church throughout the earth will be found sprouting from the "native soil" and developing steadily "until it is sufficient unto itself." Although of limited duration, the mission phase is seen as "a universal gesture of love," an "admirable proof in itself, of the divinity of the Church."

Pius XII is also noted for his statements on salvation. Salvation is "not certain" outside the visible church, even though it is theoretically possible.[8]

Toward the end of his reign Pius XII issued a final apostolic letter, *Fidei donum* (April 21, 1957), in which he called for rejoicing over the expansion of the church in Africa, and gave helpful pastoral counsel on the many problems arising from its rapid growth. He also warned against atheistic materialism and called for a renewed sense of personal and collective obligation to pour heart, strength, time, prayer, and resources into the unfinished task. This must be done in obedience to Christ's command, "Put out into the deep!" (par. 117). Luke 5:4 was one of Pius XII's favorite texts!

4. PRINCEPS PASTORUM (John XXIII—November 28, 1959)[9]

When John XXIII was crowned in 1958 he likewise confessed to having been challenged by the missionary zeal of his immediate predecessors. In his coronation sermon he pledged to give his central attention to the missions of the church. He called attention to Pius XII's sense of priority and pledged:

7. J. E. Champagne, *Manual of Missionary Action* (Ottawa: University of Ottawa, 1948), pp. 313–14.

8. *Mystici corporis,* quoted in Champagne, *Manual,* p. 318.

9. Burke, *Catholic Missions,* pp. 63ff.

We assert vigorously and sincerely that it is our particular intention to be
the Shepherd, the pastor, of the whole flock. . . . "Other sheep I have that
are not of this fold. Them also must I bring, and they shall hear my voice,
and there shall be one fold and one shepherd." These words sum up the
scope and splendor of all missionary work. This activity is certainly the
first concern of the Roman Pontiff.[10]

Early in his reign John XXIII issued *Princeps pastorum*, entitled *The
Catholic Missions*, to celebrate the fortieth anniversary of Benedict XV's
Maximum illud. He opened with a tribute to that document because it
"gave decisive impetus to missionary action in the Church" for the twentieth century. John's encyclical is largely concerned with ways and means
of raising up an indigenous clergy in each country and of mobilizing and
training the laity for the work of the missions. It stresses the importance
of missiology and abounds in quotations from the missionary encyclicals
already referred to in this chapter.

But more, the instructions of *Princeps pastorum* are specific where previous documents were content to be general. One significant illustration
will suffice. After quoting Pius XII at length on missionary adaptation,
John XXIII refers to an address he had given the delegates to the Second
World Congress of Negro Writers and Artists. He had concluded by
encouraging them to imitate "the manner of the famous Jesuit missionary,
Matteo Ricci."[11] Since Ricci is the only missionary mentioned by name in
this encyclical the implications are far-reaching. Ricci's adaptation policy
had been condemned at the highest level during the seventeenth century.

Discerning theologians immediately saw in John XXIII's endorsement
tremendous significance. Earlier that year (January 25, 1959), when he
issued his wholly unexpected call for "an Ecumenical Council for the
Universal Church," they had begun to believe that exciting possibilities
for its renewal and advance were latent in the reign of this new pope.
They had been discouraged in the months that followed by rumors that
only a rubber-stamp Curia-dominated council was contemplated. But John
XXIII's endorsement of Ricci showed that far from being a caretaker
pope, he had a genuine capacity for studying afresh Catholic teaching,
and reformulating it in contemporary terms. Was he God's man to bring
aggiornamento to the church?

Such theologians as Yves Congar, Karl Rahner, and Hans Küng thought
so. They represented a growing number of progressives who wanted the
church to develop a new theology that would be antischolastic, antitrium-
phalist, antiutopian, anti–Counter Reformation, and proecumenical. They

10. *The Encyclicals and Other Messages of John XXIII* (Washington, DC: T.P.S. Press,
1964), pp. 16–17.
11. Ibid., p. 178.

looked for an existentially relevant theology that would be loyal to tradition but free from those traditional formulations of truth that hinder understanding the gospel. Even though they knew many in the hierarchy were either puzzled or dismayed by the prospect of an ecumenical council, they hoped it would challenge the pope to make the most of his opportunity to bring the church up to date.

The Missionary Challenge to Vatican II

None saw the council's possibilities more clearly than did Hans Küng, then professor in the Catholic theology faculty of the University of Tübingen. He took pen in hand and produced (1960) *The Council, Reform, and Reunion,* a book that electrified Catholics and Protestants alike with its expansive vision for the church and its bold hopes for Vatican II. But more, it was most forthright in its proclamation of sin and error within the Holy Catholic Church. Overnight, John XXIII had become for Küng "perhaps the most ecumenically-minded pope in the history of the church." In his lecture tour of the United States (1963), Küng liked to relate an authentic story about John XXIII's response to a bewildered cardinal's inquiry as to why he called the council. The pope answered by opening the window and saying, "That's why! To let some fresh air into the church!"

It should be noted that certain external factors are often cited as responsible for the calling of the council: the church's growing awareness of isolation from the world (e.g., the failure of the worker-priest movement among the unchurched, anticlerical, Communist-leaning workers in France during and after World War II); the social backwardness of many predominantly Catholic countries; the growing interest of Catholic theologians in biblical theology and exegetical studies; the growing vigor of the lay-apostolate movement (endorsed by Pius XI and XII); the church's isolation from other churches, especially the Orthodox churches (which in 1961 had joined the World Council of Churches); the tremendous losses of the church due to the Communist post–World War II crusade (Eastern Europe, China, and Indochina); the growing awareness of the "mystical body of Christ" and the church as "the people of God"; and the increased maturation (and restlessness!) of the more than 350 indigenous bishops in the Third World. However, John XXIII said that the idea of convening the council was not so much the result of lengthy deliberation as "a divine impulse" that came to him while at prayer, as "an inspiration, as if he had suddenly been touched by God."[12]

Fresh air was needed! No one saw this more clearly than those theo-

---

12. Edmund Schlink, *After the Council: The Meaning of Vatican 2 for Protestantism* (Philadelphia: Fortress, 1968), p. 20.

logians who had found in the Protestant ecumenical movement a stimulus
to theological creativity. They became bold and started to affirm that Vatican II would be a success despite all the dark predictions to the contrary.
Perhaps this is what gave Küng such worldwide prominence in such a
short time. Hardly had Vatican II convened when it was apparent that he
had accurately predicted its spirit. Indeed, many of his concerns were
found to be shared by the majority of the council fathers.

John XXIII's opening address tacitly rejected the tired negatives: a
polemical anti-Protestantism, a southern European anti-Communism, and
a moralizing antimodernism. He stressed the positive and called for renewal
and reunion. Küng now became doubly excited. Following the first session
(October 11–December 8, 1962) he produced another book; *The Council
in Action* (1963) discussed the now rapidly enlarging possibilities before
the council. The central problem was now seen as the renewal of the
church, both inward and outward. Not enough that the church come to
a new understanding of itself, its constitution, and its liturgy; the church
must also be renewed in its mission to the world, its responsibility to other
Christian churches, and its encounter with the Jews and with the followers
of other religions. Crucial, however, was inward renewal. If inward renewal
was granted by God, everything outward would change, too. "In the missions in particular," Küng affirmed, "all of us, Catholics, Protestants and
Orthodox, are faced with a vast reshuffling of everything involved."[13] He
hoped that once Vatican II had brought inner renewal to the church, the
council would issue three calls.

1. *A Call for Cultural Identification.* The church must become "Bantu to
the Bantu, Chinese to the Chinese, Indian to the Indians." By this Küng
meant a bolder "grafting of herself (regardless of the risks of accultura-
tion) onto the national character, culture, feeling, thinking and life of the
various peoples of the world."[14] In his judgment, the church was still far
from having taken inner root in their cultural and spiritual soil. While
grateful for Benedict XV's *Maximum illud* with its strong suggestion that
the church be bolder in adapting its forms, and while particularly pleased
that John XXIII made the adaptive Jesuit, Matteo Ricci, the model of
missionaries, Küng contended that the Catholic Church had yet to attain
its full catholicity.

> The Catholic Church needs unity, but not uniformity: Ecclesia circumdata
> varietate! . . . She needs unity in multiplicity, in true Catholic fulness.
> "Unity in essentials, freedom in non-essentials." . . . One God, one Lord,
> one faith, one baptism—but in a variety of European (Italian, German,
> French, English, Greek, Russian . . .), Asiatic and African buildings and

13. Hans Küng, *The Council in Action* (New York: Sheed and Ward, 1963), p. 244.
14. Ibid., pp. 247–49.

images, formularies and chants, styles of feeling, thinking and living, of preaching and praying and practising devotion. We have all become aware of this now, and the problems are urging us on to their solution.[15]

2. *A Call for Indigenous Theology.* Closely related to the call for cultural identification is the need for Christian theology to be freed from its Aristotelian, Latin, and Teutonic molds so that it might be developed within the thought forms and experience of great peoples throughout the world. Küng argues that the council should forsake, totally and forever, "that powerful foe of all deep-level evangelization, the assimilation method, which aims at making the primitive into a European before making him a Christian."[16]

Of course, Küng recognized that theological work along these lines is "highly problematical and risky." Nevertheless the church should stimulate national Christians to reverence and love their own culture and philosophy. In a world in which Christendom is no longer dominant and the West is in political and cultural retreat, the future success of the church under God will depend on its ability, in the power of the Spirit, to become, in the most comprehensive sense of the word, "more Catholic in her character, her liturgy, and preaching, her law and custom, her doctrine and theology."[17]

3. *A Call for Christian Reunion.* As intimated earlier, not a few prominent Catholic theologians had become increasingly responsive to the stimulus that the ecumenical movement had brought to their performance of the theological task. Some, like Küng, were able to relate this ecumenical interaction to the mission of the church. He quoted the Swiss missiologist O. Niederberger with approval:

> The tragedy of the missions is that Christianity cannot show a united front in the struggle for the salvation of the world against paganism on the one hand and secularism, materialism and Communism on the other. For everyone who has the conversion of the heathen at heart, the question of Christian reunion cannot be a matter of indifference.[18]

Simply put, the success of the mission of the church depends in the final analysis on success in reuniting all separated Christian confessions. Accepting this principle, Küng was grieved that Catholic missions had been very little affected by the ecumenical movement, less so than any other segment of the life of the church. He reasoned that this was due to interconfessional competition, their polemic stance, anti-Protestant bias,

15. Ibid., p. 249.
16. Ibid., p. 259.
17. Ibid., p. 254.
18. Ibid., p. 255.

and relative isolation from Europe's ecumenical ferment. He climaxed this discussion with a call to Vatican II to labor for the renewal of the whole church of Jesus Christ throughout the world. He was encouraged by the stirrings he discerned in the Roman Church and concluded his appeal with the ringing conviction: "What lies behind us gives us courage and confidence to dare anew."[19]

The Missionary Theory of Vatican II—A Synthetic View

Before we examine analytically the specific contributions Vatican II documents made to the missiology of the church, a synthetic overview is needed to bring our discussion into focus. We begin by summarizing pre–Vatican II mission theory.

At the beginning of the twentieth century Catholic mission theory was largely built around the concept of *plantatio fidei*: the primary objective was individual conversions. Because new converts need ecclesiastical linkage, the establishment of local, self-sufficient congregations was considered the "social corollary of the primary end."[20] This led to the defining of the missionary objective as *plantatio ecclesiae*.[21] Whereas some twentieth-century "apostolic" missionary movements tended to separate the kingdom of God from the church in high hopes of seeing the gospel produce social results beyond that of multiplied congregations, these romantic efforts generally yielded to the hard realities of more traditional forms of mission. *Ecclesia peregrinans* and *ecclesia in via* quite smothered all dreams of *ecclesia triumphans*.

Over the years, however, the emphasis on *plantatio ecclesiae* resulted in the expansion of the church as a Roman institution, with papal and curial selfhood hindering the development of the selfhood of national churches. Not that Catholics do not rejoice today that Roman congregations exist all over the world. But the church's missiologists had become concerned that these thousands of congregations be less exotically Roman and more indigenous to local cultures. It was doubtless due to their promptings that the twentieth-century missionary encyclicals were drafted to bring the church around to regard its mission as "*communio ecclesiarum* existing in fraternal love and in *diakonia* for the world" after the Protestant ecumenical pattern of "the whole church with the whole gospel for the whole world."

19. Ibid., p. 276.
20. Andrew V. Suemois, "The Evolution of Mission Theology Among Roman Catholics," in *The Theology of the Christian Mission*, ed. Gerald H. Anderson (New York: McGraw-Hill, 1961), p. 124.
21. Ibid., pp. 126–29.

In a very real sense this is what Vatican II was all about. Crucial to the renewal of the church were those moments when (1) the church was defined in spiritual rather than juridical terms, and when (2) the World College of Bishops (the council) was pressed to become an episcopacy for the whole world rather than an institution to buttress papal selfhood. For fifteen hundred years the church's bishops had not been responsible for its missionary outreach. But no longer! There are those who feel that Vatican II marked the end of the Roman period in the history of the Roman Catholic Church.[22] Indeed, the key word of Vatican II was "collegiality." The era of collegiality has begun. We shall discern this revolutionary change when we examine the decisions of Vatican II itself. We shall see that in the twentieth century Roman Catholic missions have become increasingly more dynamic. The sequence is from *plantatio fidei* to *plantatio ecclesiae* to *communio ecclesiarum* to *incorporatio mundi* to a church neither Roman nor Latin nor Greek nor Protestant, but an ecumenical church with Christ as its center.

One more word is in order. The *unum necessarium* of the council was defined by John XXIII as "great cordiality of heart and the optimism that can allow everyone to emphasize what unites and overlook what seems to divide." This meant "a theology of mutual encounter in which the truth is illuminated by understanding love instead of a state-of-siege theology with love subordinated to so-called truth, a theology which is in fact a preparation for union." It was this mood created by John XXIII that made it possible for the church for the first time in its history to "see partners in those who don't belong to her."[23]

Doctrines promulgated at a council belong to the magisterium of the church. As a result they possess surpassing authority. Naturally, they are drafted with great care. Originally, some seventy schemata were drawn up ranging in topic from benefices to ecclesiastical libraries. Little by little, however, as the council struggled to find itself and its way, it began to drop some subjects, combine others, and face issues that had hardly been thought of when the bishops first met. After four years of intense study and debate, sixteen documents were adopted (103,000 words in Latin text!) dealing with three major themes: doctrinal renewal, modern society, and ecclesiastical structures. Those documents pertinent to Roman Catholic mission theory will be considered in the next two chapters.

22. Warren A. Quanbeck and Vilmos Vatja, eds., *Challenge and Response: A Protestant Perspective of the Vatican Council* (Minneapolis: Augsburg, 1966), p. 119.

23. Robert B. Kaiser, *Pope, Council and World* (New York: Macmillan, 1963), p. 256.

12

Official Roman Catholic Theology of Mission

Ad Gentes

Donald McGavran

Roman Catholic theology of mission is authoritatively set forth in *Ad gentes* ("The Decree on the Missionary Activity of the Church"). This document was promulgated on December 7, 1965, by the Twenty-first Ecumenical Council, commonly called Vatican II. "The Decree on the Missionary Activity of the Church" was written, discussed, and then revised several times. It is to be understood as the official position of the Roman Catholic Church on Christian missions and is binding on all bishops, priests, and lay members of the church. It sums up what the contemporary Roman Catholic Church, after careful deliberation, has declared mission to be. It has not been superseded or significantly changed by writings of individual Catholic missiologists in later years.

Those who desire to comprehend the full import of this excellent statement on contemporary Christian mission ought to study related Vatican II documents as well. The foundational and pivotal document of Vatican II is *Lumen gentium,* a comprehensive statement on the nature of the church. It is titled "The Dogmatic Constitution on the Church" and is full of statements which necessitated *Ad gentes* and strongly support its exposition of the missionary task. For example, *Lumen gentium* opens with the words "Christ is the light of all nations" and asserts that "God planned to assemble in the holy church all those who would believe in Christ." In section 3 we read, "All men are called to this union with Christ who is the light of the world."

All missiologists and missionaries ought to read these two documents, particularly *Ad gentes*. It clearly sets forth a high biblical view of what Christian mission ought to be. A great deal of the confusion in mission today would be cleared up if the honest way in which *Ad gentes* handles what the whole of Scripture has to say in regard to mission were to be widely copied.

A Cautionary Note

But first a digression: our endorsement of *Ad gentes* must be seen as highly qualified. We have described *Ad gentes* in its missionary dimension as a biblical document. Nevertheless, we, with other non–Roman Catholics, on reading it and other documents of Vatican II will find many statements in regard to *other* dimensions of the Christian faith which to our way of thinking are *not* biblical. Many doctrines dear to the hearts of our Roman friends do not seem to us to be in accord with the main meanings of Scripture. True, they can be defended by a verse here or there, but they do not reflect the broad central current of biblical revelation, nor were they evident in the practice of the New Testament church. The excellent theology of mission found in *Ad gentes* must not be rejected, however, because it is accompanied by what we view as erroneous understandings of the Bible in regard to some other matters.

So that our commendation of the theology of mission set forth by Vatican II may be seen as an honest evangelical evaluation, we now set forth briefly some of our disagreements. Vatican II states that it is "following in the footsteps of the Council of Trent."[1] We remember that Trent invoked curses on Protestants. Then too, Vatican II affirms again and again that the pope of Rome is Peter's successor and holds superior and final power as Christ's vicar on earth. All segments of the Christian movement should acknowledge his authority. Vatican II also states that "whosoever, therefore, knowing that the Catholic Church was made necessary by God through Jesus Christ, would refuse to enter her or to remain in her could not be saved."[2]

Chapter 8 of *Lumen gentium* is entitled "The Role of the Blessed Virgin Mary, the Mother of God, in the Mystery of Christ and the Church." It contains many statements with which evangelicals and conciliars alike will not agree. Similarly the doctrine of the eucharist (which to be authentic and effective must be celebrated only by a properly ordained priest[3] in obedient relationship to his bishop and therefore to Peter's successor, the pope of Rome) does not commend itself to the evangelical mind as in any sense a biblical position.

Perhaps the most serious deficiency is that in "The Dogmatic Constitution on Divine Revelation" (*Dei verbum*) tradition is still weighted too heavily. The full and sure divine revelation, it is held, cannot be known without seeking it through the Holy Scripture *and through tradition*. Vati-

1. *Dei verbum* (*The Dogmatic Constitution on Divine Revelation*), in Walter M. Abbott, ed., *The Documents of Vatican II* (New York: Herder and Herder, 1966), p. 111.

2. *Lumen gentium,* in Abbott, *Vatican II,* pp. 32–33.

3. "Properly ordained," i.e., by a Roman Catholic bishop on whose head *three* properly ordained bishops have laid their hands, and so on back to the apostle Peter.

can II does give precedence to the Scripture over tradition, but it must be a church-interpreted Scripture as illumined through tradition and expounded by the magisterium. While this is a new and welcome emphasis on the Bible, it is a traditionalized and specifically Roman Catholic use of the Bible. This allows Catholics to appear thoroughly biblical to Protestants, but (as ecumenicist Father Carlo Boyer writes) brings no substantial change. Paul Minear of the Yale Divinity School states it exactly when he writes, "On Divine Revelation pays respect to Scripture but does not really listen to it."

This stricture applies specifically to those formulations of Vatican II which support distinctively Roman Catholic doctrines; it does not apply to those formulations which support world mission and to those parts of "The Pastoral Constitution on the Church in the Modern World" (*Gaudium et spes*) which urge Christian action. They are thoroughly biblical. In framing them, Vatican II, to use Minear's phrase, really listened to Scripture.

We mention these *points of disagreement* (and there are others) in hopes that the luminous theology of mission set forth in *Ad gentes* not be obscured by them. They stand on one base. The Roman Catholic theology of mission stands on a *different* and biblical base. It expresses a view of God, Christ, humanity, sin, and salvation which necessitates discipling the nations. On it non-Catholic Christians may in large part agree. Indeed it is difficult to see how any honest handling of Scripture can frame any substantially different description of the main thrust of God's revelation in regard to those multitudes who do not believe on Jesus Christ. The missionary task of the church set forth by Vatican II is clearly that described in the Bible.

To be sure, different branches of the church, as they draw up their own theologies of mission, will phrase them in slightly varied ways which seem desirable at the time. This will also involve excluding certain shades of meaning which would be desirable under other circumstances. Had American Christians written a theology of mission during the war to free the slaves (1861–1865), no doubt the Christian determination to abolish slavery from the earth would have resounded at various places in the document. When sons of Christian families were facing death for that cause, and more than 250,000 of them died to free the slaves, how could it have been otherwise? Contemporary theologies of mission must allow room for similar variations in emphasis.

Nevertheless, one of the great merits of *Ad gentes* is that it was drawn up by an ecumenical council. Church leaders from every nation were there and played a part in drawing up this wide-ranging, thoroughly biblical definition of what Christian mission necessarily is. Those who formulated this theology of mission looked squarely at the different emphases proposed by various segments of the body. Those concerned for social justice were there and voiced their opinions. The social actionists were there and voiced their opinions. The bishops of the churches of Asia and Africa and Latin America were there in great numbers and spoke freely. Both advocates of indigenous theologies and advocates of universal theologies spoke. Those who felt that the renewal of cold, nominal Christians is a part of mission were quite vocal, but their views did not carry. In short, in *Ad gentes* we read the great overriding essentials of Christian mission. Variations which particular churches may wish to insert have no proper place in a worldwide theology of mission.

Today all thinking of mission is carried on, by Roman Catholics and Protestants alike, in the midst of tremendous changes. A new world is coming into being. In this new world women are held to be the equal of men, the poor the equal of the rich, and citizens of all nations equals in every respect. Tremendous changes of opinion in regard to marriage, divorce, distribution of wealth, rights of small nations, and political power seethe around us. The rights of every individual to food, health, opportunity, and ease, formerly unthinkable, are now commonly accepted by most as the very foundations of modern society. Vatican II was well aware of the tumult and formed its conclusions in regard to mission with a very accurate picture of the modern world in mind. In the following chapter we shall deal with "The Pastoral Constitution on the Church in the Modern World," which sets forth the rapidly changing social order. While seeing this clearly, however, the ecumenical council also set forth *some things which do not change*—the human race's continuing desperate need for salvation from sin, God's unswerving purpose to save them through faith in Christ and membership in His body, the unchanging command of Christ to disciple all the peoples of earth, the certainty of eternal life for the redeemed, and other foundational convictions which undergird mission. Changes are many but they must not conceal the unchanging verities.

In today's tremendous confusion surrounding the many warring theologies of mission, one must constantly seek the main current of the biblical revelation. It is not permissible to select only those passages which support a point we wish to emphasize and to make them central, thereby disregarding the main current of Scripture. Theology is always a disciplined reflection on biblical truth. The great questions are: What does the Bible say? What did the Lord Jesus teach and do? What did the New Testament churches do and teach? For example, our Lord manifested considerable concern for the physical health and well-being of others. But He also said, "Do not fear those who kill the body but cannot kill the soul; rather fear him who can destroy both soul and body in hell" (Matt. 10:21).

A theology of mission does well to include feeding the hungry and looking after refugees as duties which Christians ought to perform under today's conditions. It does not do well to substitute the performance of these duties for proclaiming the gospel and pleading with all men and women to be reconciled to God. Any responsible theology of mission must make a sharp distinction between the great underlying essentials which apply in all cultures and all ages, and the emphases which here and there, in this time and that, must be stressed. This distinction *Ad gentes* makes.

The Roman Catholic View of Mission

A large part of the confusion and crippling loss of nerve in mission today lies in the systematic attempt to redefine mission to include everything God wants done. Historically mission has been a *sending*. That is the root meaning of the word *mission*. God sent the Son. The Son sent the Holy Spirit. Christ chose the apostles and sent them out. Barnabas and Paul, sent out by the Holy Spirit, sailed to Cyprus. Classical mission has always been the church's *sending out people to proclaim the gospel, to tell others of the redemption wrought for them on the cross, and, when they are converted by the Holy Spirit, to incorporate them into the church.*

Recently under the impact of factors described in earlier chapters of this book, a large and influential minority of Christians have been insisting that such mission was valid in the days of European empires, but mission today must not give priority to evangelism and the multiplying of cells of believers. Mission must be equated with social improvement and changing the structures of society so that there will be more justice, equality, and harmony on the earth. Reconciling sinful humans to God used to be the objective of mission, but now it is reconciling humans with one another. Eternal salvation used to be the main goal; but in the modern world, it is temporal improvements, to which the biblical-sounding title of "salvation today" has been given.

It is the great merit of the Vatican II delegates that on this issue they again and again voiced a consistent biblical view. Whether one studies "The Dogmatic Constitution on the Church" and "The Dogmatic Constitution on Divine Revelation," or "The Decree on the Missionary Activity of the Church," Vatican II is quite explicit that missionary work has to do with proclaiming near and far the gospel, bringing men and women of all nations to redeeming faith in Christ, and incorporating the responsive into His body, the church. Many other good activities can engage the heart and strength of Christians, but Christian mission is not to be confused with them.

In "The Dogmatic Constitution on Divine Revelation" we read: "This . . . Council wishes to set forth authentic teaching about divine revelation and about how it is handed on, *so that by hearing the message of salvation the whole world may believe.*"[4] The whole passage in which this statement appears

---

4. *Dei verbum*, in Abbott, *Vatican II*, p. 111 (emphasis added).

affirms clearly that the constitution on revelation has been written that eternal life in Christ might be shared with the whole world.

Also significant is the opening sentence of *Ad gentes*: "The Church has been divinely sent to all nations that she might be 'the universal sacrament of salvation.' "[5] The entire decree makes it clear that universal salvation does not mean plenty to eat and wear, but rather entering into a redemptive relationship with the Savior, Jesus Christ the Lord. For example we read:

> The pilgrim Church is missionary by her very nature. For it is from the mission of the Son and the mission of the Holy Spirit that she takes her origin, in accordance with the decree of God the Father. . . . In order to establish peace between sinful human beings and Himself, as well as to fashion them into a fraternal community, God determined to intervene in human history in a way both new and definitive. For He sent His Son, clothed in our flesh, in order that through this Son He might snatch men from the power of darkness and of Satan (cf. Col. 1:13; Acts 10:38) and that in this Son He might reconcile the world to Himself (cf. 2 Cor. 5:19).[6]

Vatican II carefully guards Christian mission from being confused with other good things which the church does and ought to do. Calvert Alexander, the authorized writer of the introductory statement to "The Decree on the Missionary Activity of the Church" (*Ad gentes*), says:

> The Decree . . . defines missionary work as that which is undertaken by the Church in favor of nations or peoples who have not yet heard the gospel and into whose non-Christian culture the gospel message has never been implanted, in other words, the modern *gentes,* the more than two billion non-Christian peoples of the world who live especially, but not exclusively, in Asia, Africa, and Oceania. Efforts to expand this definition to include some de-Christianized areas of the West where the number of unbelievers and half-believers is large were rejected by the Council as rendering the term "missions" unbiblical and meaningless.[7]

The point need not be labored. The documents of Vatican II from beginning to end are clear that mission ought to be defined as intentionally persuading non-Christian men and women to believe that Jesus is the Christ, the sacrifice for sin, the Savior of the world; so that in consequence they might not perish but receive eternal life (John 3:16). In these important documents we study the universal unchanging mission of the church, commanded by Christ and demonstrated by the apostles.

5. *Ad gentes,* in Abbott, *Vatican II,* p. 584.
6. Ibid., pp. 585–86.
7. Ibid., pp. 581–82.

The Doctrinal Principles

Ad gentes in its very first chapter lays down the doctrinal principles on which Christian mission is founded. We shall take these up one by one. Before doing so, however, it is necessary to note that *Ad gentes* accepts as axiomatic the doctrines in both dogmatic constitutions promulgated by Vatican II—those on the church and on revelation. It does not repeat them. It assumes that the authority on which the church and her mission are founded is the divine revelation recorded in the Bible. No theology of mission constructed by other branches of the church is as full of references to Scripture as are the documents of Vatican II, including *Ad gentes*. It may properly be considered a most careful exposition as to what the Scriptures teach in regard to the two billion (today more than three billion) who have yet to hear and yet to believe and be saved, and in regard to the responsibility of the body of Christ to carry out God's will and Christ's command to invite them to become parts of His household.

The necessity of the church is also assumed in *Ad gentes*. God has "planned to assemble in the holy Church all those who would believe in Christ."[8] "Established in the present era of time, the Church" will call them "together from all peoples. Christ made them mystically into His own body. In that body, the life of Christ is poured into the believers."[9] In short, throughout this exposition of the classical theology of mission, a high doctrine of the church is consistently held.[10]

Evangelicals also hold a high doctrine of the church. They will, however, not limit the church to the Church of Rome. For example, the Dordrecht Confession of Faith (1632) says the church consists of those who "have truly repented, and rightly believed; who are rightly baptized, united with God in heaven, and incorporated into the communion of the saints on earth."[11] The Westminster Confession (1646) holds that "the visible Church, which is also catholic or universal under the gospel . . . consists of all those, throughout the world, that profess the true religion, and of their children; and is the kingdom of the Lord Jesus Christ, the house and family of God, out of which there is no ordinary possibility of salva-

8. *Lumen gentium*, in Abbott, *Vatican II*, p. 15.

9. Ibid., pp. 15, 20.

10. Unfortunately, with regard to the difficult problem of the salvation of men and women who through no fault of their own have not heard the gospel, Vatican II grants that such people "can attain to everlasting salvation" (*Lumen gentium*, in Abbott, *Vatican II*, p. 35). However, the following paragraph heavily qualifies the overstatement. On this point Vatican II was evasive, but that does not erase its high doctrine of the church and its essentiality.

11. "The Dordrecht Confession," in John H. Leith, ed., *Creeds of the Churches: A Reader in Christian Doctrine from the Bible to the Present* (Atlanta: John Knox, 1973), p. 299.

tion."[12] Evangelicals believe that outside the church "there is no ordinary possibility of salvation." They also hold, therefore, that the proper expansion of the church is of the highest priority if we are to meet the deepest need of the human race.

We will now recount the doctrinal principles specifically mentioned in *Ad gentes,* keeping in mind that this document accepts as axiomatic those principles of the highest order which are expounded in the dogmatic constitutions on revelation and the church.

1. *God the Father by His very nature ordains, requires, and sustains mission.* God has created all humankind. He does not wish that any should perish. He has sent His Son to be the propitiation for their sins. He ardently desires their salvation. Therefore, all mission activity of the church and, indeed, the writing and promulgation of this decree flow from that fountain of love within God the Father. From Him who is the Origin without origin, the Son is begotten, and the Holy Spirit proceeds through the Son. This is the universal design of God for the salvation of the human race.

> It has pleased God . . . to make men holy and save them not merely as individuals . . . but by making them into a single people . . . which acknowledges Him in truth and serves Him in holiness. He therefore chose the race of Israel as a people unto Himself. . . . These things . . . were done by way of preparation . . . of that new and perfect covenant which was to be ratified in Christ, and of that more luminous revelation which was to be given through God's very Word made flesh. . . .
>
> This was to be the new people of God. For, those who believe in Christ, who are reborn . . . from an imperishable seed through the Word of the living God (cf. 1 Pet. 1:23), not from the flesh but from water and the Holy Spirit (cf. Jn. 3:5–6), are finally established as "a chosen race, a royal priesthood, a holy nation, a purchased people" (cf. 1 Pet. 2:9).[13]

Thus the first doctrinal principle is that world evangelization is an activity which flows out of the very nature of God.

2. *Christ was sent by God to redeem all sinners who believe in Him.* The documents of Vatican II gleam with expressions of this doctrine:

> Christ is the light of all nations.

> [God] planned to assemble in the holy Church all those who would believe in Christ.

> All men are called to this union with Christ.

> Christ made them [His brothers called together from all peoples] mystically into His own body.

12. "The Westminster Confession," in Leith, *Creeds,* p. 222.
13. *Lumen gentium,* in Abbott, *Vatican II,* p. 25.

> The Head of this body is Christ. . . . All the members ought to be molded into Christ's image until He is formed in them (Gal. 4:19). . . . From Him, "the whole body . . . attains a growth that is of God" (Col. 2:19).

> Christ, the one Mediator, . . . ceaselessly sustains here on earth His holy Church, the community of faith, hope, and charity.[14]

The second doctrine, set forth in *Ad gentes* in careful detail, affirms that *the mission of the church is Christ at work through the church calling people in all countries and cultures to believe in Him and find eternal life.*

3. *Christ sent the Holy Spirit to carry out the divine mission. All mission from that time to this is in a definitive way the work of the Holy Spirit.* The Holy Spirit "impels the Church toward her proper expansion." The last three words are of crucial importance. Since there is no other way for sinners to be saved, but to believe on Jesus Christ and to become responsible members of His body, *the church properly expands.* The Holy Spirit impels the church toward "her proper expansion." This doctrine, thus enunciated, strikes at the root of that common but erroneous dogma of relativism, which affirms that winning people to Christ, spreading the faith, and expanding the church are all self-aggrandizement, a disreputable triumphalism. Christians, secular humanists declare, are only one of many religious bodies, each seeking God in its own way. The task is not to grow at the expense of other religions, but to cooperate with them in making this world a better place in which to live. No, says Vatican II. The Holy Spirit Himself, sent by the Son, impels the church toward its proper expansion, thrusting out missionaries from all Jerusalems to all Judeas, all Samarias, and all ends of the earth. Then the Holy Spirit, working in every tribe and tongue, gently calls men and women to saving faith in Christ and builds them into the body, the company of the redeemed, the inheritors of eternal life. Finally the Holy Spirit impels these new branches of the church to press out to all those multitudes who have yet to hear and yet to believe. "Thus, what [Christ] once accomplished for the salvation of all may in the course of time come to achieve its effect in all."[15]

4. *Christ Himself,* the Lord of the church, the risen and reigning King, in all times and places *sends out men and women to disciple the multitudinous peoples of Planet Earth.* Missionaries are perennially recruited by Christ. The missionary movement flows from the very nature of the Triune God.

> From the very beginning, the Lord Jesus called "to him men of his own choosing. . . . And he appointed twelve that they might be with him, and that he might send them forth to preach" (Mk. 3:13; cf. Mt. 10:1–42). . . . [He] sent His apostles into all the world just as He Himself had been

14. Ibid., pp. 14–22, passim.
15. *Ad gentes,* in Abbott, *Vatican II,* p. 587.

sent by His Father (cf. Jn. 20:21). He gave them this command: "Go, therefore, and make disciples of all nations, baptizing them in the name of the Father, and of the Son, and of the Holy Spirit, teaching them to observe all that I have commanded you" (Mt. 28:19f.). "Go into the whole world; preach the gospel to every creature. He who believes and is baptized shall be saved, but he who does not believe shall be condemned" (Mk. 16:15f.).

Since then the duty has weighed upon the Church to spread the faith and the saving work of Christ. This duty exists not only in virtue of the express command. . . . It exists also in virtue of that life which flows from Christ into His members: "From him the whole body (being closely joined and knit together. . .) derives its increase to the building up of itself in love" (Eph. 4:16).

The mission of the Church, therefore, is fulfilled by that activity which makes her fully present to all men and nations. . . . By the example of her life and by her preaching, by the sacraments and other means of grace, she can lead them to the faith, the freedom, and the peace of Christ. . . . This mission is a continuing one. In the course of history it unfolds the mission of Christ Himself.[16]

This fourth doctrine is of particular importance today, at a time when a considerable body of Christian opinion is that the missionary movement was a function of the centuries past, of European empires, of a world which accepted the terrible inequalities of the various nations as part of an unchangeable order of things, and so the missionary movement devoted itself to evangelism and Christianization. No, says *Ad gentes,* missionary activity arises in every age in answer to the perpetually issued call of Christ. It is He who, back of the missionary societies, the orders, and the church, calls men and women to become heralds of the gospel, ambassadors of Christ, beseeching sinners to be reconciled to God through the narrow way of the cross.

5. The fifth doctrine in the Roman Catholic theology of mission, based on the preceding four, is a beautifully clear definition of what Christian mission properly is. We cannot do better than to quote the words of the ecumenical council:

"Missions" is the term usually given to those particular undertakings by which the heralds of the gospel are sent out by the Church and go forth into the whole world to carry out the task of preaching the gospel and planting the Church among peoples or groups who do not yet believe in Christ. These undertakings are brought to completion by missionary activity. . . .

The specific purpose of this missionary activity is evangelization and the planting of the Church among those peoples and groups where she has not yet taken root. Thus from the seed which is the Word of God, particular churches can be adequately established and flourish the world

16. Ibid., pp. 589–90.

over, endowed with their own vitality and maturity. . . . They [too] can make their contribution to the good of the Church universal.

The chief means of this implantation is the preaching of the gospel of Jesus Christ. The Lord sent forth His disciples into the whole world to preach this gospel. Thus reborn by the Word of God (cf. 1 Pet. 1:23), men may through baptism be joined to that Church which, as the body of the Word Incarnate, is nourished and lives by the Word of God.[17]

Ad gentes recognizes the enormous size of the task which confronts Christians. Missionary activity is not proposed as a minor peripheral task of the church but as its most important ongoing task. "The Church is aware that there still remains a gigantic missionary task for her to accomplish. For the gospel message has not yet been heard, or scarcely so, by two billion human beings. And their number is increasing daily."[18]

6. *The human race exists today in a bewildering variety of cultural and linguistic groupings. Each of these must be approached in a way congenial to it,* so that its members may in fact hear and understand the Good News. The human race exists, *Ad gentes* says, in "large and distinct groups" which display permanent differences in cultural characteristics, religious traditions, and historical and geographical circumstances.

The Church must be present in all these groups of men through those of her children who dwell among them or are sent to them. . . . That they may be able to give this witness to Christ fruitfully, let them be joined to those men by esteem and love, and acknowledge themselves to be members of the group of men among whom they live. Let them share in cultural and social life by the various exchanges and enterprises of human living. Let them be familiar with their national and religious traditions, gladly and reverently laying bare the seeds of the Word which lie hidden in them. . . .

Thus, when the Holy Spirit opens their heart (cf. Acts 16:14) non-Christians may believe and be freely converted to the Lord, and may sincerely cling to Him who, as "the way, the truth, and the life" (Jn. 14:6), fulfills all their spiritual expectations, and even infinitely surpasses them.[19]

7. *Since the Holy Spirit through baptism and incorporation into the church transforms all believers into the people of God* (a chosen race, a royal priesthood, a holy nation, a purchased people), *all missionaries should raise up congregations.* This doctrinal principle reflects a high view of the church. The goal of missions is not simply to preach the gospel and win converts. It is much more than that. It is to *multiply congregations of the redeemed.* Article 3 of chapter 2 of *Ad gentes* is entitled "Forming the Christian Com-

17. Ibid., pp. 591–92 (emphasis added).
18. Ibid., pp. 596–97.
19. Ibid., pp. 597–600.

munity." The church among each people should be self-supporting. It should be deeply rooted in its own culture. As good citizens, Roman Catholics should practice true and effective patriotism. Lay people should play an important part in the church. They should, of course, lead exemplary lives; but leading ethical lives is not enough. "They are organized and present for the purpose of announcing Christ to their non-Christian fellow citizens by word and deed, and of aiding them toward the full reception of Christ."

8. *Allowances should be made for particular churches.* As Christianity spreads throughout the world, peoples at various levels of economic and educational advance become Christian and clusters of congregations arise which have a character all their own. Perhaps they speak a dialect or language of their own. Perhaps they are entirely literate, or very largely illiterate. Perhaps they are a proud ruler nation, perhaps a ruled nation. They may live under the shadow of Communism or some other totalitarian dictatorship. On the other hand they may have a government which they themselves entirely control. In each case, the cluster of congregations (perhaps a hundred of them or perhaps ten thousand) will look quite unlike other clusters which have formed in populations marked by other characteristics. *Ad gentes* recognizes that while all Christians are truly one in fellowship (all children of the same Father, all belonging to the one body of Christ, and all governed by the same Word), nevertheless, particular churches are in many ways quite different. They are parts of the church universal; they are at the same time particular churches. In regard to essentials, each is part of the universal church; but in regard to particulars each is unique. The dress and eating habits of the members, the kind of houses in which they live, the places of worship they erect, and their degree of political freedom will vary enormously from one particular church to another.

Consequently, *Ad gentes,* in setting forth its theology of missions, devotes seven pages, a whole chapter, to an extended discussion of the riches of the peoples that are to flow into Zion. It describes how these riches, being dedicated to Christ, will enhance the unity of the church and of the human race, and will work for the glory of God—provided that the essentials of the Christian faith are seriously and sacrificially practiced.

> Thus, in imitation of the plan of the Incarnation, the young Churches, rooted in Christ and built up on the foundations of the apostles, take to themselves in a wonderful exchange all the riches of the nations which were given to Christ as an inheritance (cf. Ps. 2:8). From the customs and traditions of their people, from their arts and sciences, these Churches borrow all those things which can contribute to the glory of their Creator, the revelation of the Savior's grace, or the proper arrangement of Christian life.[20]

20. Ibid., p. 612.

9. While all Christians have the duty and privilege of helping to spread the faith, yet *God calls some in a special way to be missionaries of the gospel.* They are selected by Christ, and sent by Him to disciple *panta ta ethne.* Among many good things Christ commissions His people to do, He sends missionaries out on a special mission, to preach the gospel to those who have not yet believed and to multiply churches. These specially chosen men and women He endows "with the appropriate natural dispositions, character, and talents. . . . He who is sent enters upon the life and mission of Him who 'emptied himself, taking the nature of a slave' (Phil. 2:7). Therefore, he must be ready to stand by his vocation for a lifetime, and to renounce himself and all those whom he thus far considered as his own, and instead to become 'all things to all men.' "[21]

Ad gentes regards the vocation of a missionary as a particularly high calling. This theology of mission at this point blazes a trail for all theologies of mission. Missionaries, especially for the last thirty years in the West, have been too often portrayed (even by some missiologists) in less than complimentary ways. Missionaries were temporary workers, soon to be replaced by nationals. They were likely to stupidly impose their own values on other cultures. They were constantly working themselves out of their jobs. Missionaries were often considered a vanishing species. *Ad gentes* rebuts this mistaken and unbiblical evaluation of the missionary. *Ad gentes* announces that Christ continuously calls missionaries to dedicate themselves to be lifelong ambassadors. They may be rejected by the world, but they are precious to Christ.

> Announcing the gospel among the nations, [the missionary] confidently makes known the mystery of Christ, whose ambassador he is. Thus in Christ he dares to speak as he ought (cf. Eph. 6:19f.; Acts 4:31), and is not ashamed of the scandal of the Cross. Following in his Master's footsteps, meek and humble of heart, he shows that His yoke is easy and His burden light (Matt. 11:29f.). By a truly evangelical life, in much patience, in long-suffering, in kindness, in unaffected love (cf. 2 Cor. 6:4f.), he bears witness to his Lord, if need be, by the shedding of his blood.[22]

Ad gentes devotes a whole chapter to missionaries. It reflects the worldwide experience of Roman Catholic missionaries who—like Protestants—have planted the church in practically all the countries of earth. *Ad gentes* stresses heavily that extensive education is necessary for this high calling.

> It is above all necessary for the future missionary to devote himself to missiological studies: that is, to know the teachings and norms of the Church concerning missionary activity, the roads which the heralds of the

21. Ibid., p. 614.
22. Ibid.

gospel have traversed in the course of the centuries, the present condition of the missions, and the methods now considered especially effective. ... Some [teachers of missions] should receive an especially thorough preparation in missiological institutes or in other faculties or universities.[23]

10. *There is a great need for united or cooperative planning in the missionary activity of the church.* This is especially interesting to non-Catholics, who generally believe that since the Church of Rome is directed from the top down, there would almost automatically be a maximum degree of co-operation among its many missionary branches. There can be no doubt that Roman Catholic missionary activity is more coordinated than that of the hundreds of almost completely independent missionary societies of the Protestant branch of the church. Nevertheless, *Ad gentes* devotes thirteen pages to cooperative planning.

Because Christian mission is to be carried out in all the pieces of the intricate mosaic of the human race, and Christians are to disciple the multitudinous *ethne* of the world, cooperation and united planning are a very high priority. It should be quite possible now to ascertain which pieces of the mosaic are highly receptive, which are mildly receptive, which are resistant, and which are positively hostile; and to plan the evangelization of each of these groups in suitable fashion. But instead, where missionary societies send their emissaries today seems to be often determined by other considerations—younger churches (which to date have little interest outside their own areas) frequently make the decision as to where the mission from abroad expends its resources. The theology of mission set forth by *Ad gentes* urges that united planning and cooperation in the carrying out of world evangelization be stressed as never before. This is excellent advice for all missionary bodies, and for every branch of the church of Jesus Christ as it seeks to carry out the divine mandate to bring all the peoples of earth to faith and obedience.

We live in a new age when we can learn from one another. *Ad gentes* says, "Catholics can cooperate in a brotherly spirit with their separated brethren, according to the norms of the Decree on Ecumenism."[24] Protestants need not be offended by the rather limited degree of acceptance which this decree gives to them. It is clear to anyone who can read the signs of the times that all those branches of the church which believe that the Bible is the inspired, authoritative, infallible Word of God and which trust in Jesus Christ as God and Savior are going to grow closer and closer together, despite differences on some points. In the urgent and enormous task of world evangelization, cooperation with Christians of other branches

23. Ibid., pp. 616–17.
24. Ibid., p. 602.

of the church and a zealous dedication to the universal command of Christ
are clearly needed.

Among the theologies of mission which are treated in this book, we
hope readers will especially study that set forth in the documents of Vatican II. In *Ad gentes* Christians have before them a well-thought-out theology and methodology of mission. It was written, revised, and finally
promulgated as the official Roman Catholic theology of mission. It will
repay careful study by all other branches of the church.

13

Official Roman Catholic Theology of Mission

Lumen Gentium

Donald McGavran

In "The Decree on the Missionary Activity of the Church," Vatican II officially laid down that "proclaiming the Gospel, baptizing such hearers as believe on Jesus Christ, and incorporating them in the Church" is essential Christian mission. But what is the church? Is it one of many instruments which God uses on occasion to bring in a more just, harmonious, and peaceful world? Or rather is it the highest purpose of God for the human race? Is it the kingdom of God? Is the church merely a means toward a higher end—or is it the highest end? Is Jesus Christ our Lord the Head of *an* instrument (one among many) which God uses to bring about His will among humans? Or does the church have an absolute value in itself?

Roman Catholic missiologists do not have to grope for an answer. They have "The Dogmatic Constitution on the Church" (*Lumen gentium*) to guide them. For Roman Catholics "The Dogmatic Constitution on the Church" has far greater authority than "The Decree on the Missionary Activity of the Church." "The Dogmatic Constitution" is official doctrine framed by twenty-three hundred bishops—*all* bishops—from all over the earth. A dogmatic constitution is what the church *must* believe.

The Essentiality of the Church

As might be expected, Roman Catholics hold a high theology of the church. The church is no accident. The church did not just happen. It was not invented by Peter and the other apostles. It did not grow up of itself as Christians multiplied. It was not started to achieve a higher end. No. The church is part of the plan of God formed at the beginning of time. The human race was to find its crown, its freedom, its salvation, its glory in the church.

The human race consists of fallen men and women who are alienated from God, and exposed to His wrath. Deceived both by Satan and by their own evil desires, they cannot achieve the glorious life of children of God, for which God created them. Consequently, God provided for them a Savior and a way of salvation. His Son paid the price for their redemption and announced clearly that all who believe on Him and determine to follow Him as God and Savior will receive forgiveness of sins, and abundant and eternal life in the sanctity of His church. Thus the church is a necessary part of the plan of salvation.

> By an utterly free and mysterious decree of His own wisdom and goodness, the Eternal Father created the whole world. His plan was to dignify men with a participation in His own divine life. He did not abandon men after they had fallen in Adam, but ceaselessly offered them helps to salvation, in anticipation of Christ the Redeemer, "who is the image of the invisible God, the firstborn of every creature" (Col. 1:15). All the elect, before time began, the Father "foreknew and predestined to become conformed to the image of his Son, that he should be the firstborn among many brethren" (Rom. 8:29).
> *He planned to assemble in the Holy Church all those who would believe in Christ. Already from the beginning of the world the foreshadowing of the Church took place.*[1]

Vatican II declared that the church is an essential part of God's eternal plan. According to that plan the world is to be saved through belief in Christ and membership in His church. Extension of the church to all peoples is therefore necessary.

"The Dogmatic Constitution on the Church" is clear that the kingdom of God is *not* some humanly achievable social order. It is *not* some just and peaceable society constructed by people of good will from all religions and ideologies. Rather the kingdom of God is *God's* rule on earth; it can be founded on no other base than men and women who believe in Jesus Christ as King and work to bring about *His* will on earth as it is in heaven.

"The Church . . . receives the mission to proclaim and to establish among all peoples the kingdom of Christ and of God. She becomes on earth the initial budding forth of that kingdom. While she slowly grows, the Church strains toward the consummation of the kingdom."[2] Note that the church is described as the "initial budding forth" of the kingdom of God. That is to say, during the course of human history (when the church will be only partially present among any people and totally nonexistent in

---

1. *Lumen gentium,* in Walter M. Abbott, ed., *The Documents of Vatican II* (New York: Herder and Herder, 1966), p. 15 (emphasis added).

2. Ibid., p. 18.

many lands), the church will serve as a partial manifestation of God's perfectly righteous, perfectly just, and perfectly pure rule. "The Church . . . will attain her full perfection only in the glory of heaven. . . . Then the human race as well as the entire world . . . will be perfectly re-established in Christ."[3]

It is impossible, according to the biblical view, for the kingdom of God to be established among those who do not believe in Christ, have not been baptized, and are not members of His body the church. "The Church," we read, "strains toward the consummation of the kingdom," toward that moment "when history will draw to a close and God's final kingdom will be inaugurated."[4] These phrases sum up the teaching of the ecumenical council as to the present and future nature of the kingdom of God. They also effectively rule out the idea that the kingdom of God which our Lord Jesus came preaching is an ideal secular social order characterized by righteousness and harmony.

The Structure of the Church

Not only is the church a necessary part of the plan of salvation, but its structure is carefully provided for in God's revelations to His apostles. In chapter 3 of "The Dogmatic Constitution on the Church," which is entitled "The Hierarchical Structure of the Church with Special Reference to the Episcopate," the ecumenical council spells out in great detail that the church is not a careless assemblage of people who call themselves Christian, but a carefully defined structure. According to the Roman Catholic understanding of that structure, the bishops, who have inherited their power directly from Peter through apostolic succession, are essential to the real church. Though Vatican II does not say, "Where the bishop is, there is the church," it expresses this thought in many other ways.

> Jesus Christ, the eternal Shepherd, established His holy Church by sending forth the apostles as He Himself had been sent by the Father (cf. Jn. 20:21). He willed that their successors, namely the bishops, should be shepherds in His Church even to the consummation of the world.

> Just as, by the Lord's will, St. Peter and the other apostles constituted one apostolic college, so in a similar way the Roman Pontiff as the successor of Peter, and the bishops as the successors of the apostles are joined together.

> Together with its head, the Roman Pontiff, and never without this head, the episcopal order is the subject of supreme and full power over the universal Church.

3. Ibid., pp. 78–79.
4. Ibid., pp. 18, 78 n.224.

The individual bishops . . . exercise their pastoral government over the portion of the People of God committed to their care.

The task of proclaiming the gospel everywhere on earth devolves on the body of pastors, to all of whom in common Christ gave His command.

To the Lord was given all power in heaven and on earth. As successors of the apostles, bishops receive from Him the mission to teach all nations and to preach the gospel to every creature, so that all men may attain to salvation by faith, baptism, and the fulfillment of the commandments (cf. Mt. 28:18; Mk. 16:15–16; Acts 26:17f.).

The infallibility promised to the Church resides also in the body of bishops.[5]

Much more has been written in this important section. Here we need note only that both the church *and* the distinctly Roman Catholic form of governing it are declared to be part of God's immutable plan. Protestants will disagree with all those passages in *Lumen gentium* which "prove" by Scripture that the church is exclusively the Church of Rome, and the governing body is exclusively that hierarchy ordained by and obedient to the pope. As Protestants we have complete sympathy with such disagreement.

Protestant and Catholic Agreement on the Church

However, we should not throw the baby out with the bath water. The Protestant theology of the church steadily maintains that the church was planned by God, founded by Christ, and destined to be the gateway to eternal life for all who believe and to endure throughout all ages. In our chapter on *Ad gentes* we quoted the Westminster Confession of Faith, which affirms that outside of the church "there is no ordinary possibility of salvation." The Protestant understanding of Scripture, agreeing with *Lumen gentium's* high view of the church, is that throughout the world the universal church is composed only of those who accept Jesus Christ as God and Savior.

Martin Luther saw that the Bible correctly interpreted does not define the church as exclusively ruled by the Roman pontiff and the college of bishops; nevertheless, the Bible does express a high view of the church. On the church, the Augsburg Confession reads:

One holy Christian church will be and remain forever. This is the assembly of all believers among whom the Gospel is preached in its purity and the holy sacraments are administered according to the Gospel. . . . It is not necessary for the true unity of the Christian church that ceremonies, instituted by men, should be observed uniformly in all places.

5. Ibid., pp. 37, 42, 43, 44, 45, 46–47, 49.

God will regard . . . faith [in Christ] as righteousness. . . . To obtain such faith God instituted the office of the ministry, that is, provided the Gospel and the sacraments. Through these . . . he gives the Holy Spirit, who works faith, when and where he pleases, in those who hear the Gospel.

Bishops do not have power to institute or establish anything contrary to the Gospel.[6]

Similarly, Calvinists make a sharp distinction between the church and the Roman Catholic governing body. The Second Helvetic Confession (1566) affirms that the church is an essential part of God's plan:

(THE CHURCH HAS ALWAYS EXISTED AND IT WILL ALWAYS EXIST) Forasmuch as God from the beginning would have men to be saved, and to come to the knowledge of the truth (1 Tim. 2:4), therefore it is necessary that there always should have been, and should be at this day, and to the end of the world, a Church . . . that is, . . . a communion . . . of them who truly know and rightly worship and serve the true God, in Jesus Christ.

Concerning the Roman Catholic governing body this confession affirms:

Christ our Lord is, and remains still, the only universal pastor, and highest bishop . . . even to the world's end. . . . Now, by taking away the Romish head we do not bring any confusion or disorder into the church. For we teach that the government of the Church which the apostles handed down is sufficient to keep the Church in due order; which, from the beginning, while as yet it wanted such a Romish head as is now pretended to keep it in order, was not disordered or full of confusion.[7]

Much more could be quoted from the creeds and confessions of faith of many Protestant churches. Here it is sufficient to note that the evangelical branches of the church have insisted in the strongest terms that the church is part of the immutable program of God. "One holy Church will be and remain forever." This emphasis is not only what Vatican II lays down as eternal truth. It is what Luther, Calvin, and all other leaders of the Protestant churches have said and taught. It is a correct understanding of the biblical witness. In this chapter we are simply saying that this high view of the church, clearly taught by Roman Catholics and Protestants alike, must be one of the foundation stones on which a biblical missiology is built.

The Church and Social Duties

Some missiologists of our day, heavily influenced by the obvious opportunity to create a more Christian social order, and the Marxist ideal of a

6. "The Augsburg Confession," in John H. Leith, ed., *Creeds of the Churches: A Reader in Christian Doctrine from the Bible to the Present* (Atlanta: John Knox, 1973), pp. 70, 69, 101.
7. "The Second Helvetic Confession," in Leith, *Creeds*, pp. 141, 144–45.

classless society or utopia which humans can build, cavalierly dismiss this biblically-based view of the essentiality of the church. Any missiology embodying it they scornfully call "ecclesiocentric" and list under "lop-sided" and outworn theories of mission.[8] Without noting that this is still the official missiology of the Roman Catholic Church and is certain to remain so, they commend the opinions of individual Catholic advocates of a theology of mission whose main thrust is effecting temporal improvements, calling these opinions "more adequate and contemporary Roman Catholic views on mission." That is, they substitute these casual pronouncements of individual theorists for the carefully constructed declarations of official Roman Catholic missiology.

One of the aims of this chapter is to point out that evangelical theology of mission is largely at one with Roman Catholic theology of mission in maintaining that, biblically, the central task of Christian mission always has been, is now, and ever will be the proclamation of the gospel and the "churching" or discipling of the multitudinous peoples of earth. The proper expansion of the church inevitably results from discipling the peoples. Proclaiming the gospel by word and deed with a view to incorporating believers in the holy church is the central priority of mission. This does not mean that Catholic theories of mission pay no attention to carrying out other parts of God's will here on earth. We shall soon see that Roman Catholics pay considerable attention to such duties, but they do not confuse the situation by calling them mission.

This is clearly seen when we consult the longest single document in Vatican II's corpus of constitutions, decrees, and declarations; namely, "The Pastoral Constitution on the Church in the Modern World" (*Gaudium et spes*). A slight majority of the bishops wanted to call the document a constitution. A large minority wanted to call it a declaration, letter, or exposition—a much less authoritative document than a constitution. In any case, the 110 pages deal with the application of Christian ethical teachings to modern conditions. Here are listed many of the crying physical, social, and economic needs of the modern world. It is clearly declared that the church ought to be doing something about them. *But nowhere in the 110 pages is meeting these needs called mission.*

Let us look at the needs of humanity which Vatican II said ought to be met: "Having probed more profoundly into the mystery of the Church, [the Council] now addresses itself . . . to the whole of humanity. For the Council yearns to explain to everyone how it conceives of the presence and activity of the Church in the world of today."[9] The council deliberately

---

8. Johannes Verkuyl, *Contemporary Missiology: An Introduction*, trans. and ed. Dale Cooper (Grand Rapids: Eerdmans, 1978), p. 188.
    9. *Gaudium et spes*, in Abbott, *Vatican II*, p. 200.

turned its gaze on the modern world, its problems, injustices, hopes, and despairs. This world the Christian sees as created by God, fallen into the bondage of sin, and waiting to be liberated through the action of Christ and Christians.

People today, "The Pastoral Constitution" declares, live in a world of hope and anguish, a world of profoundly changing conditions. The social orders of numerous peoples are not only changing, but are in most cases deteriorating, thus condemning millions to deprivation and grave loss.

> Meanwhile, the conviction grows not only that humanity can and should increasingly consolidate its control over creation, but even more, that it devolves on humanity to establish a political, social, and economic order which will to an ever better extent serve man and help individuals as well as groups to affirm and develop the dignity proper to them. . . . Many persons are quite aggressively demanding those benefits of which . . . they judge themselves to be deprived. . . . [The Church] labors to decipher authentic signs of God's presence and purpose in the happenings, needs, and desires in which the People of God have a part along with other men of our age.[10]

The first widespread characteristic of modern humanity which is spoken to by the council is atheism or secularistic materialism. This is without doubt the most widespread movement in modern times among all developed and some developing societies. It reaches a climax in the Marxist ridicule of all religions as opiates of the people. The scientific frame of mind, which counts as real and true only those things which can be weighed, measured, and known by the senses, has enormously increased the number of persons who, regardless of the lip service they pay to spiritual words, believe only in material things. Harry Blamires's *Christian Mind* describes the situation exactly:

> The Christian mind has succumbed to the secular drift with a degree of weakness and nervelessness unmatched in Christian history. It is difficult to do justice in words to the complete loss of intellectual morale in the twentieth-century church. One cannot characterize it without recourse to language which will sound hysterical and melodramatic. There is no longer a Christian mind. There is still, of course, a Christian ethic, a Christian practice, and a Christian spirituality. . . . But as a thinking being, the modern Christian has succumbed to secularization.[11]

Extensive efforts were made to get the council to denounce atheistic materialism. But the council, true to its providential nature as defined by Pope John, avoided negative measures or harsh condemnations. Thus in regard to secular materialism (atheism) it wrote understandingly and sym-

---

10. Ibid., pp. 206, 209.
11. Harry Blamires, *The Christian Mind* (New York: Seabury, 1963), p. 3.

pathetically, seeking to uncover some of the complexities behind the phenomenon.

In regard to "The Essential Equality of Men and Social Justice" *Gaudium et spes* declared:

> The basic equality of all must receive increasingly greater recognition. . . . With respect to the fundamental rights of the person, every type of discrimination, whether social or cultural, whether based on sex, race, color, social condition, language, or religion, is to be overcome and eradicated as contrary to God's intent. . . . Human institutions, both private and public, must labor to minister to the dignity and purpose of man.[12]

These sweeping pronouncements would be unexceptional today, but in 1965 they were breaking new ground. They have been quoted, illustrated, and enlarged upon many times.

"The Pastoral Constitution on the Church in the Modern World" saw the problem in the large. It clearly discerned the crucial issues in the modern mind, arising from our ever increasing control over nature.

> Today . . . with the help of science and technology, [man] has extended his mastery over nearly the whole of nature and continues to do so. . . . Hence many benefits once looked for, especially from heavenly powers, man has now enterprisingly procured for himself. In the face of these immense efforts which already preoccupy the whole human race, men raise numerous questions among themselves.[13]

Observing that the institution of marriage is breaking down, "The Pastoral Constitution" devotes a whole chapter to "Fostering the Nobility of Marriage and the Family." It thoughtfully sets forth a Christian view on conjugal love, the sanctity of marriage, and the fruitfulness of marriage. It discusses how to harmonize conjugal love with respect for human life.

A long chapter deals with "The Proper Development of Culture." Not merely the cultures of developing peoples, but (perhaps more importantly) the cultures of developed nations are discussed:

> How can the vitality and growth of a new culture [the new scientific culture of the modern world] be fostered without the loss of living fidelity to the heritage of tradition? This question is especially urgent when a culture resulting from the enormous scientific and technological progress must be harmonized with an education nourished by classical studies as adapted to various traditions.[14]

12. *Gaudium et spes*, in Abbott, *Vatican II*, pp. 227–28.
13. Ibid., p. 231.
14. Ibid., p. 261.

One thinks immediately of the cultural clash in such places as America, France, China, and India. "Progress in science and technology can foster a certain exclusive emphasis on observable data, and an agnosticism about everything else. For the methods of investigation which these sciences use can be wrongly considered as the supreme rule for discovering the whole truth. . . . Man . . . may even think that he is sufficient unto himself."[15]

Socioeconomic life is considered vital. The tremendous disparity between the rich and the poor receives much attention. The council affirms that "vigorous efforts must be made, without violence . . . to remove as quickly as possible the immense economic inequalities which now exist. In many cases, these are worsening."[16] Christians are instructed to play a very strong role in socioeconomic development and to act with charity and justice. "Whether they do so as individuals or in associations, let their example be a shining one. Whoever in obedience to Christ seeks first the kingdom of God will as a consequence receive a stronger and purer love for helping all his brothers and perfecting the work of justice under the inspiration of charity."[17]

Strangely "The Pastoral Constitution" does not mention the major causes of poverty and deprivation—human sin, laziness, the oppression which some people inflict on their neighbors, and the tremendous overpopulation of the habitable portions of the earth. Nor does it mention that the single most effective step toward economic justice and equality which any people can take is that of becoming conscious followers of Christ.

Work and leisure, investments and money, ownership and property, labor unions and the management of industry are discussed from the Christian perspective. The role of the church and of Christians in regard to all these matters is described in considerable detail.

The Christian's place in politics and the role the church should play in promoting a fair and effective political system also receive their share of attention. One thinks at once of Christian political parties and the great political role played by the Roman Catholic Church in so many lands. The rigid separation of church and state which has marked the United States, and the political powerlessness of Christians where they comprise a tiny percentage of the total population are not dealt with. Where Christians comprise the majority of the citizens, what part in the political process should they play? A great part, replies Vatican II, but also a fair part. Let them not push other people around.

As might be expected, "The Fostering of Peace" and "The Promotion of a Community of Nations" are major topics in "The Pastoral Constitu-

15. Ibid., p. 263.
16. Ibid., p. 274.
17. Ibid., p. 282.

tion." The document concludes with a long section on "Building Up the International Community." The one world, about which so many speak and which often is more a mirage than a reality, is treated very seriously by Vatican II. Its synod of bishops from all over the world was in a wonderful position to emphasize the concept of the international community. The Roman Catholic Church, with its dioceses in almost every nation, naturally and competently discussed the possibility of a peaceful and just international community.

In summing up the place of the church in the Roman Catholic theology of mission, we point out that "The Dogmatic Constitution on the Church" and "The Pastoral Constitution on the Church in the Modern World" declare in unmistakable terms that the *mission* of the church is one thing, and the *duties* of the church are something else. The mission of the church always has been, is now, and ever will be to proclaim the gospel and bring "all men to full union with Christ." The contemporary duties of the church, facing the revolutionary changes in the modern world, are many and varied. These duties must be carried out. The 110-page "Pastoral Constitution" effectively drives that point home. But such duties must not be substituted for world evangelization, which is the mission of the church. Vatican II is clear on that point.

The change in goals advocated by some Protestant churches and some missiologists—substituting "a new world order" for "discipling the peoples of earth"—is strictly eschewed in the Roman Catholic theology of mission. The kingdom of God is never confused with an improved earthly socioeconomic order. Vatican II uses the phrase "the kingdom of God" (or "the kingdom of Christ") as a virtual synonym for the church.

Yet it is clearly recognized that improved social structures are also desired by God, and that Christians ought to play a part in bringing them about. Christians must never, however, identify the improved social structure *either* with the eschatological kingdom of God, the perfect social order in which there will be no sin, no sorrow, and no death, *or* with the body of Christ, the people of God, the holy church, the kingdom of Christ. For Roman Catholics, the essential and continuing goal of mission is the founding, developing, strengthening, and spreading of the church of Jesus Christ. This high doctrine of the church is an integral part of Catholic missiology.

14

A Paradigm Shift?

Evangelicals and Interreligious Dialogue

Arthur F. Glasser

Religious encounter is a particularly crucial issue today. Some major religions are in resurgence. Islam is a case in point. Others have been deeply undermined by hostile governments. One has but to read Holmes Welch's significant article on Buddhism in China today.[1] Still others are struggling to adapt to the contemporary world. Witness the efforts of Sarvepalli Radhakrishnan, who called Hindus to strike out on more courageous lines of advance in religious reform, building on the foundations of the Vedanta.[2] Some religions, more than others, are seeking to disassociate themselves from otherworldly mysticism and are caught up in the universal concerns of war-weary humanity, struggling for world harmony and social justice. When leaders participate in interreligious dialogue the dominant note is: "We are alike despite our differences. We all seek to give meaning to our common humanity. We are all striving to affirm the worth of human values."[3] The last two decades of the twentieth century may well find interreligious cooperation growing throughout the world.

Still, all religions are in polemic opposition to Christian missions—even though these religions bear marks, in Kenneth Scott Latourette's phrase, of "mass modification" resulting from protracted contact with mission vigor throughout the modern era. Hendrik Kraemer agrees: "The great non-Christian religions have utilized the permeation of Christian ideas

1. Holmes Welch, "The Fate of Religion," in *The China Difference,* ed. Ross Terrill (New York: Harper and Row Colophon Books, 1979), pp. 119–37.

2. Paul David Devanandan, "Resurgent Hinduism," in *Christianity and the Asian Revolution,* ed. Rajah B. Manikam (New York: Friendship, 1954), pp. 132–33.

3. Paul David Devanandan, "The Shock of the Discovery of World Religions," in *History's Lessons for Tomorrow's Mission* (Geneva: World Student Christian Federation, 1960), p. 221.

and ideals for their own internal and external strengthening."[4] Understandably, this indebtedness has not been acknowledged!

In the years immediately ahead, these religions will doubtless display mounting hostility toward that segment of the church committed to the priority of beseeching men and women everywhere on behalf of Christ to be reconciled to God (2 Cor. 5:20). Evangelism will increasingly be denigrated as proselytism and church-planting slandered as religious imperialism.

In the face of the triadic prospect of unacknowledged indebtedness, hostility toward conversion-oriented evangelism, and interreligious cooperation, we approach the question, What constitutes a valid evangelical perspective on interreligious dialogue today?

What Are the Options?

Many feel that evangelicals are incapable of discussing the subject of interreligious dialogue objectively, that they too readily resort to dogmatic defensiveness. The reasoning is: those who feel they must bear witness to the gospel to one and all, with the avowed intention of pressing each and every one to embrace Jesus Christ, become His disciple, and through baptism enter His church, cannot but be negative when assessing non-Christian religions and non-Christians. Whereas evangelicals may be able to cooperate heartily with non-Christians in matters of humanitarian service and in the struggle for social justice—assuming there is freedom to name the name of Jesus Christ (Col. 3:17)—when it comes to interreligious encounter evangelicals will be incapable of rising to the demands of "reverence for reverence," scientific accuracy, and intellectual honesty.

Today evangelicals are increasingly seeking to take these criticisms seriously.[5] True, relatively few evangelical theologians have tackled this complicated subject. Few appear to have the breadth of missionary vision to sense its desperate importance to the worldwide missionary movement. Few appear to have sensed how hopelessly inadequate, from a missionary point of view, are the historic creeds whose exposition and defense have always been an evangelical priority. Besides, the more knowledgeable might ask: "What is the point in discussing the validity of interreligious dialogue? Everyone knows what the options are."

What are the options? Over the years scholars have sought—rather

4. Hendrik Kraemer, *The Christian Message in a Non-Christian World* (Grand Rapids: Kregel, 1969), p. 291.

5. E.g., David J. Hesselgrave, ed., *Theology and Mission* (Grand Rapids: Baker, 1978); John R. W. Stott, "Dialogue," in *Christian Mission in the Modern World* (Downers Grove, IL: Inter-Varsity, 1975), pp. 58–81.

simplistically, it seems—to reduce them to sharply defined approaches to other religions. They have identified at least six—two distinct groups of three. In the first group it is presupposed that Christianity is superior to other religions. These three approaches differ in degree rather than in kind.

1. *Radical Displacement.* Christianity with all its Western cultural baggage is transplanted whole, and the ethnic religion is brushed aside as valueless.
2. *Discontinuity.* The uniqueness and superiority of Christianity are assumed; though Christianity is regarded as having no real point of contact with the other religion, it nonetheless seeks to adapt itself to the cultural forms of the people.
3. *Recognition of Uniqueness.* Each religion is recognized as a unique unity to be respected; comparisons are possible, when honestly made at roughly equivalent levels of belief and practice, but Christianity is regarded as obviously superior.

In the second group it is presupposed that Christianity is on a par with other religions:

4. *Legitimate Borrowing.* Since it is granted that there are many points of contact between all religions (due to the commonality of their human dimensions), Christianity borrows freely from them in order to be truly indigenous.
5. *The Gospel as Fulfilment.* Christianity is presented as either the literal fulfilment of other religions (as the New Testament fulfilled the Old Testament), or as the capstone of the highest aspirations one finds either expressed or intimated in the scriptures of other religions.
6. *Relativistic Syncretism.* Every religion—Christianity included—is regarded as representing the spiritual quest of humankind seeking God. One finds the truth latent in all and takes the best from each. Through religious encounter and dialogue, understanding of one's own faith is enlarged and enriched by the other religion. Incompleteness diminishes and there is ongoing movement toward the ultimate truth, which may be brought even nearer by encounter with yet other religions.

As we have intimated, this classification has major shortcomings. Those scholars who feel that all six of these approaches are live options for the Christian are overlooking the nuances of the Bible and have only a limited knowledge of the non-Christian religions. They are also ignoring the crucial factor of human subjectivity. It is virtually impossible to be objective in evaluating another religion and the allegiance of its devotees. Then, too, no one is capable of truly understanding the ancient testimonies of other religions and their scriptures. Our own cultural bias is so strong that we interpret them today in terms that may be far removed from their original import. It needs to be constantly stressed that each religious system is a complex world of its own; anthropologists keep telling us how exceedingly difficult it is to separate religion from the general culture of the people who embrace its postulates.

Furthermore, each religious system is cluttered with denominational differences, and who is to say which one is normative? Although separate schools of thought can be compared and contrasted, all of us are brought to a full stop when we ask the same question of Christianity. For there is a sense in which we cannot focus just on the gospel and deliberately overlook the pluriform nature of the human response to it (the worldwide Christian movement). Karl Barth sought to make a sharp distinction between the revelation of God and the Christian religion. For a season, many of us enjoyed this dichotomy; but we now know that we cannot apprehend revelation without the human reaction. The Bible describes these two in terms of interaction within specific cultures; it does not concentrate on the development of supracultural theological propositions. Indeed, there are those like V. Chakkari who argue that unless Christians are willing to expose their churches (human witnesses to revelation) to empirical investigation and evaluation, they have no right to involve themselves in evangelistic activity.[6]

There is, then, enormous difficulty in defining precisely what we are dealing with when we encounter the other religions of the world. Yet they should not be rejected out of hand. This is neither fair nor is it respectful of the truth they contain. Even so, we find no evangelical support for the thesis that one should see these religions as sublime expressions of human nobility and creativity. Even secular anthropologists no longer hold this position. In the formative years of their crusade for cultural relativism some argued that the religious system of each culture seemed adequate and met the needs of its people. But no longer. More often than not they agree with Walter Goldschmidt's affirmation that "there are enough instances on record of primitive peoples not being happy in their own customs but like many a married couple not knowing how to escape them. . . . We must rid ourselves of the Rousseauean 'good savage,' must cease to use ethnographic data either as an escape or a vehicle for expressing our personal social discontent."[7]

6. David J. Bosch, *Theology of Religions MSR 301, Guide 1* (Pretoria: University of South Africa, 1977), p. 162.
7. Walter Rochs Goldschmidt, *Comparative Functionalism: An Essay in Anthropological Theory* (Berkeley: University of California, 1966), p. 138.

But What About Dialogue?

There is no need to reiterate the basic evangelical approach to dialogue. The church has been mandated to bear witness to Jesus Christ. The dialogic method is necessary if those who witness to Christ are to engage the minds of their listeners—they must listen and learn as well as speak and instruct. Only through such dialogue can they be assured that their witness is relevant and that the conscience is addressed (2 Cor. 4:2). After all, the issue is Jesus Christ. He is not merely to be admired. He is to be acknowledged as Lord through repentance and faith.

Indeed, the Bible is filled with endorsement of the dialogic method. God is the greatest listener and the most searching questioner. But when His servants the prophets, His Son, or the apostles engaged in dialogue, they always subordinated it to the truth they proclaimed. And in so doing they cooperated harmoniously with the Spirit, who convinces the world of sin and of righteousness and of judgment (John 16:8–11). The Spirit's objective is universal in its intent: to unmask all false religion as sin, and to call people to face the all-important question, "What have you done with God?"[8]

We have limited our remarks on dialogue for two main reasons. First, the subject has been adequately discussed by scholars who have explored its dimensions in a way consonant with evangelical presuppositions.[9] Second, nonevangelical writers have ranged widely in their presuppositions with the result that the discussion has become rather diffuse, and has often bordered on the radical. Whereas earlier writers felt evangelism to be antithetical to dialogue—"most undesirable and incompatible" is the phrase Lynn de Silva uses[10]—and conciliar conferences on the subject have only infrequently included references to "mission" and "evangelism,"[11] it should be noted that the most recent CWME gathering at Melbourne spoke otherwise: "The proclamation of the Word of God is . . . [a] witness, distinct and indispensable. The story of God in Christ is the heart of all evangelism, and this story has to be told, for the life of the present Church never fully reveals the love and holiness and power of God in Christ."[12] And even more recently, Emilio Castro, the director of

8. Johannes H. Bavinck, *An Introduction to the Science of Missions* (Philadelphia: Presbyterian and Reformed, 1960), p. 223.

9. Eric J. Sharpe, "The Goals of Inter-Religious Dialogue," in *Truth and Dialogue in World Religions: Conflicting Truth Claims*, ed. John Hick (Philadelphia: Westminster, 1974), pp. 77–95; Hesselgrave, *Theology and Mission*, pp. 227–40; Stott, *Christian Mission*, pp. 58–81.

10. See Stanley J. Samartha, ed., *Dialogue Between Men of Living Faiths* (Geneva: World Council of Churches, 1971), p. 55.

11. "Chiang Mai Statement," in *Faith in the Midst of Faiths*, ed. Stanley J. Samartha (Geneva: World Council of Churches, 1977), p. 136.

12. *World Conference on Mission and Evangelism: Melbourne, Australia, 12-25 May 1980* (Geneva: World Council of Churches, 1980), p. 193.

CWME, included an excellent statement in his monthly letter on evangelism:

> What I know as a preacher, as an evangelist, is that I must call every creature to make a personal decision for Jesus Christ with the understanding that that means conversion, forgiveness, commitment of life to the service of the Lord and hope in his mercy for life eternal. In our Christian proclamation, we confront people with the great "Yes" of God to humankind and we invite them to accept fully that offering of forgiveness, new life, passing from death to life.[13]

And What About Truth?

At this point it is necessary to shift gears. If we fail to do so, the present discussion of dialogue will end up the same as all previous discussions—with evangelicals left out in the cold, stubbornly unwilling to move forward into the full expression of fellowship with and genuine openness of mind toward all those who similarly confess Jesus as Lord, but do not buy their presuppositions.

In October 1979, a rather significant conference was convened at Union Theological Seminary, Richmond, to grapple with issues related to "Christ's Lordship and Religious Pluralism." Those who attended had their minds stretched and their hearts warmed. But I got myself into a bind that the conference failed to resolve. I sought a solution to the all-too-common phenomenon of evangelicals talking past their opposite numbers. My problem arose over the fact that some of those who readily confessed Christ's lordship (and I would not doubt the sincerity of any who confessed Jesus as Lord) were reluctant to focus on the related issue of truth.

In my formal response to Stanley Samartha's keynote address on the theme of that conference, I began by asking what is meant by the lordship of Christ, and then attempted to answer my own question. According to the witness of the Gospels, Christ's lordship is inseparably linked with the issue of truth. Jesus Himself said, "You call me Teacher and Lord; and you are right, for so I am" (John 13:13). Throughout the Gospels He unabashedly and with self-conscious authority claimed to be the Teacher and the Lord of all humankind. Hence, the test of one's submission to His lordship is the acceptance of His teaching.

I was disappointed that Samartha's paper did not raise this issue. He affirmed Christ's lordship but did not mention His teaching—even though a careful reading of the Gospels reveals that Christ was not silent about many matters related to religious pluralism. In omitting Christ's teaching Samartha runs the danger of reconceptualizing the lordship of Christ into

---

13. Emilio Castro, *A Monthly Letter on Evangelism*, January/February 1981, pp. 2–3

something bearing little resemblance to the reality described in Scripture. "My teaching is not mine, but his who sent me" (John 7:16). "Why do you call me 'Lord, Lord,' and not do what I tell you?" (Luke 6:46). John Stott summarizes for us this insistent obligation when he affirms that "we must allow our opinions to be moulded by his opinions, our views to be conditioned by his views. And this includes his uncomfortable and unfashionable teaching—of God, of Scripture, of the radical sinfulness of man, of the fact of divine judgment and of the solemn and eternal realities of heaven and hell . . . with a great gulf fixed between them."[14]

This brings up another matter: Can one be a true disciple of Jesus and not engage in the struggle for truth? This struggle largely characterized His public ministry. It is a plain fact of the Gospels that Jesus was not only controversial, He was a controversialist. He was anything but reluctant to issue warnings against the false teaching of some of the religious leaders of His day (Matt. 16:6). He repeatedly engaged them in controversy over the issue of truth. They were critical of Him and He was outspokenly critical of them. On one memorable occasion He told them they were "wrong" and then went on to state they were "quite wrong" (Mark 12:18–27). And this because they were ignorant of the Scriptures and of the power of God.

Again and again Jesus spoke His convictions without hesitation, apology, or diffidence. He taught the most profound truths with quiet, unabashed dogmatism: "His word was with authority" (Luke 4:32; cf. Matt. 7:28–29). And those who confessed Him as Lord made no attempt to substitute their opinions for His, or to adopt any other stance than to contend earnestly for the faith He delivered to them. As Floyd Filson has admirably summarized:

> The ancient world was a ferment of competing philosophies and religions. Denunciations of false teachers in the New Testament show that not every Christian teacher avoided the danger of surrendering to the world something essential. The steadying content of Scripture, the Jewish heritage of monotheism and moral obedience to God, and above all the teaching, example and work of Jesus himself enabled the church to stay clear of the swirling waters of pagan syncretism.[15]

But Samartha does not call us to follow this pattern of making Jesus' teaching and praxis of truth the center of our witness. Rather he states, "There is no reason to claim that the religion developed in the desert around Mount Sinai is superior to the religion developed on the banks

---

14. John R. W. Stott, *Christ the Controversialist* (Downers Grove, IL: Inter-Varsity, 1970), p. 210.

15. *Encyclopedia Americana*, 1975 edition, vol. 3, p. 707.

of the river Ganga." I can only reply, "The question is not superiority but truth."

If we accept the witness of the Gospels that Jesus Christ is God incarnate, there can surely be no fuller disclosure of God than is given in His person and teaching. It is the task of the church to treasure this deposit of disclosure and proclaim its mysteries. At all times the church is to be "the pillar and bulwark of the truth" (1 Tim. 3:15). The church is to hold the truth firm so that it is not moved and to hold the truth aloft so that all may see it.[16] No other religion makes such claims and endures such agonies to defend them.

Something New in Science: A Paradigm Approach

It is in connection with this unresolved issue of truth that I would like to suggest an alternative approach—one that is increasingly gaining acceptance within the scientific community, but not without intense debate. The debate was sparked by a rather erudite volume, *The Structure of Scientific Revolutions* by Thomas S. Kuhn of the Institute of Advanced Study at Princeton University. Kuhn's thesis begins with a radical postulate: we must repudiate utterly the highly idealized image of science on which all of us were brought up. He refers to the "Sunday Supplement" version— that science is the devoted and highly rational activity of a community of dispassionate experts objectively involved in the progressive discovery of truth. Kuhn shows that the history of scientific exploration records just the opposite. Through an impressive marshaling of facts he demonstrates that science has been and continues to be heavily influenced by nonrational intuitions and procedures. In fact, the record of scientific investigation is that of a sequence of peaceful interludes punctuated by violent intellectual revolutions in each of which a new conceptual world-view rises up to challenge what has gone before, but, despite its complexity and newness, does not automatically come any closer to the truth.

Kuhn then goes on to expound the nature of these revolutions in which efforts are put forth to replace the older paradigm with one that allegedly can solve the problems that brought it to the point of crisis. What is particularly stimulating is his contention that paradigm change cannot be justified by proof, but that—even so—scientists can be persuaded to change their minds.[17] In the final analysis, such decisions are inevitably made on faith, and only by those scientists who have been particularly burdened over the prior crisis.

16. Stott, *Christ the Controversialist,* p. 26.
17. Thomas S. Kuhn, *The Structure of Scientific Revolutions,* 2nd ed. (Chicago: University of Chicago, 1970), pp. 152–53.

If a paradigm is ever to triumph it must gain some first supporters, [those] who will develop it to the point where hardheaded arguments can be produced and multiplied. And even those arguments, when they come, are not individually decisive. Because scientists are reasonable people, one or another argument will ultimately persuade many of them. But there is no single group conversion; what occurs is an increasing shift in the distribution of professional allegiances. . . . If the paradigm is one destined to win its fight, the number and strength of the persuasive arguments in its favor will increase.[18]

Fortunately, Kuhn's insightful ideas have been expounded for mere mortals by Ian G. Barbour in his engaging volume *Myths, Models, and Paradigms*. In this comparative study of science and religion, he grapples with the subject before us.[19] And he establishes the thesis that although complementary models can exist within a single paradigm, paradigms themselves are not complementary. "A person can fully share the outlook of only one tradition at a time. Religion . . . is a way of life and not just a set of beliefs; it is an organic whole of which ideas are only one part."[20] So much for Kuhn and Barbour: let me recommend them both.

A Paradigm Approach to Dialogue

The concept of paradigm shift offers us a new way of looking at the contemporary debate on Christianity and other religions. Although space will prevent expounding this in detail, the following theses should suffice to mark out the new steps we might take in the current debate.

1. Each religious system constitutes an apodictic paradigm. Within itself, it seeks to provide answers to the ultimate questions concerning the origin, purpose, and destiny of the cosmos, of human society, and of individuals. The answers to these questions comprise a unique wholeness ("Truth") that is greater than the sum of its parts. And each part loses its meaning and significance when separated from the whole ("Truth").

2. No two religious systems ask precisely the same ultimate questions, nor do their answers occupy the same proportionate importance within the whole ("Truth"). For instance, Buddhists do not inquire much into the nature of sin *(pavam)*; Hindus are disinterested in eschatology, being preoccupied with fertility and renewal *(samsara)*; Muslims are concerned with faith in Allah *(Iman)* and surrender to him *(Islam)*; and animists seek safety, security, and success in the midst of a dangerous world.

3. We tend to assume that Christianity is likewise a distinct paradigm.

18. Ibid., pp. 158–59.
19. Ian G. Barbour, *Myths, Models, and Paradigms: A Comparative Study in Science and Religion* (New York: Harper and Row, 1974), pp. 119–46.
20. Ibid., p. 147.

And it is! Its concerns, which are limited to scriptural truths, are God and persons, sin and death, Jesus Christ and the cross, redemption and reconciliation, the nations and the end of the world. Its decision of faith involves the correlation of Old Testament promise and New Testament fulfilment, for Christians align themselves with a connected sequence of events (*Heilsgeschichte*) unfolding in history and belonging to it—in which the self-demonstration of God in Jesus Christ is prepared and realized. If this sequence is "demythologized, or de-historicized, or de-objectified," it is no longer a distinct paradigm.[21]

4. Within the paradigm of Christianity as we have defined it, there have often been competing theories, such as between Jewish and Gentile believers in the apostolic church (Acts 15), and later between the Orthodox and Catholic, and between Lutherans, Reformed, and Arminians. But despite their differences, all these theories have been regarded as tolerable since all have continued to give the same general answers to the basic questions. Whereas within Christianity, broadly and inclusively defined, one may find slightly different affirmations of truth, the essence remains—with the same suppositions assumed, the same questions asked, and the same sources used in the search for truth.

5. However, a new paradigm of "Christianity" will emerge when the suppositions, questions, and sources are changed. Despite the difficulty encountered in defining with precision all the fringe characteristics of evangelicalism, all evangelicals regard themselves as constituting a common paradigm of truth commitment. And this despite their awareness that they are to be found throughout the total organizational spectrum of the Christian movement. But when evangelicals ponder today's wide range of literature on religious encounter they begin to receive mixed signals. They sense with appreciation the varied ways in which many writers have sought to remain loyal to the essence of Christianity. But they have been troubled when they have perceived others making concessions on essentials—concessions without scriptural warrant. To evangelicals, this is evidence of a shift in truth commitment and it is this shift that makes it increasingly impossible for them to enter the wider circle of those who confess Jesus as Lord but who approach the issue of religious dialogue differently.

No person can serve two masters simultaneously; neither can the Christian movement serve a variety of truth commitments and at the same time claim oneness. Evangelicals will agree that true dialogue demands respect and courage along with openness to new insights about one's own religious commitment. It also necessitates the absence of coercion, the affirmation

21. Oscar Cullmann, *Christ and Time,* trans. Floyd V. Filson (Philadelphia: Westminster, 1964), p. 70.

of one's personal conviction, and freedom from intolerance. But all this does not mean that the evangelical is silent about the call to repentance and faith.[22]

> To surrender conversion as the ultimate goal is, therefore, not a consequence of modesty, but of false modesty. If, in anxiety to avoid spiritual arrogance or in our striving after solidarity with others, we should begin to "demissionize," we would rob the salt of its savour or put the lamp under a meal-tub. The surrender of conversion would, in any event, land us in a totally other spiritual climate than that of the New Testament.[23]

Christianity: A Single or Multiple Paradigm?

"A totally other spiritual climate"—this is the way David Bosch characterizes the ferment in Christianity. Kuhn and Barbour would be more specific and speak of a new truth configuration, a new *Gestalt*, a new paradigm. And the introduction of a new paradigm means an intellectual revolution of major proportions insofar as religious encounter is concerned. To put it this way may add a discordant note to ecumenical fellowship. Kuhn would argue that this is unavoidable until the reality of separate paradigms is freely acknowledged: not one Christianity troubled by internal upheavals and conflicts—but several. Have we come to this?

"Christianity is Christ." We like to affirm this, for it is essentially true. But what is the base for this affirmation? Evangelicals confess that Christianity's base must be *sola scriptura*. In their considered judgment the canonical Scriptures constitute "the only infallible rule of faith and practice." Scripture's themes are many and they are all interrelated: the Triune God (Father, Son, and Holy Spirit); the enemy (Satan and his hosts); people as fallen and lost, dead in trespasses and sins, but addressible by God; sin as demanding judgment; and salvation through Christ alone.

Another Christian paradigm would approach Scripture differently. Faith and Order Paper 99 of the World Council of Churches is a compilation by Ellen Flesseman–van Leer (1980) of studies which the conciliar movement has undertaken over the years—studies on the Bible, its authority, and interpretation. This compilation needs to be studied alongside the evaluative writings of Richard Rowe and Michael Sadgrove on the same subject.[24] The reason for suggesting this is the rather vivid way in which

22. Bosch, *Theology of Religions*, pp. 205–13.
23. Ibid., p. 211.
24. Ellen Flesseman–van Leer, ed., *The Bible: Its Authority and Interpretation in the Ecumenical Movement,* Faith and Order Paper 99 (Geneva: World Council of Churches, 1980); Richard C. Rowe, *Bible Study in the World Council of Churches,* Research Pamphlet 16 (Geneva: World Council of Churches, 1969); Michael Sadgrove, "The Bible from New Delhi to Nairobi"—a private collection from Balliol College, Oxford (1975).

these writings reflect a theological shift of major proportions. And this shift has been taking place within that segment of the church which has taken the lead in promoting the discussion of interreligious dialogue.

The issue is the authority of the Bible. Down through the years the church has held that the unity, inspiration, and authority of the Bible are intimately interrelated. Scripture is not ambiguous in its witness to itself as the Word of God and to the claim that through it God speaks to persons. It is also to be noted that when Scripture witnesses to its essential unity, the focus is not on its literary structure or on its theological coherence. The focus is not even on its record of God's redemptive acts down through history, culminating in the crucifixion and resurrection of Jesus of Nazareth. The Bible is far more a record of living persons than of doctrinal formulations. Its claim to oneness in diversity is found in "its open secret": Jesus Christ Himself, who was "manifested in the flesh, vindicated in the Spirit, seen by angels, preached among the nations, believed on in the world, taken up in glory" (1 Tim. 3:16). He is the Bible's unifying principle.

One recalls Martin Luther's comments on Psalm 40:7, "Lo, I come; in the roll of the book it is written of me." Luther asked, "What Book and what Person?" Then he answered his own question, "Scripture; and only one Person, Jesus Christ." In saying this Luther was only reiterating the witness of Christ Himself. In His encounter with the Jews He affirmed, "You search the scriptures, because you think that in them you have eternal life; and it is they that bear witness to me" (John 5:39). And He went on to say, "If you believed Moses, you would believe me, for he wrote of me" (John 5:46). Again and again Jesus referred to the Scriptures as pointing to Himself (Matt. 21:42–46; Mark 14:27; Luke 24:25–27, 44–47). And in the apostolic church this witness was confirmed (Acts 2:25–36; 3:20–22; 8:30–35; 13:32–37; 17:2–3; 18:24–28).

In the light of the Bible's christological unity, evangelicals see in it something far removed from a miscellaneous collection of diverse writings. They find it rather a corporate organism, an integrated unity—the Word of God—inspired and authoritative. Furthermore, they find the Bible not silent on the issue of the truth of God and the religions that crowd this world. Despite all the searching and critical investigation to which the Bible has been subjected over the years, evangelicals have yet to feel that they should abandon the truth paradigm that "all scripture is inspired by God and profitable for teaching, for reproof, for correction, and for training in righteousness, that the man of God may be complete, equipped for every good work" (2 Tim. 3:16–17).

In the earlier years of the ecumenical movement many things were said and written that were most encouraging to evangelicals. One recalls with appreciation the witness of Willem Visser 't Hooft, of Hendrik Kraemer, of Suzanne de Diétrich, of Robert Martin-Achard. One differed with them only on the details. As recently as New Delhi (1961) the World Council's basis was amended to include the phrase, "according to the Scriptures," as definitive of its confession of "the Lord Jesus Christ as God and Saviour." Visser 't Hooft endorsed this with the statement, "Our movement can only be a dynamic movement toward greater unity, if we listen together to the one voice which gives us our marching orders."[25] New Delhi's statements on the Bible assumed its essential unity as "a united testimony to the same saving events; and since these events are decisive for mankind as a whole, it follows that the biblical writers are addressing people of all ages as their contemporaries."[26] New Delhi reflected the "guiding principles for the interpretation of the Bible" which had been defined at the ecumenical study conference at Oxford in 1949. In fact, for almost fifteen years following the Oxford conference, the official line was, "Any teaching that clearly contradicts the biblical position cannot be accepted as Christian."[27]

By 1963, however, this position began to erode, and soon a paradigm shift of major proportions had emerged. At the Fourth World Conference on Faith and Order at Montreal, Ernst Käsemann confessed in a plenary address that he was unable to see any unified picture of the New Testament *ecclesia* emerging from the records of its various witnesses. In a very real sense this marked the end of the dominance of Barthian theology in the WCC and the beginnings of a radical turn in its approach to Scripture. When the Faith and Order Commission met in Bristol in 1967, the focus was on "The Significance of the Hermeneutical Problem for the Ecumenical Movement." The Bible was now seen as a variety of traditions and insights, some better than others. This stress on biblical diversity led to a crisis touching the Bible's authority, with its witness regarded as "only one element in a variegated complex of truth."

By the time of the Fourth Assembly of the WCC in Uppsala (1968), the question was raised as to whether it is possible to find illumination in the Bible on the ethical issues of the day. At Louvain in 1971, the Faith and Order Commission found its central question not the translation of Christian faith into action, but the actual content of the Christian faith. If the Bible represents diversity, is there not an element of provisionality in any and all suggested interpretations of it? Will this not mean that we can make the Bible say anything we choose? In the midst of this one finds theologians saying that "the Church has never expected that her members must necessarily share all Jesus' beliefs. . . . The fact of culture change is

25. Sadgrove, "The Bible," p. 2.
26. Ibid., p. 3.
27. Flesseman–van Leer, *The Bible,* p. 14.

recognized in Scripture, which itself shows how a universal faith takes different forms in different cultural settings."[28]

What can evangelicals say to this? Nothing less than that a paradigm shift of far-reaching implications is taking place. Evangelicals, by definition, approach the issue of religious pluralism from the perspective of the unity and authority of the Bible. Nonevangelicals tend to say that its authority is not a "self-contained entity, but a means whereby they may know in the present the Lordship of the living Jesus Christ."[29] This means that the authority of the Bible is in Jesus Christ—in our present encounter with Him—and not in the book as such. Such a nontraditional presupposition demands a radically different way of interpreting the Scriptures. Inevitably a "new hermeneutic" had to be devised so that despite the "very divisive literary traditions" of Scripture and the possibility of "real contradictions" and the "fading hope" of finding "one biblical message," the Bible might somehow make its contribution to the understanding of truth.[30]

This paradigm shift has brought us all to a full stop. It cannot be ignored. I read Wilfred Cantwell Smith's most recent book, *Towards a World Theology,* in order to understand his evaluation of my rejoinder to Samartha at the Conference on Christ's Lordship and Religious Pluralism. At that conference Smith had pointedly remarked:

> Dr. Glasser pled the importance of truth. For a moment I was tempted to respond by pleading for the moral injunctions, rather, of the Christian revelation. As we face Christ on the cross, and as teacher, we are made aware of imperatives toward reconciliation, brotherhood, the dignity of the neighbor, peace, concord, respect; matters with all of which denigration of others' forms of faith collides. Exclusivism strikes more and more Christians as immoral. *If the head proves it true,* while the heart sees it as wicked, un-Christian, then should Christians not follow the heart? Maybe this is the crux of our dilemma.[31]

I have quoted this statement at length because it clearly represents the position of those who confess Christ's lordship but who follow a different truth paradigm when they approach the issues of the day. In his recent book Smith's categories for truth lead him to define salvation in an exceedingly—in my judgment—subbiblical fashion. He ranges widely and includes such poignant items as being "saved from nihilism, from alien-

---

28. Sadgrove, "The Bible," p. 17.

29. Hubert Cunliffe-Jones, quoted in Rowe, *Bible Study,* pp. 69–70.

30. Rowe, *Bible Study,* pp. 71–72.

31. Wilfred Cantwell Smith, "An Attempt at Summation," in *Christ's Lordship and Religious Pluralism,* ed. Gerald H. Anderson and Thomas F. Stransky (Maryknoll, NY: Orbis, 1981), p. 202 (emphasis added).

ation, anomie, despair; from the bleak despondency of meaninglessness. Saved from unfreedom; from being the victim of one's own whims within, or of pressures without; saved from being merely an organism reacting to its environment"[32]—all of which are extremely valid. But why does he leave out what the apostolic writings present as the basic element of salvation: deliverance from the wrath of God and reconciliation to His fellowship through the blood of Christ? Related to this omission is the fact that when Smith defines faith, he speaks of a "global human quality" whereby Christians are "saved through Christ's death and resurrection," Buddhists are "saved through the teachings of Buddha," Jews are "saved through that Torah that Christians have made a point of misunderstanding," and Hindus are "saved, inspired, encouraged, and made creative, through the poetry of the Gita."[33]

Is dialogue possible across the gulf of these two distinct paradigms? We are faced with, it seems, nothing less than evidence of one of Kuhn's violent intellectual revolutions. Which paradigm will win the day? The church has known bitter and prolonged struggles of this sort in the past. And it has enjoyed some great victories. Perhaps this is why evangelicals find no alternative but to stand pat on their commitment to the Bible— "the only infallible rule of faith and practice."

32. Wilfred Cantwell Smith, *Towards a World Theology: Faith and the Comparative History of Religion* (Philadelphia: Westminster, 1981), p. 168.
33. Ibid., pp. 171–72.

15

Religious Freedom and Theology of Mission

Donald McGavran

I n a world full of other religions and ideologies, any theology of the Christian church and its mission must deal with religious liberty. The exclusive claims of the Christian religion raise thorny questions for Christian missiology. Do non-Christians have any right at all to their own beliefs? The evangelistic activities of the church and all its various agencies—missionary societies, Bible societies, evangelistic associations, and the like—seem to be an infringement of religious freedom. Serious questions concerning the basic human right of religious freedom are raised by Christian mission. They deserve honest answers.

In the first part of this chapter ("Christians and the Pluralistic World") we will look at the problem from the viewpoint of Christians committed to world evangelization and the proper expansion of the church in a world which is increasingly pluralistic. In the second part ("Religious Freedom") we will take sympathetic account of the convictions and fears of non-Christians concerning religious freedom, and try to work out a theology of mission *agreeable to Scripture* and *fair to Christians and non-Christians alike.*

Christians and the Pluralistic World

We live in a pluralistic world. Yet Christians believe that pluralism in no way cancels the lordship of Christ. It is of this pluralistic world that Jesus is Lord. In this world, without any coercion or sacrifice of religious freedom, every tongue shall confess that Jesus is Lord to the glory of God the Father. It is in this pluralistic world that Christians—by the express command of almighty God—engage in world evangelization and in Christian mission. All theologies of mission must therefore come to terms with the rapidly growing relativistic convictions that many roads lead to God

220

and no one ought, therefore, to propagate his or her own brand of religion.

At the outset, we point out that the conviction that Jesus rules over pluralism is being steadily eroded by the main currents of modern life. The people who control the media neither believe it nor announce it. The science of anthropology, proclaiming all cultures equally good, actively attacks it. The various pieces of the human mosaic demonstrate very different life styles and each claims an inalienable right to follow its own. A pluralism in which no one rules is what the modern world appears to believe in. Let us elaborate.

The six continents with their four billion residents form a very complicated mosaic. Their unity consists merely in the fact that all humans are passengers on Planet Earth and no one can get off. They have to live together; thousands of different life styles must get along with each other. Most people feel that each piece of the mosaic should be left free to do its own thing. No majority should force other pieces of the mosaic to live as it thinks right. Neither should any minority. This is a pluralistic world, and should remain such.

Christians subscribe to this doctrine, which has burst on the Western world in the last thirty years, but a bit uneasily. We believe it, but with qualifications and reservations. Apparently some cultural ways are going to be imposed on everyone. All alike will have to give up measuring in terms of quarts and miles and begin to measure in terms of liters and kilometers. All alike will be molded by educational standards laid down by the state. Many Christians are unhappy at this latter prospect. They see their children being conformed to the image which pleases a secular state and a dollar-dominated television industry. But so far Christians have done very little to combat this attempt at standardization.

Seemingly in this pluralistic world we can force the metric system, secular educational standards, health and traffic rules on all peoples, but cannot force on anyone Christian standards concerning sex, brotherhood, or the worship of God. Individuals may or may not believe what the Bible lays down as absolute truth. We are not commending all this. We are simply describing the contemporary situation.

In this permissive atmosphere how can mission survive? What happens to the lordship of Christ? The new orthodoxy of the pluralistic world forces on everyone an official dogma of secular society: that in measurable and relative matters—the world of sense and substance—through a process of consensus, uniform standards and values may be imposed; but in absolute matters, all of us must be free to follow our own desires and form our own guesses as to what truth is. Is the human being free or an automaton? Is this a mechanistic world closed to all free will? Does everything have an antecedent material cause? Is there a spirit world? Is there life after death or is death the end? Is the universe a vast impersonal process or is a righteous, loving, personal God behind it all? In these matters, the pluralistic world seems to say, "All of us are free to speculate as we wish. We are free to form our own habits, choose our associates, and adopt rules of life in conformity with our speculations. There is no absolute truth, no one way which pleases God." For many Christians, evangelism is one of the casualties of their sudden realization that all people are residents in one vast apartment house with many different life styles and must get along together. Such Christians come to believe that truth is only "what is true for me." Exactly the opposite may be "true for you."

We have been describing what happens in Western democracies. In totalitarian states (whether Marxist or Muslim) the situation is otherwise. There the beliefs of the party in control, even if it is a minority, are forced on everyone. Minorities in many nations firmly believe that the only way to a just society is through the dictatorship of the proletariat. That is one of the enduring springs of action in great sections of the global village.

This multifaceted world is complex and of fascinating interest. We and our grandchildren—unless a world government comes in by conquest—will be struggling with the implications of freedom, justice, and truth in a world where the ways of thousands of other segments of society impinge upon us. At the time of this writing the Vietnamese decision to make life miserable for the two million citizens of Chinese origin and to drive them out of the land is gravely interfering with the life of Hong Kong, Singapore, Malaysia, the United States, and other lands. Yet no one says to Vietnam, "The world community will not allow you to do this." Rather, Vietnam practices genocide before our eyes, a million die, and the rest of the world, groaning and complaining, absorbs a million boat people.

The broad aspects of pluralism are beyond the scope of this chapter. We confine ourselves to the threat pluralism poses to Christian mission. Since the foundation of the pluralistic order is the conviction that each life style is about equally valid, Christians find themselves and their children drifting almost unconsciously toward relativistic religion. This holds that no one has *The Truth*. All religions and ideologies are partly true and partly false. People say, "You know a part of the truth. So do I. Let's get together and dialogue. Perhaps we shall together arrive at a truer concept of reality. Jesus Christ was a very great man, but then so were Gautama, Krishna, Confucius, and Marx. Who knows? Eastern cults and Western scientism may have much to teach us."

This climate of thought is the antithesis of that of the New Testament—indeed, of the entire biblical revelation. Yet world evangelization and church growth today must proceed in this pluralistic milieu. What is the right attitude toward this influential contemporary dogma? What light does the Bible itself shed on this fashionable axiom?

Against this background, the thesis of this chapter may now be stated. The growth of the church and world evangelization depend on the conviction that the biblical revelation has been given by God and that, in the absolute matters concerning the human race and God, *God has revealed Himself and His perfect will authoritatively. Christians in this century or any other, this land or any other, may go forward confidently, knowing that they are basing their actions on unchanging truth.*

It is essential to remember that while Christians base their actions on God's truth, the truth which the Bible reveals is not fully exemplified in any earthly manifestation of the church. The early church in Jerusalem did not fully exemplify it. They spoke "the word to none except Jews" (Acts 11:19). The church in its days of greatest purity and glory did not fully exemplify it. The One Way is never what any given church does. Its rituals, customs, hymns, and doctrines (its wordings of biblical truth) are all imperfect human products. No culture is fully Christian. However, churches which intend to practice what God has revealed are much closer to the divine model than are others. The churches of the Reformation were much closer than the corrupt churches of the preceding hundred years. The Religious Society of Friends, which was founded by George Fox, was much closer than the Anglican churches from which the group was excluded. The culture of the Friends was better than other cultures of those days. As people turn from non-Christian faith to Christ, some (like the Mizo churches of 1950) achieve a high degree of likeness to the divine model. Others bring in so many beliefs and practices of their pre-Christian faith that they must be judged to have achieved the divine model very imperfectly.

Congregations and denominations, though they are but approximations of God's perfect revealed will, are superior to all human institutions. I think it was Thomas Aquinas who declared that the most ignorant Christian has a better grasp of God's truth than does the wisest non-Christian. The most imperfect church is closer to God's unchanging truth than is the best non-Christian society.

God's revelation, by His express order, is not to be imposed on anyone. It is to be proclaimed to the lost. God's ambassadors are to beseech lost men and women to be reconciled to God according to His one plan of salvation. They are to beseech, not to force. They are to leave men and women free to follow their own decisions. Otherwise acceptance of Jesus Christ as the Savior and God as the Father almighty becomes not acceptance by free persons, but the mechanical action of puppets.

While Christians are thus, by divine command and the example of Christ Himself, to proceed on the basis of religious freedom, they are to reject, as they would Satan himself, the slick lie that all opinions about absolute values, about God and humankind, freedom and justice, eternal life and eternal death, repentance and morality, are equally true and equally false. To this poisonous suggestion God's Word returns an unequivocal *no*. Theology of mission must say so.

There are indeed many speculations about God. There *is* a wisdom of this world. God has given human beings the ability to think and expects them to exercise it. We have been made in the image of God and commanded to love God with all our mind. Reason is a God-given ability and Christians are reasonable persons. God directs us to test the spirits, to see the difference between light and darkness, and to walk in the light. He instructs us to discern evil paths and stay out of them. It is Satan who goes up and down the land teaching people that no one is lost and all religions are about equally true. The Bible does not counsel Christians to stash their thinking ability on the shelf and believe (quite against all evidence) that all life styles deliver an equal amount of the good life and are equally pleasing to God, all cultures are equally good, all ways lead to God, and all people will ultimately be saved.

On the contrary, from Genesis to Revelation, God's Word tells of one God, the Father almighty, who created the world and then across thousands of years revealed His holy will to His people in many ways. The Bible is the inspired, authoritative, infallible rule of faith and practice. It is God's Word written. It proclaims that there is general revelation, which God gives to humans as He desires in every age and every culture. God has also given special revelation in Jesus Christ His Son, our Savior, and in the Bible. All general revelation, inevitably mixed with erroneous human ideas, must be weighed and measured over against special revelation. Everything not in accord with special revelation is either only partially true or completely false.

Is it *intolerant* to affirm this? We ask the question in the face of widespread contemporary feeling that there is no such thing as absolute truth, and therefore the position we have been advocating is an insult to the scientific outlook on life. Our position is accused of being intolerant and unfriendly. We disagree. People do indeed hold differing convictions on eternal issues. Sometimes these arise on the grounds of what the founders of the great religions have taught; sometimes on the "absolute truth," ardently proclaimed by some, that there is no absolute truth; and quite often on a person's desire for power or pleasure. It is not intolerant of non-Christians to hold to these convictions, or of Christians to believe that in Christ and the Bible God has revealed final truth concerning the eternal issues. Intolerant persons are those who not only believe they are absolutely right, but forbid others to hold beliefs which differ from theirs.

Intolerant people *force* others to believe as they do. This a Christian theology of mission would always prohibit.

Christians hold that God has made men and women in His own image,
has made them able to think. God did this, knowing that humans would
make mistakes. He gave them the right to disagree. He expects them to
cleave to what they think is right. God also expects Christians to do their
best *to persuade all people* of the objective validity of God's revelation in the
Bible and in Jesus Christ.The sinner's response to God in faith must be
free. When it comes to eternal issues, every manner of coercion should
be excluded. If this is done, then ardency of belief is in no sense intolerant.

The Christians portrayed in the New Testament were not intolerant.
Peter was not intolerant when he announced "no other name" (Acts 4:12).
Our Lord was not intolerant when He said, "No one comes to the Father,
but by me" (John 14:6). The early church never forced anyone to believe,
though they did most ardently try to persuade. It would be a sorry world
if those who believe in what they consider good ways were to be prohibited
from trying to persuade others to adopt them. All teaching of science, all
promotion of new inventions and technological improvements, and all
advocacy of human rights would be prohibited! Any such intolerance
would advance the cause neither of tolerance nor of human happiness.

Into this pluralistic world came God's Word and God's Son, bearing
authentic information about who we are and who God is, about our duty
and God's holy will, about God's plan of salvation for lost men and women
and His one way of life. God has not left us to grope in a relativistic world.
He has shown us plainly what He requires of us. Christians of many
different cultural backgrounds, languages, and degrees of technological
knowledge have studied God's Word and come to substantially similar
understandings of The Way.

If the branches of the church, with all their minor differences, were
to be represented on a single line, and on this same line Marxists, Hindus,
Confucianists, animists, secularists, and humanists were also to be represented, all the branches of the church would be grouped close together.
And all of the life styles devised by human beings would be located a
considerable distance away. Moreover, it would be found that the more
strictly the Christian denominations adhere to the Word, and the more
rigorously they exclude human doctrines which cannot be substantiated
from the mainstream of biblical revelation, the more closely they would
be grouped together. This would be the case regardless of the languages
they speak and the cultures from which they come. As a matter of fact,
Bible-reading and Bible-obeying Christians from the islands of the South
Pacific, whose ancestors 150 years ago were illiterate animists, will be seen
to be—in the essentials of faith—remarkably like believing Christians in
Scotland, whose ancestors 150 years ago were literate Christians. In short,

when God's revelation is accepted as the one authority, the unchanging Word of God, then human opinions yield and a Christian way of life results.

Under this Christian way of life, the good things in the Scotch and the Fijian cultures have been preserved. Indeed, they have been enhanced and made still more beautiful. All this has been achieved not by watering down biblical truth to fit ways of thinking about God and the human race which characterize other cultures, but rather by purging the wealth of the nations of sin, sorrow, sickness, and error, and then bringing that purged wealth into Zion. It glows more brightly. It shines more steadily. The whole church is richer because of the contributions of many purified and fulfilled cultures.

Writing in the midst of a pluralistic society suffering from an epidemic of relativism, we maintain that according to the Bible there is only one Savior and He must be made known to all. Until they believe in Christ, they are lost. The gospel was revealed to bring the lost to salvation. The Scriptures are very exclusive. When the Bible is examined as to whether it allows for many different ways of life, all about equally true and equally false, there is no question as to the outcome of the investigation. The Bible does not know of many different mediators; there is only one. The Bible does not know of many different gods; there is only one. Early Christians were known as followers of *the* Way (Acts 9:2). Eternal life is not available to any except those who have the Son. Only those who believe in Jesus Christ will never die. Thus speaks the evangelical theology of mission.

The proper Christian response to pluralistic society is to declare firmly but intelligently that God in His revelation, the Bible, has shown *the* way; at the same time Christians must grant cheerfully that other ways have much that is true and good in them. Indeed, many Christians hold that all truth, all goodness anywhere, is rooted in God's general revelation, but that no human system can save lost humanity and none is therefore equal to His special revelation in the Bible and in Christ. It stands supreme.

To be sure, more light will break from the Bible but it will be light in harmony with what God in Christ has already revealed. New light will never contradict that. The canon is closed. Christians, as long as they depend on the Bible, may be certain as to the truth of what they believe, the standards they follow, and the ultimate Rock to which they anchor their lives. Believing this, they can proclaim the gospel with power and gentle persuasiveness. Classical or biblical theology of mission insists on both religious freedom and God's clear intent that the gospel be proclaimed throughout the earth, and all peoples be given the opportunity to confess faith in Jesus Christ and to become members of His church.

We have been speaking of religious liberty as it bears upon world evangelization. We must now speak briefly on religious liberty as it concerns the different branches of the universal church. We ask, Does the drive to Christian unity among the leading denominations of the day, from Congregationalists to Roman Catholics, threaten religious liberty?

In the early days of the ecumenical movement, the World Council of Churches made some very fine pronouncements on religious liberty. But after 1968, it closed its Secretariat on Religious Liberty, merging it into the human-rights department. Simultaneously the search for Christian unity was greatly heightened. There was a tendency for uniting denominations to speak of the large new denomination as "the church." For example, we have *The* Church of South India. Other denominations were thought of as sects.

A few years ago it began to look as if half the Protestants in the United States would someday be found in one large church. While the Consultation on Church Union has fallen on hard times, and that outcome does not seem as likely now as it once did, one must ask, How will that large church (if and when it comes into being) regard the churches which maintain a separate existence? As equally valid churches entitled by religious freedom to all the courtesies and rights which the large denomination enjoys—or as divisive sects? Is a new state church coming into being?

When there was just one church in the West, its record on religious liberty was—to say the least—deplorable. For thirteen hundred years, *the* church grievously abused and denied religious liberty. Those leading the drive for Christian unity today need to make certain that the branches of the universal church which maintain a separate existence are treated as full churches.

Religious Freedom

A correct position on religious freedom is an essential part of any theology of mission. Mission is carrying out God's command to bring His salvation to all peoples (Isa. 49:6). Christ expressly commanded His followers to disciple *panta ta ethne* (Matt. 28:19). To be sure Christians have other duties, but they must not be substituted for proclaiming and discipling. World evangelization is the very heart of Christian mission. Inevitably problems and questions arise for those who believe in both evangelization and religious freedom. For example, what bearing does world evangelization have on the rights of others to hold and cherish their own religious beliefs and to carry out their traditional religious practices? Does world evangelization mean the eradication of all other religions? In a Christian world, are other religions endangered species?

Do only Christians have the right to propagate their religion? For example, have Marxists no right to multiply cells of practicing atheistic Marxists throughout the inhabited earth? They hold their beliefs to be the highest and most liberating truths known. Why should they not have the right to propagate them? Similarly, will Christians grant to Muslims equal rights—in Rome or Canterbury or Geneva—to win men and women to the Islamic faith and build beautiful and permanent mosques?

How about Nazis and Fascists and forms of totalitarian rule yet to be invented? Should the Ku Klux Klan have complete freedom to multiply its doctrines and its adherents all across the world? Have all people and all associations such rights? Does pluralistic society mean that each individual and each association has an *inviolable right* to religious freedom? These are some of the sharply worded questions which a theology of mission must answer.

What are the limits to such rights? Have all people the right to propagate error, to mislead others in any direction they wish? Few would advocate this, and yet one must ask who is to determine what is error and which paths lead in the wrong direction. Does religious freedom mean freedom in the name of religion to hijack planes? Bomb banks? And kidnap children?

What happens when my freedom clashes with the rights of society? Were Christian abolitionists who helped slaves to escape from their "rightful" masters using or misusing religious freedom? When patriots in Afghanistan carry on guerilla warfare against their "rightful" Russian rulers, are they abusing religious freedom? Is the Muslim refusal to submit to rule by atheists justifiable? On what authority can we affirm this?

What happens when rights claimed by a majority deny the rights claimed by a minority? For example, when the ruler of Chad insisted that all youth go through the traditional animistic African rites of passage—and thus become "authentic Africans"—ought Christians have refused to allow their youth to be subjected to these animistic rites? Did the ruler deny Christians religious liberty?

What about conversion? And proselytism? When is conversion sheep-stealing? Is the Orthodox Church in Greece right in prohibiting all evangelism by evangelicals? Does it do well to forbid the multiplication of Methodist, Presbyterian, Baptists, and Nazarene congregations in that country?

Do we claim religious freedom for ourselves only, or for the evangelists of all religions? If we maintain religious freedom for all, do we also maintain the right to be wrong? And the right to propagate evil—racism, drink, drugs, and pornography? When religious freedom harms society or the church, should it be permitted? Does the right to religious freedom negate all truth? Or shall we maintain that no one may plead "rights" in the face of the truth, or claim "freedom" from the moral law? And then comes Pilate's famous question, "What is truth?"

These are some of the problems raised by the clash of the command of Christ to disciple the peoples of earth and the right of every individual, so heavily stressed in the modern world, to do as he or she thinks best, wise, profitable, or pleasant. To answer these questions we now present certain principles which will help Christians pick their way carefully through this mine field. We enunciate these principles as part of our theology of mission, believing that they will help us to carry out Christ's command (to proclaim the gospel to all and to disciple all peoples) in such a way as to enhance genuine religious freedom.

1. *Religious freedom is a universal human right based on both revelation and reason.* To be sure, revelation does not explicitly declare that there is to be no coercion in matters of religion. But the teaching of Christ and the practice of the early church abundantly support religious freedom. Christ called all who labor and are heavy-laden to Himself. He did not force them. He invited them. Many rejected Him. Many of His disciples fell away. They evidently were free to do so. The apostles preached the gospel, and boldly announced that all who believe in Jesus as Messiah will be saved; but they had no power to force listeners to become followers. Indeed they showed no inclination to force them. Paul writes, "We are ambassadors for Christ, God making his appeal through us. We beseech you on behalf of Christ, be reconciled to God" (2 Cor. 5:20). In this there is not the faintest hint of force. Full religious freedom of the individual is the ground of all such entreaty.

The Bible demands that belief in the Triune God and obedience to Him must be free acts. God Himself invites; He does not compel. In the third chapter of Revelation we hear the Savior say, "Behold, I stand at the door and knock; if any one . . . opens the door, I will come in" (v. 20). We can never forget that Adam and Eve were free to disobey the express command of God. Disobedience entailed certain consequences, but Adam and Eve were entirely free to obey or not as they desired.

Reason also declares that if humans are to be human, not puppets, then in regard to matters of religion, their decisions must be free. In every piece of the mosaic, every individual, as an integral part of personhood, has the right of religious freedom.

2. *All are bound to seek and embrace the truth.* Everyone must abide by the moral law. We live in an orderly world, not a chaos. The universe is bound together by law and by truth. No one may plead "rights" in the face of the moral law or assert freedom to believe contrary to the truth. In the use of all freedoms, personal and social responsibility and the rights of others must be observed. We are not free to rob and kill, to oppress and destroy. If we have deposited a hundred dollars in the bank, we are not

free to draw out a thousand. The truth that we have only a hundred dollars controls us. We have no freedom to distort or disregard that truth.

Similarly we are free to bring or not to bring children into the world; but once we have brought children into life, we are not free to declare, "You are none of mine. I will neither feed nor clothe you." The Bible from beginning to end gives abundant illustration of this principle.

3. *All Christians are straightly charged to be heralds of the gospel.* "And [Jesus] said to them, 'Go into all the world and preach the gospel to the whole creation. He who believes and is baptized will be saved; but he who does not believe will be condemned'" (Mark 16:15–16). Religious freedom, though demonstrated abundantly in the earthly life of our Lord and His apostles, must not be so understood as to cancel this clear directive, stated and illustrated repeatedly in the New Testament. A proper theology of mission emphasizes principle (3) as well as principle (1). Under some circumstances dialogue or a joint search for truth may be a good way to proclaim. As Christ's ambassadors we may use many ways to present His message. We must, however, always remember that we are not sent out merely to dialogue, or to tell others that they may have as much truth as we do. Rather we are sent out *to announce the King's message.* Religious freedom can be observed in proclamation. But it must not cancel proclamation of the Good News.

4. *Governments, in matters of religion, may not coerce their citizens or deny them freedom.* Rather governments must maintain the inviolable right of religious freedom. Government has been instituted by God to insure that citizens are treated like human beings, and that religious liberty is guaranteed to them. In particular instances where a whole nation considers itself to belong to a given religion, government properly recognizes that fact; but at the same time government ought to protect the rights of all citizens, especially the rights of small minorities so easily coerced. In countries where most of the citizens are Christians, government will protect the rights of Jews, Marxists, animists, Muslims, and Hindus. In countries like Iran where the vast majority is Muslim, government ought to protect the rights of Christian and Marxist minorities. The great nation of India when it drew up its constitution in the early fifties declared itself to be a secular state affording equal protection to all religions. It guaranteed the right to practice and to propagate one's religion to Hindus and Parsees, Christians and Sikhs alike. Since the huge Hindu majority, swayed by emotion, often press for local and state laws which discriminate against Christians and Muslims (in some cases Hindus have actually burned churches and destroyed mosques), the central government and the Supreme Court have occasionally had to overrule discriminatory laws passed by municipalities and state legislatures.

Just as governments ought to guarantee religious freedom, it is also the God-ordained duty of Christians to obey government regulations.

> Let every person be subject to the governing authorities. For there is no authority except from God, and those that exist have been instituted by God. Therefore he who resists the authorities resists what God has appointed, and those who resist will incur judgment. For rulers are . . . God's servant for your good. [Rom. 13:1–4]

However, this obedience is to be rendered only up to a point. When the commander of the temple guards brought the apostles before the Sanhedrin and the high priest said angrily, "We strictly charged you not to teach in this name," Peter replied, "We must obey God rather than men." Peter "did not cease teaching and preaching Jesus as the Christ" (Acts 5:24–42). The record also states that the apostles rejoiced to be counted worthy to suffer for the sake of the name. Those who, impelled by conscience, disobey the law, who "obey God rather than men," may suffer for doing so.

5. *The rights of different religions must be recognized and protected by governments.* In the United States this principle is well illustrated by the commotion concerning prayer in public schools. Jews, atheists, agnostics, Buddhists, and Hindus claimed that the reading of the Bible and prayer in public schools forced a Christian view of life on their children and were therefore an infringement of their religious freedom. The United States government with the active assent of many Christians ruled that prayer therefore could not be offered in public schools. Since in many cases all the children in a given school are the children of Christians and of nonchurchgoers who want their children to hear the Bible and pray to God every day, this government order in effect has forced on these Christians a secularist ruling favoring non-Christians. The hot battle continues today.

In India, Christians protested the use of a third-grade reader which included a lesson about "The Cow Our Mother." They maintained that the Hindu majority was forcing Christian children to regard the cow as a goddess, a view quite contrary to Christian religious beliefs. While the application of this principle is fraught with difficulties, the principle itself is easily defensible. Non-Christians as well as Christians must be granted religious freedom.

6. *The inviolable human right to persuade and counterpersuade must be affirmed and protected in matters religious.* Persuasion is the basis of all learning, progress, and commerce. Students have laid before them lessons which persuade them of the truths of history, science, mathematics, or sociology. They do not easily believe. Repeated persuasion, illustration, emphasis, and examination are usually required. Similarly progress would be gravely

handicapped if we were not free to advocate that better methods be followed and to persuade people to buy a better pencil or razor, a better cooking utensil or sewing machine. All commerce depends on a ceaseless process of persuading people to buy this product rather than that. As soon as sufficient numbers are persuaded, factories making the outmoded article are dismantled at considerable cost and new ones which make the improved model are built, again at substantial cost. A free market in ideas is essential to normal human life. This is what Principle (6) affirms.

No one need fear that people will be pushed around and coerced by persuasion. Human beings have abundant defenses against persuasion. They do not easily believe. They watch the most interesting advertisement on television and quietly resolve never to buy that article. The Christian preacher standing in the marketplace speaks eloquently to passersby, but almost all of them pay no attention. Even those who pause to listen to the wandering "babbler" (Acts 17:18) have no intention at all of believing the nonsense they hear. To be sure, persuasion must not be accompanied by bribery, force, or unworthy means. The patient in the Christian hospital must not be told, "If you accept the gospel, you will get good medicine. If you do not, you will get bad medicine." Food must be distributed to adherents of all religions alike, provided that they are all hungry.

Evangelism and religious freedom is a field bristling with problems. The more firmly a religion is believed, and the more ardently it is propagated, the more likelihood exists (1) that it will be persecuted, and (2) that it may violate the right of others to religious freedom. A proper theology of mission, therefore, maintains that (1) on the basis of God's revelation in the Bible and of reason, the right to propagate the highest and best one knows must always be asserted and defended, and (2) Christians must make sure that their methods of proclamation and persuasion are free of any trace of coercion.

When facing prohibitions and persecutions (and they are not uncommon), theology of mission will appeal to the universal right of religious freedom. It will claim that under such circumstances, governments ought to protect the right of all peoples to change their religion if they wish to do so. Governments should protect Christian minorities and guarantee them a right to believe and worship as they choose. Moreover, religious freedom always includes the right to propagate one's religion.

Conclusion

Donald McGavran

B y this time the reader will have acquired a wide acquaintance with the extensive theologizing currently going on in regard to the missionary enterprise, which has proven to be a unique and costly undertaking. From countless Christian churches over the years many streams of personnel and money have gone forth—not to conquer, not to add territory to the sending nations, and not to bring back wealth to the sending congregations and denominations. Missions have cost the sending bodies hundreds of thousands of their choicest sons and daughters, and hundreds of millions in money. The constant goal has been the establishment of independent national churches. Each of these—missionaries expected—would help the nation in which it expanded to achieve the high standing intended for it by God.

While other factors have been at work, the missionary movement has exerted, and continues to exert, a transforming and humanizing influence wherever it has gone. This has not financially benefited the sending nations. Rather, as mission was carried out at enormous cost to the sending churches, the profitable empires of the sending nations collapsed.

This vast enterprise has strong theological roots. Christians believe God wills it. Otherwise they would neither begin nor continue it. However, in the last half of the twentieth century, great differences of opinion have arisen as to what God intends to accomplish by Christian mission. What are God's goals? How have these been described in the Bible? How are the biblical mandates for world evangelization and for doing "good to all men, and especially to those who are of the household of faith" (Gal. 6:10) to be weighed? Which is heavier? On these points very different mission enterprises and theologies have been and are being constructed. The theologies fall into two groups. On one side are the evangelical and official Roman Catholic theologies of mission. On the other side are the conciliar and liberationist theologies of mission.

The process by which these theologies have arisen is not simple. The

233

historical chapters in this volume point out in detail, with abundant documentation, the long winding paths by which these four main theologies
of mission have reached their present campgrounds. The interpretative
chapters, presenting the core arguments of these clusters of theological
opinions, are built on the historical chapters. Reading both is necessary
to achieve real understanding. A tremendous Christian searching has
been going on in the midst of the greatest revolution ever to envelop the
human race. The historical chapters help us see something of the depth,
breadth, and intensity of that search. The interpretative chapters point
out in as brief a form as possible the contemporary conclusions of the
searchers.

This analysis of contemporary theological opinion on world evangelization has not been an easy task, because each main theology has been
stated in many slightly different ways. Back of each way is a doctrinal
stance—a view of God, Christ, revelation, the Bible, humankind, sin, salvation, the kingdom of God, and eternal life. These doctrinal stances
(with the single exception of Vatican II's "Decree on the Missionary Activity of the Church") have *not* been officially formulated and published.
This is because in most denominations are found adherents of all four
schools of thought. Consequently rather than pointing out that there are
at least four main schools of thought, missiologists have been assuming
(as I myself did until 1968) that the many positions expressed amount to
but minor differences on isolated issues. All these viewpoints deal with
the same thing—Christian mission. The vague word *mission* with its many
meanings covers them all. As a result the world of mission is in the midst
of great confusion as to what "mission" essentially is.

We have spoken of the "present campgrounds" of the four main theologies of mission. Any true delineation of the current scene must show
both the contemporary conclusions reached by the main parties *and* the
continuous change going on. Advocates of the main theologies of mission
often change their formulations—move on to new campgrounds. Sometimes this is done to hold in orbit some segment of their constituency
which appears likely to bolt. Sometimes it is because a new team is elected
to administer mission activities and invariably emphasizes its own understanding of the situation. Sometimes a need (it may be for God, or for
something to eat) stalks to the center of the stage and demands attention.
The main theologies of mission as we have stated them must therefore
be understood as temporary resting places—campgrounds.

True, they may become permanent. A campground of the Roman
legions in Britain did become London. The doctrinal stance back of each
theology, arising as it does from convictions concerning inspiration, revelation, and the authority of the Bible, does not change easily. A convinced
critic cannot take eternal life seriously. An adherent of Barthian theology

cannot believe in propositional revelation. Yet good Christians are continually adjusting their positions (making concessions, some would say) to bring about as large a degree of peace and agreement as possible.

Readers must not be misled by the multitude of peripheral writings. It would be easy to gather a dozen publications from the evangelical camp demanding that social action become the central focus of mission. But this does not mean that evangelicals as a whole are now substituting social action for evangelism. A few eminent Roman Catholics may voice opinions markedly different from those promulgated in *Ad gentes,* but the official Roman Catholic position remains that announced by Vatican II. The contemporary conclusions we have described are the *mainstreams* of missiological thought of very large bodies of Christians. Regardless of what an eminent person here or there says, the mainstreams are likely to continue flowing in the same direction for some time to come.

We believe that Christ's cause will be better served if the four mainstreams of theological thought about Christian mission are clearly set forth. Since they are stressing very different ends and are built on very different biblical bases, all cannot be believed by anyone. If this one is true, then that one is not. If the priorities demanded by one are correct, then the diametrically opposite priorities demanded by the other cannot be held to be God's will. Painful though it is, those who carry out and teach Christian mission ought to recognize the four diverse streams, back the one which to them seems truest and most clearly God's will, see what priorities and policies it demands, and act accordingly. We stand in the midst of a great debate. The cause of truth will be furthered as we recognize the various positions, examine with care the biblical foundations on which each is built, and then decide which is in fact God's will. Good stewards of God's grace must administer His gifts (their talents) in view of the actual situation and the clearly revealed will of God.

We trust that our statements of the various positions are fair. They were formed after voluminous reading and much discussion with national leaders, missionaries, and church officials from every continent. Many revisions which take into account the thought of such mission thinkers have been incorporated. While the statements in the historical chapters were framed by Glasser, and those in the interpretative chapters were framed by McGavran, they also passed the scrutiny of the other. They come to the reader as the considered opinion of both authors.

If any reader differs with us either in regard to some sequence of events or our summary of classical or some other theology, we hope these descriptions of the contemporary scene will nevertheless be found valuable. They may lead that reader to attempt his or her own statement of the historical background and conclusions of the tremendous movements of thought through which the church of Jesus Christ is now passing.

The authors have written from the point of view of the classical theology of mission. We beg any brothers or sisters who hold a liberationist, Roman Catholic, or conciliar theology of mission, and who feel that the classical position is outmoded, to set forth their own idea of a theology of mission adequate for today. We shall read it with interest.

Any description of contemporary theologies of mission should rigidly eschew the easy solution of saying, "A pox on your polarization. We all believe the same thing." That helps no one. It simply urges that the search go on with both eyes shut.

To those who differ with the classical evangelical position and wish to set forth their own description of contemporary theologies of mission, we give the following advice: illumine the whole field, state the various positions competently, and espouse the one which seems truest. In addition, be sure your position is based on the authority of the entire Bible. That means keeping various ends in view: (1) discipling *panta ta ethne*—three billion have yet to believe; (2) serving the household of faith; and (3) making provision for social, economic, and political improvements.

As this book goes to press, we anticipate that there will be many years, possibly many decades, of these four different emphases. The overwhelming authority of the biblical revelation, the terrible spiritual destitution of those who know not Christ, the uniqueness of Christ's atoning death, and the absolute exclusiveness of both Old and New Testaments in regard to "other gods" will continue to convince most of those who carry out Christian mission to adhere to the classical position. They will adhere to it not because it is classical but because it is irrefutably biblical. World evangelization will continue.

At the same time the terrible destitution, poverty, oppression, and hunger of rapidly mounting multitudes will persuade Christians and churches to devote very considerable portions of their time, prayers, money, and personnel to achieving temporal improvements of all kinds. Direct relief of poverty will be accompanied—we hope—by tremendous efforts to limit the population to what the land will support. In sovereign nations, oppression from outside is less likely to be the real cause of poverty than are overpopulation, interior sins, and injustices—witness the rampant corruption in Zaire and other lands and the millions killed in China, in Russia, and only yesterday in Cambodia.

Conciliar, liberationist, Roman Catholic, and evangelical forces will weigh carefully the physical needs of humanity and their causes. Each force will also weigh the spiritual destitution of people: their alienation from God and their misplaced dependence on fallible human wisdom. Each force will then assign a different value to the many kinds of want and deprivation. All will see that, when everyone has enough to eat and wear, enough freedom and enough political responsibility, jealousy, hate, lust, pride, and other sins will remain, along with attendant sorrow, pain, and fear. Indeed they will not only remain but will be fatter and more vigorous because they are exercised by well-fed men and women. All will see this, but each will assign a different value to it. The essential problem is weighing the amount of sorrow and suffering caused by various factors and proportioning the sacred resources committed to Christians by the Lord, *so that the maximum relief of suffering occurs.*

Many value judgments must be made. Is eternal separation from God more disastrous than going to bed hungry? Is going to bed hungry the cause of more suffering than are widespread illiteracy and a sociopolitical system which guarantees that education will be of no economic importance to most people? Is it more important to wipe out yaws and malaria or to increase rice production? Which is more important for the benefit of the population of a Third World country—to multiply food production, to keep the population down at a manageable level, to stop a baby-food company from selling substitutes for mother's milk, or to lead a third of the citizens to become sincere committed Christians? Is it really beneficial to a population to turn from animism to the Christian faith? If so, how is such conversion to be measured against the crying need to build up labor unions which will limit the power of local capitalists?

How are these value judgments made? What is the final authority? The decision of a few leaders? Or the consensus of the population concerned? Or a majority vote in the United Nations? Or is it the revelation of God's will in the Bible and in Jesus Christ, applied by the church in the light of the actual situation? All theologies of mission are answering these questions and others like them.

Conciliar and liberationist theologies of mission agree in effect that the most grievous suffering known is an unequal distribution of land, food, wealth, learning, and security. According to conciliars and liberationists, any judgment that people are spiritually destitute and alienated from God depends on such a narrow view of Scripture that it cannot form the basis of action by Christians in general. There are so many varying convictions about God, sin, salvation, and release (*moksha* or *nirvana*) that it is unfair to impose Christian convictions on the whole world.

This mind-set fosters a relativistic outlook which eventuates in a conclusion that, whatever one's ideas about God and eternal life are, ignorance, physical hunger, and deprivation must be eliminated *first.* What Christians say about God will seem incredible to people suffering from physical hunger unless and until their hunger is satisfied. "You cannot preach the gospel to hungry people." On this shaky foundation the conciliar and liberationist theologies of mission are erected. These value judgments determine the entire framework of that wing of theological opinion.

The evangelical and official Roman Catholic theologies of mission, on the contrary, agree in effect that the most grievous suffering known is living, at any economic level, separated from God, subject to sin and Satan, with no hope of life beyond death, and no sure basis for ethical action. Physical deprivation—such as Paul suffered for years in jail, and Jesus Christ suffered in His incarnation in a poor home and in His death on the cross—is painful to be sure; but it is not the greatest pain. "If your hand causes you to stumble, cut it off [that will be painful and a terrible deprivation, but not the worst deprivation]; it is better for you to enter life crippled, than having your two hands, to go into hell, into the unquenchable fire" (Mark 9:43, NASB). Our Lord also said, "Do not fear those who kill the body but cannot kill the soul; rather fear him who can destroy both soul and body" (Matt. 10:28; cf. Luke 12:4).

Paul's entire argument, his gospel, was definitely not, "Hear the good news. We Christians are going to treat you Gentiles more justly and see that you get more of the good things of life." No. Rather it was:

> You Gentiles are slaves to gods which in reality do not exist. Turn to Jesus Christ who bore your sins on the cross. He is the propitiation for your sins. The gospel is God's power for the salvation of everyone who believes. The righteousness *you* do is not what counts. Salvation is not by works, but by faith. You can gain acquittal from guilt by trusting God's free grace through the deliverance which is found in Christ Jesus. There is no condemnation for those who are in Christ Jesus.

Passages like these resound like a refrain throughout the apostolic writings.

In those days the earth was full of demeaning social structures: slavery, flogging and crucifixion as ordinary forms of punishment, making the conquered pay for the Roman occupation, huge land holdings for the rich and tiny plots or none at all for the poor, no voice for women, gladiatorial games, condemnation to the galleys, and many more. Yet neither our Lord nor His apostles single out any one of these evil structures for comment. We are not pleading that Christians should today make no effort to change evil social structures. Times are different. Christians now have political power. What good they can do, they should do. We are saying, however, that the Bible clearly estimates spiritual destitution as more grievous than material and social deprivation.

In effect the whole Bible says that while physical sufferings and deprivations are real, while God's people should do justly and love kindness, while Christ did come to preach to the poor, and while Christians are to feed the hungry, entertain guests, care for widows and orphans, and give cups of cold water in Christ's name, *still* the first duty of Christians and of the church is to preach Christ, to call men and women from darkness to light, and from death to life. The greatest deprivations, the most demeaning, are spiritual, not physical. Furthermore, if spiritual needs are met, if persons become new creatures in Christ Jesus, material needs can be met more effectively. Social engineering exercised on non-Christians yields a small trickle of advance, but on practicing Christians it yields a broad, deep river of social well-being. Not only *can* we preach the gospel to the hungry, but often hungry, deprived, and shaken people are the very ones who listen most eagerly to it.

Convictions like these are the foundation of the evangelical and official Roman Catholic theologies of mission. These value judgments voiced in the Gospels and Epistles are the framework of the theological opinion about mission which almost all Christians held till about 1950. Till then, what we have called the evangelical theology of mission was also the universal or classical theology of mission.

In the titanic struggle between theologies of mission going on today, what is really at stake is the view of the relationship between the spiritual world and the physical world. Indeed, it is really a struggle between those who believe the Marxist/secular view that the physical is the only real world, and those who believe that the eternal verities are spiritual not physical. One who accepts the secular conviction that the supreme values are physical and economic will certainly adopt either the conciliar or liberationist theology of mission. On the other hand, one who accepts the conviction so clearly set forth in the Scriptures that "God gave us eternal life, and this life is in his Son. He who has the Son has life; he who has not the Son has not life" (1 John 5:11–12), will adopt the classical theology of mission.

The purpose of this book is to encourage Christians to work toward a theology of mission which takes the whole Bible with utmost seriousness. This will incorporate the position that humans are created in the image of God but fallen, and that permanent amelioration of the human lot will depend on increasing acceptance of God's grace through Jesus Christ and an increasingly responsible membership in His body, the church. On that firm foundation a great deal of social reconstruction has been, is being, and will be mounted. The longest single step which human beings can take toward the better world where God's will is done on earth as it is in heaven, is taken when they become believing and responsible members of the church of Jesus Christ. Social concern then arises from beliefs for which they will die and by which they intend to live.

Bibliography

Abbott, Walter M., ed. *The Documents of Vatican II*. New York: Herder and Herder, 1966.

Alves, Rubem. *A Theology of Human Hope*. New York: Corpus Books, 1968.

Anderson, Gerald H., ed. *The Theology of the Christian Mission*. New York: McGraw-Hill, 1961.

_____, and Stransky, Thomas F., eds. *Christ's Lordship and Religious Pluralism*. Maryknoll, NY: Orbis, 1981.

_____. *Mission Trends No. 4: Liberation Theologies in North America and Europe*. Grand Rapids: Eerdmans, 1978; New York: Paulist Press, 1979.

Barbour, Ian G. *Myths, Models, and Paradigms: A Comparative Study in Science and Religion*. New York: Harper and Row, 1974.

Bassham, Rodger C. *Mission Theology, 1948–1975: Years of Worldwide Creative Tension—Ecumenical, Evangelical and Roman Catholic*. Pasadena: William Carey Library, 1979.

Bavinck, Johannes H. *Introduction to the Science of Missions*. Translated by David H. Freeman. Philadelphia: Presbyterian and Reformed, 1969.

Berg, Clayton L., and Roberts, W. Dayton. *Ten-Year Horizon (1981–1990)*. Background Briefing Paper 12 (1980).

Berkhof, Hendrikus. *Christ, the Meaning of History*. Richmond: John Knox, 1966.

Bethge, Eberhard. *Dietrich Bonhoeffer: Man of Vision*. New York: Harper and Row, 1970.

Beyerhaus, Peter. "The Ministry of Crossing Frontiers." In *The Church Crossing Frontiers*, edited by P. Beyerhaus and K. Hallencreutz, pp. 36–54. Uppsala: Gleerup, 1969.

_____. *Shaken Foundations: Theological Foundations for Missions*. Grand Rapids: Zondervan, 1972.

Blamires, Harry. *The Christian Mind*. New York: Seabury, 1963.

Bock, Paul. *In Search of a Responsible World Society: The Social Teachings of the World Council of Churches*. Philadelphia: Westminster, 1974.

Bocking, Ronald. *Has the Day of the Missionary Passed?* London: London Missionary Society, 1961.

Bosch, David J. "Crosscurrents in Modern Mission." *Missionalia* 4 (August 1976): 54–84.

————. *Theology of Religions MSR 301, Guide 1.* Pretoria: University of South Africa, 1977.

Braaten, Carl E. *The Flaming Center: A Theology of the Christian Mission.* Philadelphia: Fortress, 1977.

Brown, Robert McAfee. "Liberation Theology and the Coming of the Kingdom." Ventnor Conference of Evangelical Mission Executives (April 20–21, 1979), pp. 1–14.

————. *Theology in a New Key: Responding to Liberation Themes.* Philadelphia: Westminster, 1978.

Burke, Thomas J. M., ed. *Catholic Missions: Four Great Missionary Encyclicals.* New York: Fordham University, 1957.

Castro, Emilio. Editorial. *International Review of Mission* 64 (July 1975): 237–42.

————. *A Monthly Letter on Evangelism.* January/February 1981, pp. 2–3. Geneva: World Council of Churches, 1981.

Catholic Missions: Four Great Missionary Encyclicals. Edited by Thomas J. M. Burke. New York: Fordham University, 1957.

Champagne, J. E. *Manual of Missionary Action.* Ottawa: University of Ottawa, 1948.

"The Christian Community in the Academic World." *Student World* (WSCF) 3 (1965): 233–35.

The Christian Life and Message in Relation to Non-Christian Systems of Thought and Life. Volume 1 in the series *Jerusalem Meeting I.M.C. 1928.* New York and London: International Missionary Council, 1928.

The Church for Others and *The Church for the World.* Geneva: World Council of Churches, 1968.

Cochrane, Arthur C. *The Church's Confession Under Hitler.* Philadelphia: Westminster, 1962.

Cragg, Kenneth. *Sandals at the Mosque: Christian Presence amid Islam.* New York: Oxford University, 1959.

Creeds of the Churches: A Reader in Christian Doctrine from the Bible to the Present. Edited by John H. Leith. Rev. ed. Atlanta: John Knox, 1973.

Cullmann, Oscar. *Christ and Time.* Philadelphia: Westminster, 1950.

————. "Eschatology and Missions in the New Testament." Translated by Olive Wyon. In *The Theology of the Christian Mission,* edited by Gerald H. Anderson, pp. 42–54. New York: McGraw-Hill, 1961.

————. *Salvation in History.* Translated by Sidney G. Sowers. New York: Harper and Row, 1967.

————. *The State in the New Testament.* London: SCM, 1957.

Damboriena, Prudencio. "Aspects of the Missionary Crisis in Roman Catholicism." In *The Future of the Christian World Mission,* edited by William J. Danker and Wi Jo Kang, pp. 73–87. Grand Rapids: Eerdmans, 1971.

de Diétrich, Suzanne. *God's Unfolding Purpose: A Guide to the Study of the Bible.* Translated by Robert McAfee Brown. Philadelphia: Westminster, 1960.

Deist, Ferdinand. "The Exodus Motif in the Old Testament and the Theology of Liberation." *Missionalia* 5 (1977): 58–69.

Devanandan, Paul David. "Resurgent Hinduism." In *Christianity and the Asian Revolution,* edited by Rajah B. Manikam, pp. 123–37. New York: Friendship, 1954.

————. "The Shock of the Discovery of World Religions." In *History's Lessons for Tomorrow's Mission,* pp. 217–24. Geneva: World Student Christian Federation, 1960.

The Documents of Vatican II. Edited by Walter M. Abbott. New York: Herder and Herder, 1966.

Drafts for Sections: Uppsala '68. Geneva: International Review of Mission, 1968.

Edwards, David C. "Signs of Radicalism in the Ecumenical Movement." In *Ecumenical Advance: A History of the Ecumenical Movement,* edited by Harold E. Fey. Volume 2, *1948–1968,* pp. 371–409. Philadelphia: Westminster, 1970.

Ellul, Jacques. *Violence: Reflections from a Christian Perspective.* Translated by Cecilia Gaul. New York: Seabury, 1969.

Fey, Harold E., ed. *Ecumenical Advance: A History of the Ecumenical Movement.* Volume 2, *1948–1968.* Philadelphia: Westminster, 1970.

Flesseman–van Leer, Ellen, ed. *The Bible: Its Authority and Interpretation in the Ecumenical Movement.* Faith and Order Paper 99. Geneva: World Council of Churches, 1980.

Frey, Harold Christian Andreas. "Critiques of Conciliar Ecumenism by Conservative Evangelicals in the United States." Ph.D. dissertation. Boston University, 1961.

Gibellini, Rosino, ed. *Frontiers of Theology in Latin America.* Translated by John Drury. Maryknoll, NY: Orbis, 1979.

Goldschmidt, Walter Rochs. *Comparative Functionalism: An Essay in Anthropological Theory.* Berkeley: University of California, 1966.

Goodall, Norman. "First Principles." *International Review of Missions* 39 (July 1950): 257–62.

————, ed. *Missions Under the Cross.* London: Edinburgh House, 1953.

Gort, Jerald D. "Jerusalem 1928: Mission, Kingdom and Church." *International Review of Mission* 67 (July 1978): 273–98.

Gremillion, Joseph. *The Gospel of Peace and Justice: Catholic Social Teaching Since Pope John.* Maryknoll, NY: Orbis, 1976.

Gutierrez, Gustavo. *A Theology of Liberation.* Translated by Caridad Inda and John Eagleson. Maryknoll, NY: Orbis, 1973.

Hamilton, Kenneth. "Liberation Theology: Lessons Positive and Negative." In *Evangelicals and Liberation,* edited by Carl E. Armerding, pp. 120–27. Nutley, NJ: Presbyterian and Reformed, 1977.

Henry, Carl F. H. *The Uneasy Conscience of Modern Fundamentalism.* Grand Rapids: Eerdmans, 1947.

Hesselgrave, David J., ed. *Theology and Mission.* Grand Rapids: Baker, 1978.

Hoekendijk, Johannes C. "Notes on the Meaning of Mission(ary)." In *Planning for Mission,* edited by Thomas Wieser, pp. 37–48. New York: U.S. Conference for the World Council of Churches, 1966.

Hoffman, Ronan. *Pioneer Theories of Missiology.* Washington, DC: Catholic University of America, 1960.

Hollenweger, Walter J. "The Roots and Fruits of the Charismatic Renewal in the Third World: Implications for Mission." Unpublished paper. University of Birmingham, 1979.

Jackson, Eleanor M. *Red Tape and the Gospel: A Study of the Significance of the Ecumenical Missionary Struggle of William Paton (1886–1943)*. Birmingham: Phlogiston Publishing/The Selly Oak Colleges, 1980.

John XXIII. *The Encyclicals and Other Messages of John XXIII*. Washington, DC: T.P.S. Press, 1964.

Kaiser, Robert B. *Pope, Council and World*. New York: Macmillan, 1963.

Kraemer, Hendrik. *The Christian Message in a Non-Christian World*. Grand Rapids: Kregel, 1969.

Krüger, Hanfried. "The Life and Activities of the World Council of Churches." In *Ecumenical Advance: A History of the Ecumenical Movement*, edited by Harold E. Fey. Volume 2, *1948–1968*, pp. 27–62. Philadelphia: Westminster, 1970.

Kuhn, Thomas S. *The Structure of Scientific Revolutions*. 2nd ed. Chicago: University of Chicago, 1970.

Küng, Hans. *The Council in Action*. New York: Sheed and Ward, 1963.

Latourette, Kenneth Scott, and Hogg, William Richey. *Tomorrow Is Here*. New York: Friendship, 1948.

Lehmann, Paul L. "Willingen and Lund: The Church on the Way to Unity." *Theology Today* 9 (January 1953): 431–41.

Leith, John H., ed. *Creeds of the Churches: A Reader in Christian Doctrine from the Bible to the Present*. Rev. ed. Atlanta: John Knox, 1973.

Let the Earth Hear His Voice. Edited by J. D. Douglas. Minneapolis: World Wide, 1975.

Lindsell, Harold, ed. *The Church's Worldwide Mission*. Waco, TX: Word, 1966.

Loffler, Paul. *The Layman Abroad in the Mission of the Church*. London: Edinburgh House, 1962.

McGavran, Donald A., and Wagner, C. Peter. "Will Nairobi Champion the Whole Man?" *Church Growth Bulletin* 11 (July 1975): 459–64.

Míguez Bonino, Jose. *Doing Theology in a Revolutionary Situation*. Philadelphia: Fortress, 1975.

Miranda, Jose. *Marx and the Bible: A Critique of the Philosophy of Oppression*. Translated by John Eagleson. Maryknoll, NY: Orbis, 1974.

Mosothoane, Ephraim. "The Liberation of Peoples in the New Testament." *Missionalia* 5 (1977): 70–80.

Neill, Stephen. *The Interpretation of the New Testament: 1861–1961*. New York: Oxford University, 1964.

————. *The Unfinished Task*. London: Morrison and Gibb, 1957.

Newbigin, Lesslie. "Call to Mission—A Call to Unity?" In *The Church Crossing Frontiers*, edited by P. Beyerhaus and K. Hallencreutz, pp. 254–65. Uppsala: Gleerup, 1969.

————. "Mission and Missions." *Christianity Today*, 1 August 1960, p. 23.

————. "The Mission and Unity of the Church." Ainslee Memorial Lecture. Grahamstown, South Africa, 1955.

————. *The Open Secret.* Grand Rapids: Eerdmans, 1978.

Percy, Jack O., and Bennett, Mary. *Facing the Unfinished Task.* Grand Rapids: Zondervan, 1961.

Potter, Philip. "Evangelization in the Modern World." *International Review of Mission* 64 (July 1975): 314–18.

Quanbeck, Warren A., and Vatja, Vilmos, eds. *Challenge and Response: A Protestant Perspective of the Vatican Council.* Minneapolis: Augsburg, 1966.

Ramalho, Jether Perlira, ed. *Signs of Hope and Justice.* Geneva: World Council of Churches, 1980.

Recker, Robert. "The Concept of the Missio Dei and Instruction in Mission at Calvin Seminary." *Calvin Theological Journal* 11 (1976): 181–98.

Ridderbos, Herman. *The Coming of the Kingdom.* Nutley, NJ: Presbyterian and Reformed, 1976.

Rosin, H. H. *Missio Dei.* Leiden: Interuniversity Institute for Missiological and Ecumenical Research, 1972.

Rowe, Richard C. *Bible Study in the World Council of Churches.* Research Pamphlet 16. Geneva: World Council of Churches, 1969.

Sadgrove, Michael. "The Bible from New Delhi to Nairobi." Private collection from Balliol College (Oxford), 1975.

Samartha, Stanley J., ed. *Dialogue Between Men of Living Faiths.* Geneva: World Council of Churches, 1971.

————. *Faith in the Midst of Faiths.* Geneva: World Council of Churches, 1977.

Schlink, Edmund. *After the Council: The Meaning of Vatican 2 for Protestantism.* Philadelphia: Fortress, 1968.

Schmidlin, Joseph. *Catholic Mission Theory.* Techny, IL: Missions Press, 1931.

Schmidt, William John. "Ecumenicity and Syncretism: The Confrontation of the Ecumenical Movement with Syncretism in Special Reference to the International Missionary Council of the World Council of Churches." Ph.D. dissertation. Columbia University, 1966.

Schrotenboer, Paul G. "The Bible in the World Council of Churches." *Calvin Theological Journal* 12 (1977): 144–63.

Scott, Waldron. *Bring Forth Justice.* Grand Rapids: Eerdmans, 1980.

Segundo, Juan Luis. *The Liberation of Theology.* Translated by John Drury. Maryknoll, NY: Orbis, 1976.

Sharpe, Eric J. "The Goals of Inter-Religious Dialogue." In *Truth and Dialogue in World Religions: Conflicting Truth Claims,* edited by John Hick, pp. 77–95. Philadelphia: Westminster, 1974.

————. "New Directions in the Theology of Mission." *Evangelical Quarterly* 46 (1974): 8–24.

————. "The Problem of Conversion in Recent Missionary Thought." *Evangelical Quarterly* 41 (1969): 221–31.

————. "The Spirit and the Religions." In *The Church Crossing Frontiers,* edited by P. Beyerhaus and K. Hallencreutz, pp. 111–23. Uppsala: Gleerup, 1969.

Smith, Wilfred Cantwell. "An Attempt at Summation." In *Christ's Lordship and Religious Pluralism,* edited by Gerald H. Anderson and Thomas F. Stransky, pp. 196–203. Maryknoll, NY: Orbis, 1981.

————. *Towards a World Theology: Faith and the Comparative History of Religion.* Philadelphia: Westminster, 1981.

Stott, John R. W. *Christian Mission in the Modern World.* Downers Grove, IL: Inter-Varsity, 1975.

————. *Christ the Controversialist.* Downers Grove, IL: Inter-Varsity, 1970.

Suemois, Andrew V. "The Evolution of Mission Theology Among Roman Catholics." In *The Theology of the Christian Mission,* edited by Gerald H. Anderson, pp. 122–34. New York: McGraw-Hill, 1961.

Taylor, John V. *The Uppsala Report 1968.* Geneva: World Council of Churches, 1968.

Van Engen, Charles E. *The Growth of the True Church.* Amsterdam: Rodolphi, 1981.

Verkuyl, Johannes. *Contemporary Missiology: An Introduction.* Translated and edited by Dale Cooper. Grand Rapids: Eerdmans, 1978.

Vicedom, Georg F. *Mission of God.* St. Louis: Concordia, 1965.

Visser 't Hooft, Willem A. "The General Ecumenical Development Since 1948." In *Ecumenical Advance: A History of the Ecumenical Movement,* edited by Harold E. Fey. Volume 2, *1948–1968,* pp. 1–26. Philadelphia: Westminster, 1970.

————. *Has the Ecumenical Movement a Future?* Atlanta: John Knox, 1976.

Warneck, Gustav. *Outline of a History of Protestant Missions.* New York: Revell, 1906.

Warren, Max A. C. *Social History and Christian Mission.* London: SCM, 1967.

Welch, Holmes. "The Fate of Religion." In *The China Difference,* edited by Ross Terrill, pp. 119–37. New York: Harper and Row Colophon Books, 1979.

Wieser, Thomas, ed. *Planning for Mission.* New York: U.S. Conference for the World Council of Churches, 1966.

World Conference on Mission and Evangelism: Melbourne, Australia, 12–25 May 1980. Geneva: World Council of Churches, 1980.

World Missionary Conference, 1910. New York: Revell, 1910.

Index